A HEALTHY HORSE
THE NATURAL WAY

A HEALTHY HORSE
THE NATURAL WAY

THE HORSE OWNER'S GUIDE
TO USING HERBS, MASSAGE, HOMEOPATHY,
AND OTHER NATURAL THERAPIES

CATHERINE BIRD

THE LYONS PRESS
GUILFORD, CONNECTICUT
AN IMPRINT OF THE GLOBE PEQUOT PRESS

First Lyons Press edition, 2002

First published in Australia in 2002 by
New Holland Publishers (Australia) Pty Ltd

The Lyons Press is an imprint of the Globe Pequot Press.

ISBN 1-58574-576-6

10 9 8 7 6 5 4 3 2 1

The adoption and application of the information in this book is at the reader's discretion and is their sole responsibility. This book is not a substitute for professional veterinary advice. The publisher expressly disclaims all liability to any person arising directly or indirectly from the use of, or for any errors or omissions in, the information in this book.

Publishing Manager: Anouska Good
Project Editor: Jennifer Lane
Designer: Nanette Backhouse
Production Controller: Wendy Hunt
Veterinary Consultant: John Saxton

Reproduction by Sang Choy International, Singapore
Printed and bound in Singapore by Tien Wah Press (Pte) Ltd, Singapore

Library of Congress Cataloging-in-Publication Data is available on file.

CONTENTS

ACKNOWLEDGMENTS

Putting this book together has been a wonderful adventure. With the increased interest in natural therapies, I have been fortunate to find fellow equine therapists I now value as friends. These people have proved themselves to be very special in their desire to help horses and have supported my quest to get this information 'out there'. Without their help and consultation this book would have been difficult to write; Sharon May Davis—Equine Therapist and Researcher (AUS), Lyn Palmer—Equine Aromatherapist (UK), Patti Duffy Salmon—Equine Herbalist (USA), Tanya Nolte—EquiHomeopath (AUS), and Maggie Moyer—TTOUCH/TTEAM (USA). With vibrational healing I have an amazing teacher in Larayne Porter. Her channelling of St John the Baptist as my spiritual mentor has made this dream become a reality.

Thanks go to our gorgeous model in the massage chapter, Northern Lights, and my friend (his human) Prue Spurrett, along with Liz Sugar for providing Elizabeth Park for our photographs.

I am grateful to David Vella for his foreword; I truly appreciate his support of my work from a veterinary perspective.

There have been many people who have helped me so much, and I know these people know who they are. I hope they will read this and know their friendship has contributed to the pages within this book. It is through their friendship I have grown in my convictions and had the courage to put my thoughts on these pages.

Writing a book involves its own challenges. My friend, author Anne Rennie, prepared me well for each of these, and introduced me to literary agent Selwa Anthony. Selwa made things happen with New Holland, who in turn provided Jennifer Lane, editor, who helped to shape this book into a publication I am proud to offer to the world.

FOREWORD

Catherine's work is remarkable, both for what she accomplishes and the pleasure she takes in performing it. Her endeavours have seen her embark on a journey of endless discovery—a journey that she has pieced together patiently and professionally.

I was both honoured and privileged to observe Catherine's work during the early days of her career, when I accompanied her on her weekly horse massage sessions at Sydney's Mounted Police Horse unit. Here I glimpsed the realm of 'what they didn't teach us in vet school'. At the end of the day I also had the added bonus of carrying home with me the smell of horses and wonderful oils!

Witnessing a horse's response to Catherine's massaging hands when they find the 'right spot' is truly amazing. I've seen flighty horses remain completely at ease during and after their massage. Some horses literally stretch out just like cats do when they rise after a sleep! This is truly astonishing to see—you don't need any further convincing that the horse is enjoying its massage when this happens.

When addressing horse health, we can often be conditioned into only considering the physical aspects. Natural therapists believe that aspects other than the physical also need to be addressed if the horse is to achieve 'whole' health. Numerous natural therapies are available to help address the wider health picture.

There's an exciting marriage of horse health disciplines in this book. Catherine has put together a wealth of experience and information, drawing on her strong foundations of experience with treating people and horses. Her work reveals a deep understanding of the many modalities available to assist in healing. She has applied the principles of these modalities in detail, while always bearing the whole horse in mind.

Catherine emphasizes the importance of the qualified veterinary aspect in treating horses and advises her readers to seek veterinary assistance for their horses whenever it is necessary. The use of natural therapies is complementary and not meant to replace veterinary medicine.

Traditional veterinary medicine and natural therapies are not mutually exclusive; both disciplines have boundless areas in which they can and do enhance each other, and Catherine highlights this throughout her book. This interface is neither a straight line nor a matter of 'east meets west'. I think the relationship is more like an interwoven whole, with a dynamic interface that grows with an infinite connectedness. If we remain open-minded to what is available, if we accept the wisdom and knowledge of these offerings and exercise due care in their use, then I feel we have the responsibility and opportunity to employ these in our desire for healthier horses.

A Healthy Horse the Natural Way is presented in a concise, user-friendly format and contains practical, useful information throughout. The old adage, 'above all, do no harm' is well heeded, as is the fact that we should never underestimate horses' innate ability to heal themselves and even ourselves as their companions, too.

It takes dedication and hard work to achieve what Catherine has achieved with this book. Her commitment to improving horse health has meant many a sacrifice. Her first book, *Horse Scents*, and her website and newsletter devoted to natural horse health are all examples of this commitment. Catherine's motto has always been 'healthy happy horses naturally'—a fitting portrayal of the expert guidance she offers in this book.

Dr David Vella BSc BVSc (Hons)

INTRODUCTION

CONSIDERING THE WHOLE HORSE

Having horses in your life is very special. Working with a horse to make sure he is as healthy and happy as possible can prove to be like putting together a jigsaw puzzle with many intricate pieces, but the horse can give you the most amazing insights along the way. Many horse owners commonly consult a veterinary surgeon about one piece of this jigsaw. We refer to a farrier and a dentist about other pieces, and then there are the many other trainers and professionals who may be called in to see where their respective pieces fit. This book aims to show you how to bring the jigsaw pieces together and consider your horse as a whole entity, rather than just looking at any one piece of the puzzle at a time.

This jigsaw puzzle can become very complex. A large piece of the puzzle concerns how your horse is shod, as the balance of the hoof can affect your horse's whole body, and your horse relies on his feet to keep him sound. Your horse's dentist holds yet another piece that is always vital to your horse's health. If your horse cannot eat his feed properly or has an uncomfortable jaw, he cannot perform at an optimum level. Do you ride your horse? Then your saddler also holds a colourful piece of your jigsaw, as an ill-fitting saddle can create many problems. Sometimes the missing piece of the puzzle lies in training, and you may need a trainer who can help you adjust how you ride or instruct your horse.

All of these pieces of the jigsaw rely on someone else to place them in the correct place in the puzzle. When a horse is 'not right', these are often the first areas to consider. If the horse still doesn't have 100 per cent health after these factors have all been considered and checked, you need to look for other missing pieces of the puzzle which may lie in areas that have traditionally been overlooked. With the right knowledge, you can step in to help—you may even find that you hold the missing piece or the key to the problem yourself.

Your horse's muscle health can be affected by all of the above factors, so your horse may need a massage to relieve any strain. Your horse's immune system may need boosting with herbs to help him recover from the illness your veterinary surgeon has diagnosed. Silly behaviour or slow-healing injuries may respond well to aromatherapy. Homeopathy may be able to 'bring up' a suppressed disease that is underlying the disease state, or, in a first-aid situation, it could trigger a positive response in your horse's body to help him overcome a critical moment while waiting for your veterinary surgeon to arrive. Your horse may also be reflecting certain emotions that need to be faced by you or someone else in your family.

The exciting part is putting all of these jigsaw pieces together. When you understand what each piece means and how it relates to other pieces, you can work towards a complete picture of a healthy horse. This is what I want to share with you. Let's discover the pieces that can help our horses and learn about the importance of these when considering the whole horse.

Many natural therapists who in the past have only ever treated human clients are now being approached to treat animals. Working with animals is a rewarding experience, and it appeals to many therapists who want a change. As a natural therapist I am often interacting within a triangle of communication formed by the animal, the owner and myself. This triangle could become weak if I was to enter into judgement of the owner—it is much more satisfying to be able to enhance the relationship between the owner and his or her animal by giving positive input.

Veterinary Surgeons and Natural Therapists— two distinctly different pieces of the puzzle

Under most legislation, only a qualified veterinary surgeon on the appropriate register is legally able to diagnose any health problems your horse may have. This part of the law is very clear. As a natural therapist, I am often called in as 'the last resort'. At this point I'm often asked 'What's wrong with my horse?' but this is a question I must avoid answering, instead referring the owner to a vet.

The protection granted by this legislation is a valuable safeguard for every horse owner. Working with animals is difficult, as they are not able to verbalize how they feel. Your veterinary surgeon is trained to follow a disciplined line of thought that bears this in mind. A veterinary surgeon is therefore the most qualified person to find any health problems and provide answers to your questions. As a natural therapist I may offer suggestions, but always with the proviso: 'Ask your vet'. Therapists usually inform their clients that they are not allowed to give a diagnosis and then focus on things that may be secondary to the veterinary surgeon's observations.

As the horse's owner you may not agree with your vet's diagnosis, but don't pressure a natural therapist to provide the diagnosis that you think is correct. In this case you should search out another veterinary surgeon's opinion until you are satisfied with a diagnosis. Remember whenever you find your horse has a health problem and you need to look at the jigsaw puzzle of his health, the first piece always lies in the domain of your veterinary surgeon. There may be many people making a guess at the illness or imbalance your horse may be suffering from, and offering their advice. This can often point you in the right direction—a discussion of a perplexing condition with your vet—but never trust something as valuable as your horse's health to the self-confessed 'expert' from the stable block or local riding club.

Some veterinary surgeons do not accept the use of natural therapies on horses. In general this is not their fault, or something to be judgemental about, it is simply that they are not educated in the philosophy or the application of herbs or essential oils. Some veterinary surgeons are hostile to their use—others dismiss them. But there are also many veterinary surgeons who now acknowledge the possibilities to be explored. If natural therapies are already being used on your horse, or if you plan to administer natural therapies in conjunction with a veterinary surgeon's treatment, it is important that you advise your veterinary surgeon of this when he or she attends to your horse. It could have a crucial bearing on the diagnosis or on the prescription of pharmaceutical drugs.

Sometimes it is the horse owner who gently educates the veterinary surgeon about the benefits of natural remedies. Don't be too harsh on your veterinary surgeon if he or she shows little interest—though if your veterinary surgeon is dismissive or rude, seek out a vet who will work with you and not condemn you for using therapies that do not fall into the orthodox paradigm of veterinary medicine.

For all of us, the horse's welfare is the first consideration, always.

THE VETERINARY SURGEON—YOUR FIRST CALL

The role of your veterinary surgeon is to be the team leader when it comes to your horse's health. It is fair to expect your veterinary surgeon to work with you. You should feel comfortable enough to ask any questions; however, you also need to be observant and able to give a clear and accurate list of symptoms when asking your veterinary surgeon to assess your horse.

Cooperation between both you and your veterinary surgeon can help find the right answer to your horse's problem sooner. Get to know your horse on a physical health level. Record any changes you notice in your horse's appearance or behaviour. It is helpful to note changes in feed or training, any medications or vaccinations you have given, how often you have your farrier visit and any other professional attention you seek in regard to your horse.

Another useful way of recording your horse's development is by taking photographs on a regular basis. By comparing photographs you may notice when your horse first developed a problem, as we often don't notice problems developing when we spend time with our horses every day.

Often the way veterinary surgeons are trained leads them to perceive or consider worst possible scenarios. If your horse's ailment is minor, this approach allows your vet to eliminate nasty possibilities quickly. If your horse has a serious condition, though, your vet will be able to inform you early on about what you are dealing with.

In an emergency, always contact your veterinary surgeon immediately. Any suspected case of colic, for example, requires veterinary consultation. It is not worth jeopardizing your horse's life. A telephone call in the early stages of colic may see your horse eased of his symptoms with a simple solution. If you put off that telephone call by being indecisive, it could mean risky surgery is the only remaining option for your horse. It is worth having your veterinary surgeon show you how to take your horse's temperature, pulse and respiration rate. Having this skill means you could provide this information to your veterinary surgeon should he or she need to determine whether your horse is in need of emergency care.

The normal body temperature of a horse is approximately 38°C (100°F). To take a horse's temperature the thermometer is usually lubricated and inserted gently into the horse's rectum. This must be done with extreme care, and it is very important that your veterinary surgeon has shown you how to do this safely before you attempt to do it yourself. A horse's body temperature can vary slightly. It may be slightly higher in foals and yearlings, during the day or hot weather, after exercise, and in the presence of fever or infection. A mild fever is 38.5°C (102°F), a moderate fever 39.5°C (104°F) and a high fever is 40.8°C (105°F).

To take your horse's pulse you need to find one of the major arteries. The most easily located main arteries are those under the jaw, above the knee and behind the fetlock. When you take your horse's pulse, it is easier to count the number of beats occurring over 15 seconds and multiply this figure by four to get the number of beats per minute. Often when people attempt to count the pulse over a minute, they lose count or get confused. The average adult horse has an average resting heart rate of 28–48 beats per minute (bpm). This is faster in younger horses and can also be faster in mares than it is in stallions or geldings. Keep in mind that a very fit horse may have a slower resting heart rate.

Your horse's respiration rate is the number of times your horse either inhales or exhales per minute. Your veterinary surgeon can often use this to get an indication of your horse's stage of illness. The easiest way to determine your horse's respiration rate is to count the rise or fall of the flank or ribs. At rest, a healthy, relaxed adult horse will have a respiration rate of between 8–16 breaths per minute. Younger horses may have a resting respiration rate of between 12–20 breaths per minute. Exercise, hot weather, fever, shock and poor condition are all factors that may elevate the respiration rate.

Your veterinary surgeon will also find it useful if you can describe the mucosal colour inside your horse's mouth (particularly the underside of the lips and the gums).

Salmon-pink is a healthy, desirable colour, whereas any tinge of blue or purple indicates that your horse is not getting enough oxygen. Blotched colouring could be a possible toxic reaction, pale pink may mean anaemia, dark pink could mean dehydration (but don't confuse this with bright red, which indicates highly oxygenated blood from exercise), and yellow could indicate a kidney disorder or jaundice.

If you suspect your horse is ill or injured, list the warning signs that are causing you concern, then call your vet. With the above information your veterinary surgeon can prioritize how quickly he or she may have to get to you, and rearrange appointments if your horse's condition requires urgent attention.

Sometimes the cost of a consultation makes a horse owner reluctant to call out a vet. At least make a phone call and get a qualified opinion from a trained vet, who can then decide if a visit is necessary.

THE FARRIER—A NEED FOR SOUND FOOTING

In the event of a horse's lameness it is always best that a veterinary surgeon assesses your horse. There are many reasons why a horse may go lame. He may have a bruised foot, changes within the bones of the leg or soft tissue injuries. Your veterinary surgeon is always the best person to decide what is happening in this case. If you ask anyone other than a veterinary surgeon about a lame horse, you may be relying on incorrect information and cause more damage to your horse.

When a horse is lame, determine the cause by starting at the hoof and working your way up through a process of elimination. The old saying 'no hoof, no horse' is indisputable—never underestimate the importance of correct foot care.

There are many theories concerning how to trim a foot, what sort of shoes to use, or whether to just go barefoot. That is a decision to be made with each individual horse. If you don't think your horse's feet are important, remind yourself how it feels when you buy a pair of shoes that don't quite fit. Your feet hurt, you get blisters, you limp around, and you can't wait to rest your feet. To get this point across to a teenage client one day, I insisted that she borrow one of her mother's shoes and walk around the house for half an hour so she could feel what it would be like for her horse. When a horse's shoes are unsuitable or they have been left on for too long, the horse may develop corns or bruising. A horse can also get a bruised foot by standing on a stone, so be careful you don't automatically blame poor or incorrect shoeing. It is important for you to attend to any bruising, as an abscess may develop and this would mean your horse is out to rest until his hoof has healed.

When I massage a horse and find there is unevenness in the shoulders, very often I can note a difference between the two front feet. Sometimes it is a minor difference and can be corrected easily on the farrier's next visit. Other times it may be something that cannot be fully corrected, but the owner can work with his or her farrier over time to get the horse as even as possible. Other front feet imbalances may give your horse sore muscles over the point of the shoulder, chest or top front of his leg.

A horse that has soreness in his back or hips that is not easily resolved with massage often has problem feet. This can often be traced from the back to the stifle, then to the hock and down to the feet. When a horse has sore feet he may adapt the way he stands to change the weight distribution. If your horse is continually suffering a sore shoulder or hip, or back pain, do not forget to consider his feet and discuss them with your farrier.

Always be wary of making radical changes. One unfortunate incident I witnessed was at the 2000 Paralympic Games. A medal contender on a balloted horse went through stressful days worrying if her horse would be pronounced fit enough to ride after the owner had misread the guidelines set out by the organizers and did not have the horse shod two weeks before arriving at the equestrian centre. She decided to use the onsite farrier, who declared this horse's feet were all wrong. The farrier radically changed the way the horse's feet were trimmed, with the unfortunate result that the horse was laid up with sore feet throughout the competition. You can understand the panic the rider must have experienced after working for four years to get herself selected.

THE DENTIST—CHEWING OVER IDEAS

I am still surprised when owners know little about dental care for their horse. A well-cared-for mouth will make sure this piece of the jigsaw falls into place and contributes to the whole picture. Poor teeth can affect your horse's health by affecting the way chewed

food reaches the stomach for processing, or in some cases may see the horse not get enough digestible food. Teeth can also affect your horse's performance and behaviour.

One useful indicator is smelly breath. If your horse is storing stale food in his mouth, or if food is trapped there by misshapen teeth, he will have stale breath. If you recoil when your horse kisses you, it may be time for a visit from the horse dentist. Another sign is if your horse drops food from his mouth or obviously chews to one side. An indicator that your horse may not be able to chew his feed properly is seeing it undigested in his manure. Oats demonstrate this well.

If your horse moves away when you go to place the bit in his mouth or rub the side of his face, he may have sharp teeth that are cutting into his gums. If your horse begins to resist going on the bit, bending to one or both directions or throwing his head, get his teeth examined. If he begins to hang on the bit or is difficult to collect up, instead tucking in behind the bit leaving you with the sense of having nothing in your hand, this may also indicate a tooth is hurting him somehow. Also be suspicious if your horse begins to constantly mouth the bit while riding, or starts chewing anything within reach when in the stable.

Physical indicators of teeth trouble include a tight banding over the temporal mandibular joint behind the eye towards the jaw line. One of the auricular muscles (on his forehead and under his forelock) may also be more developed than the other, indicating that your horse only uses one side of his jaw when eating. I like to see a horse's teeth assessed yearly or every six months if possible.

THE SADDLER— HOW COMFORTABLE IS YOUR SADDLE?

A well-fitting saddle for your horse is as important as a pair of comfortable walking shoes for you. A saddle can create great discomfort for a horse and cause the development of unwelcome behavioural changes. Pain is often the reason a horse objects to something. Remember, horses are herd animals with a strong instinct to flee danger. Pain caused by a saddle may be equivalent to a predator attacking that part of the horse's body, so his natural reaction is to flee and not be a willing ride.

When you take the saddle off your horse's back after a ride, observe if there are any dry spots or patches of hair sitting awkwardly. Run the flat of your hand across your horse's back and see if you can feel any change in texture, heat or swelling specific to the odd areas. Sometimes a crinkling under your hand can indicate this area of skin is not getting enough blood flow, and this may be because the saddle

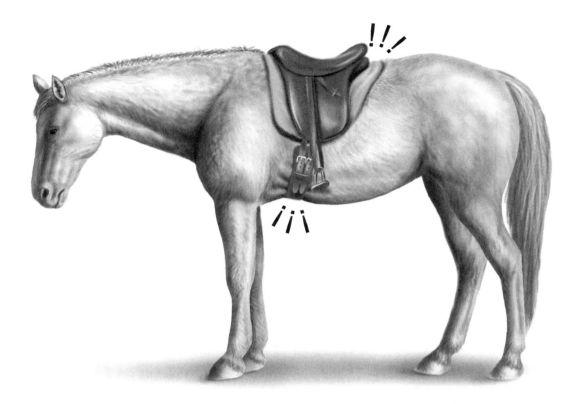

does not fit correctly. If your horse develops white spots on the wither or along his back, you may have ignored the warning signs for too long. Your saddle is definitely placing the wrong sort of pressure on your horse.

The saddle should sit flat on the back of your horse without rocking back and forth or sideways. It should fit comfortably without a saddlecloth, and there should be no need for padding or gel pads. Saddle blankets were only designed to absorb sweat and act as a slight shock buffer. It is important that the saddle fits your horse's ribcage so that, when riding, your weight is distributed evenly. If, however, the saddle feels like it is pinching into any area of the horse, it is too firm. If your horse begins to develop muscle spasms behind his shoulder blade or around his ribcage and girth line, your saddle may be pinching too tightly under the saddle flaps, especially if the horse has put on weight recently. The saddle should sit well back from the shoulder and rest along the Longissimus dorsi muscle that reaches along both sides of the back beside the spine.

Behavioural problems like nipping when girthing-up, rearing or pulling away when you go to mount, refusing to collect, and making poor canter transitions or disuniting when ridden, may all be signals that you need to check the fit of your saddle. Checking your saddle may not mean you need to purchase a new one; it may simply indicate a need to have your flocking checked and redone. One of the biggest frustrations I have with saddles is finding someone who will fit the saddle he or she wants to sell you. There are still some saddlers who will measure your horse and then return to fit the saddle, often in stages. If you find a saddler like this, then you have found a gem.

The saddle should also be comfortable for you. If you are not sitting comfortably your balance will be affected, and this in turn will affect how much your riding will 'ouch' your horse.

THE TRAINER OR INSTRUCTOR— AN INFLUENTIAL ROLE

Trainers usually focus more on educating the horse, while instructors place a greater emphasis on educating the rider. I have seen many trainers and instructors push on through physical problems, stating that the problem is simply a training issue. I believe the best approach is to ask a veterinary surgeon to check whether your horse is suffering from pain in his feet, mouth or back. If your horse continues to misbehave after the vet has ruled out possible medical problems, you probably do have a training issue. Always keep in mind, though, that horses rarely say 'I won't'. Usually horses are only too willing to do what we ask of them, but do not respond to training because they physically can't due to conformation or pain, or won't because they do not comprehend what is being asked of them.

I do not believe in a blanket approach to every horse. Horses are individuals, and as such they often require different keys to open up their potential. Gone are the days where cruelty was deemed a necessary part of getting a horse to submit. Today's training techniques aim to develop a partnership between you and your horse. Successful trainers and instructors encourage the rider to be able to recognize when his or her horse is prepared to give, and help develop a relationship where the horse will respond willingly to what is asked of him.

Trainers can be very helpful when you are working with a new horse. The best horsemen and horsewomen I have seen are body language experts. They watch and observe the horse and then use their body language and presence in a gentle way to get a willing response and a positive result. If your trainer needs gimmicks or refuses to let you participate with your own horse, beware. If a trainer does not show you respect, it is unlikely he or she will have respect for your horse.

If you decide to use a trainer choose one that makes you feel good and likes your horse. You should also make sure that the techniques the trainer teaches you can be applied afterwards, when you are working with your horse on your own. Your aim is to work independently with your horse and not become dependent on your trainer.

If you are serious about your riding, you will need an instructor who will help you continue to progress through the levels as your own ability improves. Signs that you may initially interpret as a physical or behavioural problem in your horse (for example, resistance) can often be more accurately interpreted and corrected by an instructor. An instructor with a good eye will spot any faults in your riding that may be contributing to this resistance. For instance, you could be sllipping off to one side of the saddle or your hands could be saying one thing to the horse while your seat says another. With the help of an instructor or trainer you can quickly eliminate a sloppy right side or a rigid rein, allowing you and your horse to move forward with your style of riding.

I often work with trainers, instructors and owners and find that—if a horse is suffering with a recurrent muscular problem that doesn't respond to my massage—it may be due to the rider's position on the horse or a weakness the rider has in his or her own body.

YOU, THE OWNER

All the professionals already mentioned in this chapter play a key role and hold a vital piece of the jigsaw puzzle that is your horse's health. It is important that you are able to communicate your needs to them and work with them to achieve the healthiest outcome for your horse. Veterinary surgeon, farrier, dentist, natural therapist, saddler and trainer—you need them all. Their jobs are highly specialized and horse owners do not serve their horses well by dabbling in these areas in a do-it-yourself manner. It is worth educating yourself, though, so you can converse with these professionals. Be fair to any natural therapist you turn to for advice—do not ask people who are not veterinary surgeons to diagnose your horse's health. They can offer an opinion and work with what is presented to them by your horse, but if the horse does not respond to physical therapy or natural supplements, you must get a veterinary surgeon's diagnosis.

What this book can do is add another dimension to the way you care for your horse. I have chosen natural therapies and listed natural remedies that you can use on your own horse. In each chapter I have listed helpful herbs or homeopathic remedies that you can use in most situations. However, if you find you need to take the treatment further, please consult a specialist health care professional.

When working with any professional, you and your horse have a right to be treated with respect; however, this goes both ways. Don't verbally attack a veterinary surgeon because he or she doesn't understand how a herb can help your horse. If you want your veterinary surgeon to accept that you are using herbs with your horse, educate him or her on the properties and benefits of those herbs.

We are all learning as we grow in our understanding of horses. As a wise old stockman told me, people who think they know all about horses rarely know anything. Horse people who are always learning will realize they have a lot more learning to do, even after working with horses for fifty years. Here I will share with you what I have learned so far. I intend to keep adding to these pages for the next fifty years, and I hope you regard this as a starting point when it comes to using natural therapies with your horse.

Listen to your horse

Now having said all of the above, here is a simple secret about horses: Your horse knows when and where he hurts and when someone is not treating him properly. Listen to your horse and remember that actions speak louder than words when it comes to the equine world. If you pull on the reins and he fights you, is he really fighting you or showing you his mouth is sore? It is unwise to presume your horse is fighting you, because a healthy, happy horse is usually only too willing to give.

Being a flight animal, your horse reads the body language of those around him and picks up many subtle hints of communication that we humans often miss. If your horse refuses to behave for a certain farrier, or becomes difficult to handle when the chiropractor comes back to check on him, take note and question how this person handles your horse. Your horse's responsiveness should improve with each visit of a massage therapist, trainer or anyone you entrust with your horse's welfare. Initially a horse may be agitated during his first massage or when tasting his first dose of herbs, but if he feels better and likes the way he is treated, then he will welcome the next opportunity to feel good. Another therapist once told me a story about a rough chap from the Australian bush who, after claiming to work on horses with some form of physical therapy, asked her how to get near them again for the second treatment! This clearly illustrates that horses know what is right and proper, and what is not.

Don't ignore signs that seem incidental. Often when I attend to a horse, he will nibble an area that needs addressing or push a body part towards me. Nine times out of ten, something there needs to be addressed. I was once asked to massage a racehorse that had inexplicably lost form. The manager was concerned about the horse and knew that something was wrong, though several veterinary examinations had failed to find the cause. The manager was very fond of this horse and went to watch his racing assessment. As the horse walked past, he appeared to hold his offside fore hoof up to the manager. This was reason enough for the manager to request another examination, this time with a specific focus on that leg. Happily, the root of the problem was found—a chipped sesamoid bone in the offside fetlock.

NATURAL IS NOT ALWAYS SAFE

Pardon? Yes, you read correctly—natural is not always safe. Please do not blindly assume that something is safe for your horse just because it derives from a plant or nature. Before the development of modern-day pharmaceuticals, many of the herbs used by veterinary surgeons were not safe and were in fact strong purgatives or narcotics that often caused the death of the horse. Because the general role of the horse was different in that era—a menial necessity used for transport and labour— veterinary surgeons were under pressure to administer dramatic treatment, get a fast recovery, and get the horse back to work as soon as possible. This treatment sought to violently expel the symptoms and induce a 'heroic' response, rather than simulta- neously dealing with the problem and strengthening the horse's whole body. Veterinary medicine and knowledge have come a long way since then, and today professionals use much gentler herbs.

Modern herbal practices, however, focus on the use of gentle herbs that act in a more systemic way and are kinder to the horse when administered with due care. Herbs are a valuable tool and have an important role to play in the health care of your horse. The philosophy of herbalism seeks to build and nurture the horse's state of health and can be used to treat specific symptoms or to treat the whole body in order to prevent illness. Just remember to exercise sound knowledge and due care when using herbs and essential oils, as they have a strong physiological action on any human or horse body.

Precautions with herbs

Some sceptics argue that herbs are not scientifically tested. In a sense the herbs have been tested—through many centuries of folk use. Today we can analyze herbs to identify their major constituents; however, the synergistic effects of these constituents can make results erratic. The conditions under which the herb has been grown can determine the potency and the relative proportions of the active constituents within the plant. Therefore test results of the concentrations of those constituents can be inconsistent, and it is difficult to standardize doses.

Many people refer to herbs by their common name, which can lead to confusion. It is important that you know the botanical name of a herb before you use it on your horse. For example, the common name 'milk thistle' may refer to completely different plants depending on which country you live in and which books you read. *Silybum marianum* (sometimes known as St Mary's thistle) is a popular remedy for liver problems and is often called milk thistle. *Sonchus oleraceus* (sometimes known as sow thistle) is eaten in salads in Europe and fed to budgerigars, but it is also commonly called milk thistle. See how confusing it can be?

Never harvest and use a plant—on either your horse or yourself—that you cannot positively identify. Many herbs have look-alike relatives that are actually extremely toxic weeds. Nor should you pick plants from alongside heavily travelled roads to use on your horse. These plants are almost certainly polluted with exhaust fumes, and are not healthy.

Whether herbs are fresh or in a dried form often determines their potency. For example, Skullcap (*Scutellaria laterifolia*) is a herb that is only effective if you use a fresh plant tincture. Few people realize the properties of Skullcap are greatly reduced if a dried plant is used to obtain the fluid extract, or if they use capsules of dried plant matter. Garlic (*Allium sativum*) is a good winter herb as it strengthens the immune system; however, raw Garlic can irritate a sensitive gut. Dried, granulated Garlic is preferable to raw Garlic, which can irritate the sensitive gut wall of a horse. While some studies have shown that long-term use of raw Garlic can cause anaemia in small dogs, no similar studies have been done on horses.

Herbs are drugs. When herbs are selected properly, the risk of dangerous side effects, drug interaction and other hazards is very small. However, it is important that you know all the actions of any herb that you use on your horse. For example, diuretic herbs have the potential to deplete your horse's stores of potassium, and the body system may need to be buffered with a high potassium herb or feed.

Precautions with essential oils

Your horse's skin may react to some of the skin irritants in essential oils that only tingle your own skin. Water actually increases the irritability of essential oils to the skin, so if your horse begins to have an adverse reaction to essential oils you have applied to him, use plain oil or milk to relieve the skin. The essential oils Peppermint and Orange are both very irritating to the skin in water, so these are best avoided in any wash downs for your horse—or for that matter in a bath for yourself.

Different horses can react differently to skin applications. Thoroughbreds seem to be the most sensitive, being what is often termed 'thin-skinned'. Furthermore, chestnut-coloured thoroughbreds appear to be more sensitive than bays, while grey horses generally seem to have the least sensitivity. Avoid using citrus oils on grey horses, though, as they are more prone to photosensitivity. This is especially true of Bergamot oil, which was responsible for the perfume stains on many sun-bronzed people during the 1970s. It is important that you always use a good quality vegetable oil as the 'carrier' for your essential oil (see page 111). The olive oil from your kitchen will be too acidic for this purpose and could irritate your horse's skin.

Herbs as drugs in competition

Often competitors who would like to use illegal, performance-enhancing drugs which show up in tests at competitions (for example, Federation Equestre Internationale level competitions or on the racetrack) use herbs as an alternative. However, many of the herbs one would select to replace steroidal compounds, painkillers or anti-inflammatories contain similar constituents to these drugs.

Responsible herbal medicine suppliers and practitioners are aware of this and will explain it to their customers—but it is the owner's responsibility to ensure the products do not test positive. Ignorance is no defence with most ruling bodies. Laboratory drug test results only identify the presence of a constituent in your horse's body, and do not differentiate between sources. For example, salicylic acid will test positive regardless of whether you have used an aspirin or Willow bark. No matter what the source is, it is illegal to use certain substances.

Another risk you must be aware of before using herbal preparations and essential oils on a competition horse is that they may contain substances that can 'mask' the presence of prohibited drugs. Laboratories test for such masking agents, which are just as illegal as the substances they can conceal. 'Vicks Vapour Rub', for example, can't be used on a competition horse because its camphor content can mask the presence of other drugs in a drug test. Many essential oils contain camphor.

Liniments that contain Eucalyptus, Peppermint or Rosemary should be avoided close to a competition. All are considered to be performance enhancing by the associations that adhere to FEI regulations, and will show positive in a test. Some liniments also contain camphor and menthol, which would test positive as masking agents.

Complementary and adjunctive

Always be mindful of any drugs your veterinary surgeon has prescribed or treated your horse with. Check with both your veterinary surgeon and herbalist to ensure that any herbs you intend to use will not be antagonistic to your veterinary surgeon's treatment of your horse. Some herbs and essential oils (such as Juniper and Grapefruit) detoxify and purify the bloodstream. Avoid using these essential oils if your horse is being treated with pharmaceutical drugs, as the essential oils may flush the drugs out of your horse's system before they have performed their function.

Upon discovering natural therapies, many people become evangelical with their newfound knowledge. This approach is dangerous, particularly when natural therapies are being used on horses. For one thing, you may not have enough knowledge to recognize symptoms that mean you've chosen the wrong herb and be able to administer another herb to remedy the situation. As humans we have the ability to realize that a certain herb we have treated ourselves with may, for example, have upset our bowel function. We can then find ourselves another remedy to ease the discomfort. Your horse can't yell out from the stable, though, and tell you when your herbal treatment has given him a tummy ache and he needs a soothing, mucilaginous herb instead.

The best way to use natural therapies on your horse is to incorporate them into his routine and to use them only as an adjunctive to any veterinary care. Again, it is vital that you inform your veterinary surgeon of any herbs you are using on your horse, and it is always essential you have your veterinary surgeon do any diagnosis of your horse. Veterinary surgeons are the only ones qualified to do so.

Now you have been warned severely. Natural remedies can be very useful in helping you and your horse achieve a happier and healthier life together, but they are still medicine. Just because they may work more slowly than traditional medicine doesn't mean they are any less potent. Our horses are much too valuable to experiment on.

What natural remedies can do for your horse

Let us look at what we can achieve with the therapies offered in this book. After you have consulted with your veterinary surgeon and been given a diagnosis which rules out any serious disease states, you can then decide if the use of natural therapies is appropriate.

Therapies that fall under the banner of 'natural' do not employ the use of man-made products. Instead they draw on nature and natural life cycles to help the body to heal itself, or find a level where it can achieve optimum function. What most pharmaceutical products do is suppress symptoms so that it appears your horse is cured or better. This is necessary in an emergency situation, and will often save your horse's life where natural therapies alone could not. It is also essential in the treatment of chronic disorders where symptoms need to be suppressed before the problem can be managed. Once the symptoms have been brought under control there is often no need to continue with long-term drug use, and this is where natural therapies can come into play. Their function will help the horse continue the healing process and restore tone to the whole horse.

This book explores the use of herbs, homeopathic remedies, Bach flower remedies, essential oils and massage to treat a horse's health problems, and also discusses how our own thoughts and emotions interplay with our horse's health.

Herbs are useful for addressing problems that have established themselves in your horse's body. The herbs discussed in this book are slow and steady in their action with an emphasis on a gentle action. Homeopathy is a therapy that can address both chronic and acute states of illness. This book will look primarily at homeopathic first-aid remedies, to treat acute states. Chronic conditions are more complex and need the discernment of a professional. When you reach the stage where you feel comfortable and proficient with the use of these first-aid remedies on your horse, you may wish to explore homeopathic remedies that are suited to long-term use. In this case I suggest you begin by consulting a professional.

Bach flower remedies are used to relieve underlying emotional states of diseases. They can be used immediately after an incident occurs, or to peel back emotional layers of an old 'stuck' behaviour which may be the root cause of a chronic disease state or stubborn training issue. Essential oils can be used to treat physical conditions and overcome any emotional memories that may be blocking the development of your working relationship. Massage provides you with a physical tool to help your horse overcome muscular injuries or conformational faults that may be restricting his movement, thereby improving his performance. The correct application of your hands can also create a closer relationship between you and your horse, build your horse's emotional trust and draw his affection. This book also looks at the environment you create for your horse and how, together with your own thoughts and emotions, it can affect your horse's health.

We will then address the common health conditions and behavioural problems many horse owners will be faced with. Together we will discover how these approaches and philosophies provide a layout of the final jigsaw pieces. When all the pieces of your horse's health that have been discussed in this book have been discovered, considered and placed in the correct part of the picture, you may still find that there is a piece missing here and there. However, by this point, you will be well equipped to search further.

The key to you and your horse enjoying a healthier lifestyle with natural therapies is common sense. Do yourself a favour and treat the therapies as additional, complementary suggestions to what is already available to you through consultation with your veterinary surgeon. If you explore this book with a modicum of common sense, you will enjoy the experiences that natural therapies have to offer both you and your horse.

HERBS

HERBS AND HORSES

Using medicinal herbs with horses is not new. The use of herbs has been well documented in old veterinary and herbal texts. Traditionally, many cultures have used herbs to keep their horses healthier and happier. Several Native American tribes used Echinacea for treating viral infections in horses, while the Romany Gypsies of Europe were accomplished horsemen and women who combined their training methods with the use of herbs. In Ancient Greece, Xenophon noted the importance of feeding an overworked horse a barley surfeit (a mash of barley and green herbs) to restore the horse's strength.

Veterinary science has progressed greatly in the last fifty years, but prior to this veterinary surgeons relied heavily on herbs, particularly those with a strong narcotic effect such as opium and cannabis (see page 22). Today's herbalists focus on using herbs that have a gentle action, and have moved away from treating the symptoms to treating the whole horse.

Herbs are largely misunderstood in today's world of quick fixes. They cannot be prescribed for a horse in the same way that phenylbutazone can be. The philosophy of herbalism aims to gently restore the horse's body to good health.

The best ways to use herbs to help your horse are, firstly, in a preventative programme if your horse has a predispositon to a specific complaint. Secondly, herbs can be used to restore tone and integrity to the body after an illness and to aid your horse's recovery. Thirdly, herbs may be used in a nutritional approach to managing a long-term or chronic illness or condition. Herbs can also be used in acute situations, but only after your veterinary surgeon has made a diagnosis and prescribed the necessary 'quick fix'. Then, with the horse safely out of the crisis, you can use herbs to restore homeostasis in your horse's body.

The use of herbs in health care is often maligned through ignorance. It is often much easier for people to criticize due to a lack of understanding, than it is for them to be open to learning. Natural health care is a philosophy that must be embraced in its entirety, not taken in dribs and drabs in the hope of sedating a horse or masking lameness. To get the most out of herbs, start broadening your perceptions on life. If your horse shows a symptom that worries you, firstly get it diagnosed by a veterinary surgeon, then begin to look at the bigger picture.

Generally, the aim of herbalism is to cleanse the body of the irritant causing the state of disease and then restore tone to the whole organism. One mistake I often see, however, is people relying on their knowledge of how herbs interact with humans to decide what herbs to use on a horse. Please do not make this mistake. Many herbs that are safe to use on humans can cause harm when used on horses. If you are in any doubt, consult your veterinary surgeon or equine specialist—do not rely on information written for another species.

Make sure you know what you are treating and never diagnose a horse yourself—your veterinary surgeon must do this. If you see any reaction that is not pleasant for your horse, stop administering the herb immediately. Also be aware that if you are giving your horse more than one herb, this combination or the individual herbs may interact with pharmaceutical medications. Do not underestimate the power of herbs, and only use herbs that are classified as having a gentle action.

How herbs work

It is not always clear how herbs cause changes in the body. It is the combination of all the constituents of a herb that makes its action complete. Scientific analysis can isolate active constituents within the herb, though this only gives a partial picture of the herb's effect. Scientists tend to disregard the interaction of all the constituents of the herb, including the minor ones, and overlook the unique character and spiritual nature of that herb, which contribute to its healing properties.

Centuries of use in many cultures have validated the use of herbs today. The 1900s saw a developing mistrust of anything natural emerge. With the beginning of this new century, we have an opportunity to combine the use of modern pharmaceuticals with the ways of old. This way we will benefit from thousands of years of collective knowledge and not just a hundred years of clinical trials.

Herbs can be allocated to certain classes of actions, according to their main active constituents. These active constituents have been duplicated synthetically in pharmaceutical drugs such as aspirin, which is based on salicylic acid, a major constituent of Willow bark.

Scientific isolation and duplication of individual constituents of herbs has done some damage to the reputation of medicinal herbs. Scientists have looked at the active constituents of a herb and extracted the constituent they believe to rule the action of that herb. Then, when this active constituent does not work as effectively when isolated from its other constituents, or when it causes serious side effects, blame is placed upon the original herb. This is not fair. Mother Nature designed herbs to be of benefit to man and horse. If the whole plant is used as a raw herb, it rarely creates the same problems its active constituents alone may create. Willow bark is again a good example. Scientists have isolated one of the main constituents of Willow bark to create today's quick-fix pain relief. Long-term use of this constituent results in humans and horses developing ulcers and kidney problems, whereas healers since the Middle Ages in fact prescribed Willow bark to heal stomach ulcers. This is because they used the entire herb, and the synergy of all constituents within the herb acting on the body together creates the greatest benefits.

Many herbs contain constituents that, when isolated and used intensely in scientific experiments on rats, can cause cancer. This has seen many valuable medicinal herbs listed as scheduled substances and restricted in their use. Again this is to the benefit of a few parties that have something to gain by these herbs being unavailable to the general public. An example of this is Comfrey, which contains pyrollizidine alkaloids. When isolated, these alkaloids are toxic to the liver and encourage cancer. However, by eating certain brands of peanut butter or honey, you are consuming more pyrollizidine alkaloids than you would in a prescribed dose of Comfrey.

Common sense has to prevail when using herbs medicinally, as some are toxic for horses or can have serious adverse reactions. If you stay within recommended doses and consult your veterinary surgeon to have your horse's condition diagnosed correctly before you begin any herbal treatment, herbs will only enhance the quality of your horse's life.

I use herbs primarily in two ways with horses: in a dried or powdered dose to treat physical problems and as a fluid extract administered in drop dosages to treat the underlying spiritual cause of the physical problem. Sometimes only one approach is needed; at other times a combination of both is required.

How much do I give my horse?

The doses given for each herb listed in this chapter will provide an optimum result. These doses are based on the suggested amount that may be safely given to a full-sized horse weighing about 600kg. When giving any herbs to a small horse, reduce the dose by a half or even two-thirds for a small pony.

You can use herbs in several different forms, and in many instances the form you use will depend on what is readily available to you. Be careful if texts written for human therapy are your only source of reference, as the effects of many herbs can vary greatly between horses and humans. You will discover that many different methods other than those mentioned in this book are advocated for using herbs to treat illness. Each is valid in its application and philosophy, and it takes a wise person's careful consideration to decide how these can be applied to horses.

Herbalism can become a way of life, especially when herbs are incorporated into a nutrition-based lifestyle. Decisions have to be made about whether you will use alcohol-based extracts or the dried herb. In order to avoid using alcohol, you may decide to use cider vinegar to extract the active constituents from the plant matter, or you may decide to purchase extracts where glycerin has been used to extract the active constituents. Generally it becomes a philosophical decision. Some herbalists will never use an alcohol-based tincture for fear of causing fermentation in the gut of a horse, or because they do not believe alcohol is a suitable carrier. Other herbalists insist that alcohol is necessary to trigger a catalytic response within the body.

For the purposes of this book, written for the horse owner who wants to be able to help his or her horse, my focus is on the use of fresh or dried herbs—either cut, powdered or in a hot water infusion. The disadvantage of using some herbs this way is that the active constituents may be weak or not soluble in water, and a stronger substance will be required to extract what you need. In this situation it is safer to consult a professional and obtain fluid extracts or tinctures.

One of the easiest ways to get your horse to take herbs is by making an infusion or a decoction. An infusion is simply a cup of tea made from the soft parts of a plant (the leaves or flowers). If you have limited resources you can purchase the tea bags of specific herbs from a health food store. You can make your infusion by simply pouring boiling water over the fresh or dried plant matter as you would when making yourself a cup of tea. Cover with a tight lid and steep for 5–20 minutes. This short exposure to heat minimizes any loss of volatile elements so the benefits of the herb are not destroyed. Then strain, place in a container to take up to the stables and simply add 1–2 cupfuls to your horse's feed. Infusions can be taken over a period of days; however, it is best to make the infusion fresh each day. The cumulative daily dose ranges from 1–4 cupfuls, depending on the potency of the plant and severity of your horse's condition.

A decoction is similar, but is used to prepare denser plant material. Take the root, bark or seed of a herb you need and simmer in a pot for about 20–30 minutes. Steep for a further 15 minutes to draw out the active constituents. It is important you do not boil the mixture, as this may damage the medicinal properties of the herb. Strain the mixture and administer it to your horse as you would an infusion.

If you have enough of the fresh plant available, you can make a juice. This is usually done in a blender using leafy herbs. The easiest way to use fresh herbs to treat your horse is to simply add a large handful of leaves to his feed (do not do this with the root or woody parts of a herb, though).

When it comes to using dried herbs, the dose depends on the cut of the herb. If the herb is cut (i.e., chopped in small pieces) and looks like potpourri which is made from the leaves and/or flowers, you can usually administer the herb by the cupful. A cupful of dried herbs is usually the maximum dose, though you should always be guided by the dose recommendations for each individual herb; the maximum dose for some of the stronger herbs is much less than a cupful. Whether you are using only one dried, cut herb, or a combination of dried, cut herbs, the total dose you can add to your horse's feed is 1 cup. Store the herbs in an airtight container and add the cupful to your horse's feed up to three times a day depending on the severity of your horse's symptoms and the strength of the herbs you have chosen.

Dried roots or bark need to be ground into a powder so your horse can digest them safely. Just a teaspoonful or a tablespoonful of the powdered herb will have a therapeutic effect on your horse.

Do not combine dried, cut herbs with powdered herbs, as it is very difficult to keep the proportions of the mixture consistent and keep track of the concentrations safely.

Some horses don't like it when you add a mixture of dried herbs to their feed. You may need to halve the dose initially and let the horse get used to the taste of the herb. Increase the dose over a couple of days as the horse gets used to his new feed, until you reach the therapeutic level.

Fluid extracts are herbal preparations made by percolating the plant matter in a 40 per cent alcohol solute. The most common prescription is what is referred to as a 1:1 FE. This means that every millilitre of fluid from your bottle is equivalent to one gram of the herb. There is strong debate as to whether it is safe to give horses alcohol-based products, and each side of the debate is emphatic that it is correct. I believe most horses tolerate alcohol in very small doses, and that it can act as a useful catalyst to trigger the body's use of the herb and assimilate the benefits of the herb. However, the dose must be accurate, so using alcohol extracts is best left to professionals. These days you can obtain many herbs which are made in a similar way, but contain glycerin instead of alcohol. These preparations are referred to as glycetracts. They are used on small animals that cannot tolerate alcohol (such as cats and dogs) and on people who have a moral or physical objection to alcohol.

Another method that may be used with horses is to steep the dried herb in apple cider vinegar. This may be particularly useful for an older horse or a horse that has been neglected and is having trouble assimilating the nutrients from its feed or herbs. Apple cider vinegar acts as a catalyst for the herbs that are to be assimilated, much like alcohol, but the preparation method is more time-consuming. Soak the dried herbs in apple cider vinegar overnight. Do not strain. It is important that the mixture stays fresh and does not ferment, so do not make up more mixture than you can use over a 3-day period.

A note on using more than one herb at once

The recommended dose for each individual herb in this chapter is the amount that may be used when no other herb is being given at the same time. When herbs are used in combination, it produces a synergistic effect that increases the dynamic properties of those herbs, so smaller amounts of each herb should be used.

When combining dried, cut herbs that each have an individual recommended dose of 1 cupful, combine the herbs in equal parts but only to a total amount of 1 cupful. If one of the cut herbs within the blend has a dose recommendation of ½ a cupful, keep the proportion of this herb to half the amount of the other herbs being used.

When combining a selection of herbs where one herb is obtained from bark or a root, and therefore must be used in a powdered form, it is best to use the powdered form of all the herbs you have selected so they can be combined evenly in the blend. Combine the herbs in equal amounts, but only give up to 1–2 tablespoonfuls of the blend of herbs in total as the dose.

If you ever feel that you need to increase a dose beyond the recommended guidelines, remember it is safer and more desirable to increase the number of times a day you give the recommended dose than it is to increase the size of the dose. You should rarely need to increase any herbal treatment to three times a day unless you really need to boost the action of the herbs. Never give your horse more than three doses a day without consulting a professional.

Using herbs externally—poultices and infused oil compresses

Herbs do not always have to be administered internally to benefit your horse. Wounds, swelling or muscle soreness can be treated with a poultice or an oil infused with herbs.

To make a poultice you can use dried or fresh cut herbs, but don't apply the plant matter directly to the skin. First mix the cut herbs with enough hot water to soften them. Place the wet herbs in the centre of a large, clean piece of gauze, folding the sides of the fabric inwards to enclose the herbs and stop them falling out. The poultice should be warm when placed on the horse, but check that it's not too hot before you do this. If you are treating a leg the poultice can be bandaged in place and left on overnight. If you are treating a part of the body that cannot be bandaged, hold the warm poultice in place until the temperature has lowered to body temperature, then moisten again with hot water (but take care not to burn your horse).

A poultice can also be made using powdered herbs. To do this, select enough powdered herb to cover the area on the gauze, add a small amount of boiling water to the herb to make a paste, then spread the paste on the gauze and bandage to hold against the horse.

As an alternative to a poultice, you can apply an infused oil compress, which is less messy as you do not have to contend with plant matter or paste. Note that infused oils are different to the essential oils used in aromatherapy. To make an infused oil, take fresh herb flowers such as Chamomile or plants such as Chickweed, place them in an airtight container and cover the fresh plant with a good quality olive oil. After about 3 days, strain the oil. Make a compress by dipping a piece of gauze or soft fabric into the infused oil and apply as you would a poultice.

Herbs to avoid using on horses

There are some herbs which are commonly and safely used for human consumption, though they are dangerous to give to your horse. Never presume that a herb is safe for your horse to ingest simply because it is safe for you.

A popular herb for managing stress in humans is St John's wort (*Hypericum perforatum*). This herb contains a toxic constituent called hypericin. Once ingested, this constituent is spread through the body via the circulatory system. While it is unlikely that humans will have an adverse reaction to this herb, horses can have a severe reaction—with symptoms including photosensitivity and peeling skin conditions that are extremely uncomfortable, slow to heal and prone to infection. The horse often rubs constantly until his skin is raw. If your horse grazes on St John's wort, or if you accidentally feed it to him, he may suffer a loss of appetite, mild fever and diarrhoea, and his gait may become irregular. In extreme cases a horse can suffer blindness or go into a coma.

Clovers are also toxic to horses. White clover (*Trifolium repens*) can cause laminitis, so if your horse begins to display tenderness, swelling or inflammation around the hooves, check for clover in his paddock. Aliske clover (*Trifolium hybridum*) contains toxic nitrates and can cause blindness, depression and severe nephrosis as well as affecting your horse's gait and triggering photosentivity. If a sensitive horse consumes enough of these first two types of clover, your vet may need to treat him for colic. Red clover (*Trifolium pratense*) can be fed in moderation and not cause harm. However, if a horse ingests this clover over a period of time, he may start slobbering and experience digestive problems. It can even induce abortion in mares. When mixed with other grasses in hay, this clover is the first to go mouldy, creating even more problems to deal with.

Melilot (*Melilotus alba*) is closely related to clover. It contains chemicals such as dicoumarol and melilotside that may be responsible for anaemia and haemorrhage in horses.

Buckwheat (*Fagopyrum esculentum*) has historically been used to add bulk to pig feed, and some manufacturers have used this idea to extend horse products. Buckwheat has caused photosensitivity in animals that are exposed to sun or have light-coloured skin. All parts of the plant are toxic to horses; the toxic component is fagopyrin, which may cause blistering or peeling of the skin.

Horsetail (*Equisetum arvense*) is a herb I have seen suggested elsewhere as a horse herbal remedy. This is a concern because the plant contains thiaminase, which causes a thiamine deficiency in horses. Toxic levels are higher in young green plants than in older mature plants, and younger horses are more likely to be affected. Hay can easily contain horsetail grass and, if fed to your horse for about 2 weeks, symptoms such as weakness, staggering, muscle problems and diarrhoea would appear. If you see any of these symptoms, stop feeding the suspect hay and call your veterinary surgeon. Death may result if the symptoms are left unchecked.

Wild and cultivated onions (*Allium* sp.) are to be avoided with horses. They are not as toxic to horses as they are to cattle, and you may only observe a loss of weight and decreased appetite. However, your horse would also have developed urine discolouration, muscle weakness, rapid breathing and a rapid heart rate.

Some herbalists use Cherry bark (*Prunus virginiana*) to flavour the more bitter cough and flu remedies. I personally disagree with this herb being used on humans and horses and strongly advise you not to use it. The leaves and seeds of this plant contain cyanogenetic glycosides and could release cyanide into your horse's bloodstream, causing death. In this instance death would be rapid with hardly any visible symptoms. Peppermint is a safe, pleasant tasting alternative to Cherry bark.

There are many herbs that may be used quite safely on humans, though they can cause serious illness or even death in your horse. Please ensure that your horse's herbalist does not prescribe herbs as though your horse is a human patient.

Horses (and, in some cases humans) may have severe reactions to caster bean, pokeroot, black walnut, white oak, bracken fern, the nightshade family, rhubarb, false hellebore, mistletoe, tobacco, yew, columbines, monkshood, poppies, lupins, hemp, rhododendron, foxglove, ragwort, lily of the valley, irises and some of the rue species, among others—so beware.

Herbs as drugs in competition

One of the most popular reasons for using herbs on a competition horse is to gain the 'nervine' effect that many herbs possess, which calms the horse. Some associations regard the use of herbs that have this quality as cheating, so check with the ruling body of your chosen riding discipline before using any herbs that are known to have a calming effect, such as Chamomile or Valerian. Willow bark, another herb that competitors often turn to, is anti-inflammatory and pain-relieving in its action. Its main constituent, however, is salicylic acid, which is the base for the pharmaceutical aspirin and is therefore a prohibited substance at FEI (Federation Equestre Internationale) events and racecourses.

Competitors must take extreme care if using herbs on their horse. Competition rules vary and are often unclear. For example, an FEI newsletter printed in 2000 suggested that the use of any reputedly calming substance would be considered unsportsmanlike, whether the substance was proved to be effective or not. Within the racing industry it is not always clear which herbs are banned and which ones are permitted and therefore safe to prescribe. The ruling bodies claim that if owners and competitors were openly informed as to what is banned and what is not, then the system would leave itself open to cheating. Unfortunately, observing the ways of human nature, I have to agree with them. But what they fail to understand is the philosophy of herbalism and its affiliated therapies. When the true philosophy is embraced by people who want to use herbs to benefit their horse, we do not have these problems. If more owners were to look beyond the next race or competition, and the ruling authorities were to understand when a lifestyle decision for the horse may not necessarily indicate 'cheating', there would not be a problem. Again, we have to get past the 'quick fix' or 'magic pill' mentality—then we may see a greater acceptance of herbs being used on competition horses. Until we reach this level of understanding en masse, you are entirely responsible for the herbs you choose to use on your competition horse and any illegal constituents they may contain.

Some herbal suppliers claim that their blends of herbs will not test positive if your horse is swabbed, when really they have no idea what will happen. Do not put your reputation at risk—do your own research. Herbs are drugs in terms of their action on the horse's body, and those that are stimulating, calming or even narcotic should be considered illegal in competition. Basically, most herbs fall into these three categories, so you must cease using herbs at least 1 week before a competition at this level. Herbs that have fat-soluble constituents take longer than a week to disappear from your horse's system. If there is a chance you may be tested in the lead-up to competition or during training, herbs may not be a viable option for you. You may be using Ginger as a harmless additive to your horse's feed, intending to ward away winter ills, without realizing that it is considered to be a stimulant at high-level competition. Ginger was in fact a popular additive used to 'pep' up a racehorse in the early 1900s. Before the sophistication of laboratory tests, racing officials would lift the tail of each competing horse and sniff for the scent of Ginger. Thankfully you have the protection of more reliable tests today if you find yourself challenged for using herbs which are prohibited substances.

Herbs including Valerian, Kava kava, Guarana, Peppermint, and even Chamomile are listed as banned substances with various horse associations. There is always a provisional clause to include any herb that shows a positive result, however, and any herb may be added to the list without notice.

Please rely on common sense when using herbs on a competition horse. I cannot guarantee that the herbs mentioned in this chapter will not test positive, as constituents that are currently permitted may be ruled illegal by racing boards or equestrian associations at any time.

The classified actions of herbs

Herbalists classify the herbs they use by their action on the body. When deciding what herb to use on a horse, they assess the level of healing or illness the horse has reached, then prescribe herbs to help the body get back to a state of balance. This state of balance is referred to as homeostasis.

The philosophical basis of herbal healing presumes a body, be it horse or human, is always trying to achieve homeostasis. Herbalists attempt to cleanse the body of what is creating the imbalance, then restore tone to the body, thus getting it back to its optimum operation.

As you read through the herbs presented in this chapter, you will come across terminology that refers to the action of the herb. Each individual plant has many different actions, and you will see different herbs listed in several categories—each of these actions may be altered by combining different herbs.

A guide to the terminology:

Adaptogenic	a herb that helps the body adapt to stress.
Alterative	also referred to as a blood purifier, this herb helps the metabolism of the body to utilize nutrition and eliminate wastes.
Analgesic	a herb that helps reduce pain.
Anthelmintic	a herb that discourages or expels intestinal parasites.
Astringent	a herb with a high tannin content, and a constricting action on tissue.
Anti-inflammatory	a herb with an action that helps reduce inflammation.
Anti-catarrhal	a herb that helps the body address excess mucus, usually from the respiratory tract.
Antispasmodic	a herb that relieves or prevents muscle cramps or spasms.
Bitter	a herb with a bitter taste that triggers digestive processes, and acts primarily on the liver.
Cardiac tonic	a herb that supports the heart and circulation.
Carminative	a herb that relieves gas and flatulence.
Demulcent	a herb that has a soothing effect on internal membranes.
Diaphoretic	a herb used to increase elimination of toxins through sweating.
Digestive tonic	a herb that aids digestion.

Diuretic	a herb that increases the flow of urine.
Emmenagogue	a herb that stimulates menstrual flow and the uterus. Herbs that have this action must never be given to pregnant mares.
Eliminative	a herb that encourages the body's eliminative functions.
Emollient	a herb that soothes when applied to the skin.
Expectorant	a herb that helps to remove excess mucus from the upper respiratory system.
Febrifuge	a herb that reduces fever.
Galactagogue	a herb that promotes lactation or the flow of milk from the breast.
Haemostatic	a herb that slows the flow of bleeding.
Hepatic	a herb that acts on the liver.
Nervine	a herb that tones and strengthens the nervous system.
Purgative	a herb with drastic laxative action, not recommended for use with horses.
Relaxant	a herb that appears to relax the whole body, not just mentally, but particularly in terms of visceral neuromuscular functions.
Sedative	a herb that will help to calm the nervous horse and also relieve tension throughout the entire body. (Sedatives can include antispasmodics and nervines.)
Stimulant	a herb that increases the ability of body function and potential in activity. Used indiscriminately, stimulants can cause adrenal overload and exhaust a horse.
Tonic	a nourishing, supportive and restorative herb that restores tone to the horse's system.
Vulnerary	a herb that promotes the healing of wounds and cuts.

THE HERBS

Listed below are some herbs that have been used safely with horses. Suggested doses are listed alongside. Please stay within these recommendations—more is not better, and what is recommended here will achieve results. Some herbs are not listed in this book because they are toxic to your horse (such as St John's wort, Blue cohosh or Horsetail). Others have been excluded because they have become rare and endangered, and thus are either very difficult to obtain or so expensive that most horse owners would find the cost prohibitive (such as Golden seal and False unicorn root, which were some of the most valuable herbs available to us for treating both horses and humans). Herbs that must be used fresh or as a tincture made from the fresh plant have been excluded as well, as it is often difficult to obtain fresh herbs. Skullcap (*Scutellaria laterifolia*) is one of these herbs. It is not easy for the novice to harvest Skullcap, and once it is dried it loses most of its actions.

I have listed the specific indication for each herb. This refers to a condition or situation that professionals associate most closely with the healing qualities of that herb. For example, St Mary's thistle is the herb of choice for any condition requiring liver support.

BLADDERWRACK KELP (*Fucus vesiculosus*)

SPECIFIC INDICATION: OBESITY ATTRIBUTED TO HYPOTHYROIDISM.

This demulcent herb is potent in its ability to balance the metabolism. If you are giving your horse a prepared feed that contains iodine, do not 'double dip' by adding Bladderwrack to his feed, as iodine is a major constituent of this herb. You can add Bladderwrack to the diet of any pony exiled to the diet paddock by slowly introducing the herb with a teaspoonful of the powdered herb in each feed for 3 days. Once the pony has acquired a taste for this herb, work up to a tablespoonful dose. When using Bladderwrack as a weight-loss helper, your pony's weight should stabilize within 6 weeks. If you don't see this result, seek veterinary assistance to ensure that no other medical condition is the root cause, and to devise a programme that will help.

For an overweight, full-sized horse you can give up to 2 tablespoonfuls of powdered Bladderwrack in each feed every day. It will condition your horse's coat and hooves and is an excellent spring supplement when your horse is shedding his winter coat.

Bladderwrack may be included in a blend of herbs to treat rheumatism in the older horse (see page 211). It also supports developing muscles in young performance horses beginning training, or performance horses resuming training at a higher level. A course of Bladderwrack added to your horse's feed after he has expelled a worm infestation helps rid your horse's intestines of remaining toxins and encourages a quick recovery.

BURDOCK (*Arctium lappa*)
SPECIFIC INDICATION: A CLEANSING ALTERATIVE IN TOXIC CONDITIONS.

Burdock is classed as a bitter herb, and it will stimulate your horse's digestion. I primarily use Burdock to treat skin conditions from the inside. If a skin condition does not clear up with topical applications, you need to cleanse the inner workings of your horse, including the blood, with herbs such as Burdock. You will find this approach useful with dry, scurfy skin conditions, eczema, or recurrent sores.

You do not need to use much of this herb to obtain results. As it is sourced from the root of the plant, use it in a powdered form so that your horse can assimilate it easily. Begin with 1 teaspoonful added once or twice a day to your horse's feed and, if necessary, increase the dose to 2 teaspoonfuls morning and night.

As with any bitter herb, reduce the dosage if your horse's bowels become loose. If your horse continues to show intolerance to the powdered herb, make a gentle decoction by placing a handful of the sliced root in 6 cupfuls of water, then pour 1 cupful of the strained fluid over his morning and evening feed.

Burdock has a mild diaphoretic action which assists in eliminating any build up of toxins via the skin, and disperses excess nervous energy in a hot horse.

CELERY SEED (*Apium graveolens*)
SPECIFIC INDICATION: RHEUMATOID ARTHRITIS WITH MENTAL DEPRESSION.

Celery seed has a warming effect on your horse's body. I once considered celery an old horse's herb until I worked with horses off the racetrack. If you are rehabilitating a thoroughbred prone to tying-up,

1 tablespoonful of bruised Celery seeds added to your horse's morning and afternoon feed is an excellent supplement. Many racehorses come off the track already showing signs of arthritic changes, despite their youth. Celery seed will help support this condition and will also help to cleanse your horse's body of the toxins remaining from drugs that were administered while your horse was a racehorse. Administer Celery seeds for at least the first 3 months after a horse has retired from the track.

An infusion of Celery seeds is useful in stimulating milk flow in the lactating (but not pregnant) mare. I usually discard the seeds if the infusion has a strong colour; though when I am treating an older mare showing signs of age, I include 1 tablespoonful of the seeds from the pot when pouring a cup of the tea onto her feed to help relieve joint stiffness.

One caution to observe is Celery seed's diuretic action—do not give this herb to a pregnant mare or a horse suffering a serious kidney disorder. When sourcing Celery seed ensure it is organically grown, as the seed sold for agricultural activity may be coated in a fungicide.

CHAMOMILE (*Matricaria chamomilla*)

SPECIFIC INDICATION: GASTRO-INTESTINAL DISTURBANCE ASSOCIATED NERVOUS IRRITABILITY.

Many people are aware of Chamomile's calming qualities. As a result, some associations are currently discussing whether these properties make it a prohibited substance—so take care if your horse is likely to be tested (see page 37).

This herb is useful for the horse prone to nervous colic. Adding a cup of strained Chamomile infusion to your horse's morning and night feed is one way to manage your horse's predisposition at stressful times. If making your horse a cup of tea is inconvenient, you can add a handful of dried flowerheads to each feed to achieve the same results. The strained infusion is also useful for the horse recovering from a colic episode, as it is gentler to a distressed gut when given in this form.

If you are using Chamomile to address your horse's nervousness and there is no history of colic, you can add the flowers from your brew to his feed as well.

Limit the use of this herb to a period of less than 3 months of continuous use. Chamomile has a strong action on the liver, which will need to be given a break to avoid a toxic reaction. Some horses may show signs of allergic reactions to the pollen from the flower heads—in this case, an infusion is the safest, most effective form to administer.

The cooled tea is very soothing when used as a wash for inflamed skin conditions.

CHICKWEED (*Stellaria media*)

SPECIFIC INDICATION: ASTRINGENT, SOOTHING TO SKIN CONDITIONS.

Chickweed is an excellent stomach tonic and a cheaper alternative for disturbed digestion when Slippery elm bark powder is difficult to obtain. The best time to give Chickweed to your horse is half an hour before feed time, as it soothes the intestinal tract and prepares it for digestion. It is a good herb to add fresh to your horse's feed when changing his diet, as it supports the intestinal environment and increases the absorption of nutrients.

Chickweed grows in abundance in most temperate areas and is best harvested fresh, when needed, as the whole plant. Simply collect a couple of handfuls and bruise the plant before offering it to your horse.

Externally you can apply infused oil of Chickweed to skin disorders or inflamed joints. Simply steep the leaves, stems and flowers of Chickweed in enough high quality olive oil (cold pressed and preferably organic) to cover it for 3 or 4 days. Strain and apply to the areas that would benefit. A Chickweed poultice will remove heat from an infected wound or injury and draw out poisons from swollen bites.

CLEAVERS (*Galium aparine*)

SPECIFIC INDICATION: LYMPHATIC CONGESTION THAT BENEFITS FROM DIURETIC AND ALTERATIVE HERBS.

This herb has traditionally been used to treat skin complaints, as it cleanses the blood to help the body find relief from eczema and greasy heel.

Cleavers can be easily grown in shady corners and is best added fresh by the handful to your horse's feed. It stimulates the lymphatic system, so a horse with an overload of lymph fluid or congested, swollen legs will benefit from this herb along with light massage techniques. If you can only access the dried herb, add 1 cupful of the cut herb or 2 tablespoonfuls of the powdered herb to your horse's feed daily.

It is a useful herb for the horse with a sluggish elimination system that develops tight muscles while in work, and for the horse prone to tying-up for an unknown reason. Because it helps the body eliminate toxins, it is also useful for horses with allergies.

Cleavers has a high silica content and can be given freely to your horse if he has a hoof abscess, or in a tonic formula to improve a dull coat or promote regrowth of the mane and tail.

COMFREY (*Symphytum officinale*)

SPECIFIC INDICATION: A SOOTHING DEMULCENT TO GASTRIC ULCERS. STIMULATES BONE REPAIR.

Comfrey has many useful qualities. A few crushed leaves can be added to your horse's feed to encourage cell growth after any injury. It will help the body heal broken bones, cartilage and connective tissue. A cooled infusion of Comfrey will also soothe internal ulcers or bleeding anywhere in the body—and will assist your horse if he is suffering from respiratory congestion, or recovering from a colic episode or a lifetime spent in the stressful world of racing. Very few racehorses escape this career without having developed an ulcer at some time.

Fresh leaves whisked in your food processor can make an effective poultice for damaged bones, arthritic changes in joints and haematomas.

You will need to grow this herb yourself, as its sale is restricted to topical applications. You can purchase Comfrey ointment, but Comfrey suffered an unfair propaganda campaign that left it much maligned and its availability restricted. If you are able to purchase the dried leaf, ½ a cup of the cut herb may be added to your horse's feed up to three times a day.

DANDELION (*Taraxacum officinale*)

SPECIFIC INDICATION: TOXIC LIVER AND DIGESTIVE CONDITIONS.

Adding a handful of fresh Dandelion leaves to your horse's feed throughout spring helps flush out any toxins that have accumulated over the cooler winter months. After any long rest this is an excellent herb to help get your horse's body back into work. The herb is also a useful springtime preventative for horses prone to flatulent colic, laminitis and tying-up. It cleanses the blood and rebalances your horse's metabolism by acting on the liver, helping him to adjust to the change of season.

The root is even more powerful than the leaf in its hepatic action. You can use it powdered and add up to 2 tablespoonfuls to your horse's feed daily. I find it extremely effective with horses recovering from an illness or a reaction to a vaccination, as well as the side effects of long-term pharmaceutical drugs. I make a decoction of the root daily, strain it (as I prefer the horse not to attempt to digest the root) and then pour it over his feed.

The white sap is said to be effective if applied to warts daily.

I advise against harvesting this plant yourself as it is difficult to distinguish between this herb and Catsear or Flatweed (*Hypochaeris* sp.), which is believed to contribute to stringhalt.

DEVIL'S CLAW (*Harpagophytum procumbens*)

SPECIFIC INDICATION: INFLAMED JOINTS AND CONNECTIVE TISSUE.

This herb has an unfortunate name, as the results owners get from using this herb are often described as miraculous. Devil's claw's anti-inflammatory properties make it useful for treating arthritic changes and degenerative joint diseases. This herb is also useful for the rehabilitated horse who has suffered tendon or ligament damage in the past. It will aid digestion and is useful for the horse who is adjusting to a new diet after a period of neglect.

The pain relieving action of Devil's claw is so effective, however, that you must take care that it does not mask a more serious problem underneath the pain you are relieving. It is a natural replacement to phenylbutazone; however, this is not always the wisest way to use herbs. Always consult your veterinary surgeon if the pain persists. This herb is very potent; always advise your veterinary surgeon if your horse has been given this herb within 48 hours of an examination, as it may affect his diagnosis.

Devil's claw will also address chronic muscle pain. If you are massaging your horse while administering this herb, though, the above warning applies; some spasms may be dulled and you may not notice painful sites.

As the qualities of this herb come from the root, use it in a powdered form and begin with 1 tablespoonful added to your horse's feed twice daily. If circumstances call for it, increase your horse's dose to 2 tablespoonfuls twice daily in feed, but do not do this for more than a week at a time.

Avoid using this herb with pregnant mares or on a horse you suspect has ulcers.

DONG QUAI (*Angelica senensis*)

SPECIFIC INDICATION: MUSCLE DAMAGE AND FEMALE REPRODUCTIVE DISORDERS.

Dong quai is specifically useful for mare problems. Its warming qualities make it useful for any mare with joint pains, especially during the damp winter months, and it is a useful tonic for mares that have difficulty in conceiving. It regulates the oestrus cycle, not due to any hormone-like action, but because it targets smooth muscle and enables contractions of the uterus.

This herb is also useful when a horse is recovering from an injury where there has been muscle damage or wastage. It helps these muscles and also helps the horse recover from weakness and debility that is often experienced after a trauma.

Dong quai is also useful for dry constipation caused by physical or emotional tension, as it relaxes the visceral muscles of your horse's gut.

You only need to dose Dong quai by the teaspoonful, and you may give your horse up to 3 teaspoonfuls per day in feed. However, 1 teaspoonful is often sufficient.

Do not give this herb to a mare once she has been served or during pregnancy.

ECHINACEA (*Echinacea angustifolia, Echinacea purpurea*)

SPECIFIC INDICATION: ANY SEPTIC OR INFECTION CONDITION OR WHERE IMMUNE SYSTEM IS DEBILITATED.

This herb is one of the most popular in modern herbalism. You can use Echinacea as a pre-winter immune booster, or after an illness to help rebuild your horse's immune system after it has been depleted by a virus or a debilitating illness. Echinacea is an excellent support for any infection from abscesses, wounds or respiratory illness. Use the herb if your horse has thrush or an abscess in his hoof. Echinacea is also a good system support if your horse has carbuncles or boils that are slow to heal.

If your horse is kept in a livery stable, add Echinacea to his feed if there is an outbreak of any contagious disease. It has a systemic antimicrobial effect that is effective as an antiviral and antibacterial agent. The effectiveness of Echinacea diminishes after about 3 weeks of continuous use, so it is best to only dose for up to 3 weeks at a time.

There are some excellent Echinacea/Garlic proprietory products now available. If you obtain the powdered root, you can add between ½–1 tablespoonful to your horses feed up to three times daily, or ½ a cup of the dried leaf or shaved root up to three times daily. Alternatively, you can make an infusion and administer it throughout the day if your horse requires it.

There is a debate about whether it is best to use the root or the plant. The root is usually sourced from *Echinacea purpurea*, and is more expensive because the plant has to be removed from the ground and replanted each year. The leaf and flower are usually sourced from *Echinacea angustifolia*. As the plant is perennial and there is no need for replanting each year, it is less expensive. Often your choice will be based on availability and budget, but whichever form you choose to use, your horse will benefit.

The only time I would avoid using this herb is if your horse has a weak or irregular heart beat, as Echinacea can exaggerate these problems.

EYEBRIGHT (*Euphrasia officinalis*)

SPECIFIC INDICATION: EYE CONDITIONS AND IRRITATED MUCOUS MEMBRANES.

This herb is astringent and antibiotic, which makes it cleansing to the eyes.

To make an eyewash, use one part dried herb to four parts water. Boil for 30 minutes, strain and add one part vegetable glycerine. This is a basic stock, and it should be stored in the fridge. Daily take 1 tablespoonful of Eyebright stock, add 1 cup of boiled (sterilized) water and set aside to cool before using it to wash your horse's irritated eyes. You can use this safely on the hour if desired.

For chronic watery eye conditions, rinse your horse's eyes with an infusion made from the dried plant daily. This is a little more inconvenient than the eyewash, as it must be made fresh each day.

Taken internally, Eyebright will address excess mucous in the upper and lower respiratory tract. You can also use it if your horse suffers seasonal allergies. The dose ranges from 1 teaspoonful of the powdered herb to ½ a cup of the dried cut herb morning and night. You could also pour a cup of the tea over your horse's feed.

FENNEL (*Foeniculum vulgare*)

SPECIFIC INDICATION: FLATULENCE IN FOALS AND MARES. THIS IS THE DIETER'S HERB.

Fennel will suppress your horse's appetite and help your horse's metabolism find balance. Fennel is a good general tonic herb that you can add to any general tonic blend of herbs. The tea is good for the horse prone to or recovering from flatulent colic. It helps the bowels re-establish healthy intestinal flora.

This herb can be fed to your horse on a regular basis. The fleshy part from the stems of the plant can be cut and liberally added to feed. An infusion can be made from the seeds, and it can be added to your horse's feed by the cupful. If you are trying to trim down a horse in the 'diet paddock', you can add a cup of Fennel tea to his drinking water every time you top it up. Two cupfuls a day would be effective given this way.

Externally, Fennel can be used fresh, as a poultice, to draw out toxins from insect bites and allergic skin reactions.

Fennel seed is also safe to feed lactating mares and mares in late pregnancy. One tablespoonful of seeds given twice daily is a sufficient dose.

FENUGREEK (*Trigonella foenum-graecum*)

SPECIFIC INDICATION: DEBILITY AND CONVALESCENCE WHERE DIGESTION AND NUTRITION ARE POOR.

Fenugreek is a conditioning herb. It is a must for any horse that has lost condition after a rest or serious illness. It is a good general tonic that will address every body system. You may see your horse's hooves strengthen and the shine come back to his coat within 3 weeks.

The most nutritional part of this herb is the seed. One caution to observe is that the seeds swell when they become moist. Because of this it is best to make a paste by soaking 2 tablespoonfuls of seeds in 1 cup of water and crushing to form a paste that can be added to your horse's feed.

If this is too time consuming for your situation, up to 3 cups of the dried cut plant can be added to your horse's feed; however, 1 cupful daily is usually sufficient. If you opt to use the powdered seed, limit your dose to 1 teaspoonful initially and blend it with other powdered herbs such as Peppermint or Fennel to disguise the taste.

Do not give Fenugreek to a pregnant mare, as it is a uterine stimulant.

FEVERFEW (*Chrysanthemum parthenium*)

SPECIFIC INDICATION: WORM INFESTATION AND ARTHRITIS IN AN ACTIVE INFLAMMATORY STAGE.

This herb is useful for managing intestinal worms. While it is useful to support your horse's health with herbs between pharmaceutical preparations, it is not wise to rely on the herb alone and forego any pharmaceuatical pastes. If, however, you are determined to try managing worms using herbs alone, ensure your vet does an annual faecal count to make sure you are not endangering your horse's health.

Feverfew is also an effective herb to help restore tone to the bowels after an episode of colic. It is warming and is therefore an excellent winter herb to add to your horse's feed. It is also a useful herb to give a mare that is slow to recover from foaling, as it helps to tone and cleanse the uterus.

This herb has a salicylate-like action which acts as a strong anti-inflammatory when your horse is experiencing arthritis in an active stage.

You can feed a small handful of fresh leaves up to three times a day, or 1 cupful of the dried, cut herb daily. This is one herb that loses a lot of its qualities when dried, so try to obtain freeze-dried stock as the potency is better maintained that way.

Be aware that some horses may suffer unpleasant side effects including mouth ulcers and soreness of the mouth when given too much of this herb. Avoid giving Feverfew to pregnant mares, as it is considered to be a uterine stimulant.

GARLIC (*Allium sativum*)

SPECIFIC INDICATION: ANY INFECTION.

Garlic can be used as a preventative if your horse is prone to laminitis, arthritis, skin problems or respiratory ailments. It is also reputed to help minimize intestinal worm populations. Some horses secrete Garlic through their skin, helping to repel insects. Unfortunately, if your horse has plenty of green pasture to eat, the chlorophyll in the grass will nullify the bug-repelling effect of the Garlic.

Externally, an infused oil made from one part crushed Garlic and one part olive oil, sealed and stored overnight, then strained, can be applied directly onto the skin to manage mange or Sweet Itch.

Fresh Garlic is the most medicinal form, though some horses may not like the taste initially. As a general tonic you don't need to feed much to your horse—a clove every alternate day is plenty to help your horse maintain his health. If you prefer to use granulated Garlic you can give doses of up to 1 tablespoonful once or twice daily for 3 weeks with 1 week off every cycle.

During an illness you can give up to 2 fresh cloves a day, but it is not wise to do this for more than 2–3 weeks as you can upset sensitive stomachs. I have seen higher doses recommended in some books, but I have found that any dose higher than 2 cloves a day can irritate a horse's gut. Many reputable herbal suppliers have compounds of Echinacea and Garlic that are safe to give your horse to ward off winter ills.

If a veterinary surgeon gives your horse sulphur paste to treat an infection, stop giving your horse Garlic immediately and do not resume using it until 2 weeks after the sulphur treatment stops. Some horses have been known to develop an intolerance to Garlic if they have had repeated prescriptions of sulphur drugs.

GINGER (*Zingiber officinale*)

SPECIFIC INDICATION: FLATULENT INTESTINAL COLIC AND ANY 'COLD' CONDITION.

Ginger is another herb that can be used to support a horse that is prone to or recovering from colic. It addresses the respiratory tract and is a useful maintenance herb for the older, arthritic horse. Ginger is also useful with horses that do not travel well and go off their feed when they have been transported by box to an event. A cup of tea over his feed before travelling will settle a horse for the trip; alternatively, you can pour tea over some feed on arrival to encourage eating.

Ginger can be added fresh to your horse's feed either as 1 tablespoonful of the grated root or 1 cupful of a strong brew poured over the feed up to three times a day. If fresh Ginger is inconvenient, 1 tablespoonful of the powdered root can be added to your horse's feed once or twice daily instead.

One simple way to use Ginger with your horse is to place 3–4 thin slices of the fresh root in the bottom of his water bucket each day. It is a warming support to the older horse that is a little stiff during the colder months of the year, or when there is a sudden change in the weather.

It is very difficult to obtain Ginger in a consistent strength—it will vary each time you use it. Remember that Ginger is a strong herb. Without realizing it, you may get a root that is particularly high in volatile oils, so always stay within recommended doses to ensure your treatment is not too stimulating to your horse's digestive system.

GINKGO (*Ginkgo biloba*)

SPECIFIC INDICATION: ANY PROBLEM THAT CAN BE TRACED BACK TO POOR CIRCULATION OF THE BLOOD.

This herb is useful for the horse going back into work after a rest. It has a direct action on the capillaries of the veins and arteries, so it can support the muscles by redeveloping tone as they adjust to being worked again. Ginkgo stimulates the immune system and is useful to treat a horse suffering from any chronic inflammatory disease such as rheumatism. It also helps with respiratory disorders such as heaves or difficulty of breath, especially if these are suspected to be associated with an allergic reaction or a particular season.

Ginkgo is an excellent herb for older horses that are slowing down but are still sound for riding. As it is associated with peripheral circulation, it can help maintain a healthy blood supply to all the limbs and the eyes and ears. It is sometimes given to the older horse, where it brings about increased alertness by improving the blood supply to the brain. Ginkgo also supports the heart of the ageing horse.

The cut leaf is easiest to obtain, and you can give your horse about 1 cupful twice daily, added to feed.

GINSENG (Siberian ginseng) (*Eleuthericoccus senticosus*)

SPECIFIC INDICATION: A DEPRESSED IMMUNE SYSTEM.

If you decide to use Ginseng with your horse, it is important that you use the botanical name listed here for Siberian ginseng—it is the one whose qualities are referred to here. It is a stimulating adaptogen made from the root of the plant. There is also *Panax ginseng* and *Panax quinquefolium*, but these ginsengs are usually too hot and stimulating and could make your horse overexcited.

Siberian ginseng (*Eleuthericoccus senticosus*) is an excellent balancer of the immune system. Use it to help your horse resist or recover from a viral or bacterial infection, and to protect your horse if a contagious disease has been reported in your area. This herb will improve vitality after exhaustion and be helpful if your horse has had a demanding season and is looking tired or sometimes even depressed from his efforts. Siberian ginseng supports the lungs and the cardiovascular system and is also useful on the horse that has been suffering long-term chronic illnesses.

You can give your horse 1 teaspoonful of the powdered herb, in feed, up to three times a day for 3 weeks. It is another herb that you should stop using for a week after you have used it for 3 weeks, or the effect in any ongoing treatment will be diminished. Pause and observe your horse's condition during his week of abstinence and then resume if necessary. Ginseng is not a herb that should be used for long-term, preventative treatment. It is much more effective if only used when needed.

HAWTHORN BERRY (*Crategus oxyacanthoides*)

SPECIFIC INDICATION: A HEART AND CIRCULATION TONIC.

The powdered berry stimulates blood flow, acts as a heart tonic and helps improve blood flow to the limbs. This makes Hawthorn very useful with horses suffering navicular syndrome or recovering from laminitis. Hawthorn will support an older horse suffering from dropsy, by increasing blood flow to the brain and supporting the function of the heart.

Hawthorn is also useful for treating a racehorse recovering from a bleeding episode or being rehabilitated after coming off the track permanently. It would be wise to assist any horse recovering from the rigours of the track by dosing with Hawthorn for 6 months.

The recommended dose is 2 tablespoonfuls of the powdered berry, two to three times daily, mixed in with feed. Alternatively, some horses really enjoy the taste of this herb and will happily lick it directly from your hand.

Hawthorn can also be used to treat pregnant mares that have a history of slipping foals prematurely, and for supporting foals during weaning. Use half of the recommended dose when treating a foal.

LEMON BALM (*Melissa officinalis*)

SPECIFIC INDICATION: TENSE BEHAVIOUR REFLECTED IN UNCOMFORTABLE DIGESTION.

Lemon balm addresses all states of anxiety, including those experienced by young horses while they are learning how to meet the expectations of training and competition. As it is a pleasant tasting herb, you can make a tea to add to your horse's evening feed. This will help your horse relax and adjust to a new environment—for example, it will help him adjust to the stable if he is accustomed to a paddock. Lemon balm also helps a horse that has suffered spasmodic colic to recover with less discomfort, and restores tone to the bowel.

Lemon balm has a delightful scent and provides a wonderful, but very expensive, essential oil. The herb is more easily obtained than the oil, so it has been included in this chapter.

One cupful of the dried cut herb can be added to your horse's feed twice daily, for up to a month after symptoms are no longer present.

LICORICE (*Glychrrhiza glabra*)

SPECIFIC INDICATION: GASTRIC UPSETS AND HEAVES.

This herb should not be confused with the commercially available confectionery known as licorice. The herb Licorice was once used as the original flavouring for this confectionery, but this is not the case today.

The herb Licorice has an anti-inflammatory action similar to pharmaceutical steroids and is useful for treating allergic respiratory problems and heaves. It can also assist a horse that is recovering from steroid abuse, particularly a show horse that has been bulked-up unnecessarily. One teaspoonful given daily, in feed, is a sufficient dose.

The medicinal part of this plant is the root, so Licorice is best used in a powdered form. One teaspoonful given daily will help address systemic skin problems, especially those of unknown origin that manifest with an itch and lead to constant rubbing and raw skin.

If your horse has stomach ulcers, give him 1 teaspoonful of Licorice powder mixed into a handful of feed before he eats his main meal. The herb is more effective if taken before eating, and it will prepare his inflamed stomach for what is about to eaten.

Licorice may also be used to assist infertile mares, due to its mild steroidal properties. The herb is an emmenagogue, however, so do not give it to a pregnant mare.

Licorice is a very potent herb that should not be given to a horse for more than 3 months continuously, as it can alter the potassium levels in your horse's body and cause water retention. Supplement Licorice with fresh or dried Dandelion leaves to minimize this possibility and limit the amount you give your horse to no more than 1 teaspoonful daily.

MARSHMALLOW (*Althaea officinalis*)

SPECIFIC INDICATION: GASTRIC OR DUODENAL ULCER (ROOT). RESPIRATORY CATARRH ASSOCIATED WITH DIGESTIVE WEAKNESS (LEAF).

Marshmallow has the ability to bind and eliminate toxins, allowing the body to cleanse itself. It is a useful herb for treating arthritis, infections, worm infestations, or when included in a general cleansing tonic. Marshmallow root will also calm inflammation of the stomach and bowel, urinary inflammation and spasm—and help if your horse is having difficulty urinating.

Two tablespoonfuls of the powdered root can be used two or three times a day. Alternatively, a decoction can be made from the root, and 1 cup of this, strained, may be poured over feed three times a day.

The action of the leaf is milder than that of the root. If you only have access to the fresh or dried leaf, an infusion can be made which is useful for treating respiratory problems and to soothe an irritated throat. To make an infusion, simmer 1 or 2 handfuls of the fresh herb or 1 cupful of the dried herb in enough water to cover generously, for 5 minutes. The recommended dose for the infusion is 1 cupful given twice daily. Stomach ulcers respond to preparations of the leaf or the root, as both address inflammation in the stomach and bowel.

Marshmallow has a secondary healing response in treating respiratory catarrh, a condition which often reflects a stomach/intestinal imbalance.

MEADOWSWEET (*Filipendula ulmaria*)

SPECIFIC INDICATION: DAMAGED GASTRIC MUCOSA AND BODY ACHES AND PAINS.

Meadowsweet is useful to treat a horse that has suffered or is suffering chronic stomach complaints and ulcers. It also addresses diarrhoea by calming inflammation of the intestines.

Meadowsweet is also useful for soothing the hot-blooded horse, cooling tempers and fevers. It can also be added to a blood-cleansing blend of herbs and will help to remove toxins that may be contributing to the horse's disposition. It is a handy first-aid herb to add to feed when your horse has a snuffly nose, minor injuries, swellings, or joint and muscle pain. One cupful of dried flowers can be added to your horse's feed twice daily or 1 cupful of the infusion, made from 1–2 cupfuls of the fresh flowers and/or leaves, can be poured over feed morning and night.

MOTHERWORT (*Leonurus cardiaca*)

SPECIFIC INDICATION: THE ANXIOUS AND NERVOUS MARE UNABLE TO CYCLE OR IS BADLY BEHAVED WHEN IN SEASON.

This herb is useful for treating the mare whose behaviour becomes unmanageable during her season. It is antispasmodic and eases the discomfort that some mares experience at this time. It is also very beneficial for the horse whose heart races when he sees a shadow or is unnerved in an unknown environment.

It is safe to give to a mare during pregnancy, but avoid using it during the first 3 months of gestation. It can be used to ease the discomfort of a mare suffering from colic or flatulence during pregnancy, but always call your vet if the mare is suffering gut pains, as you do not want to put the life of the mare or foal at risk.

The recommended dose is 1 cupful of the dried, cut leaf given daily for mares that are not in foal, or ½ a cupful daily for pregnant mares.

MULLEIN (*Verbascum thapsus*)

SPECIFIC INDICATION: IRRITATION TO THE AIRWAYS AND FOR PAINFUL, DRY COUGHS.

Mullein addresses most disorders of the respiratory tract. Most coughs will improve with 1 cupful of the dried plant and flowers added to your horse's feed once or twice a day, depending on the severity of your horse's symptoms. Alternatively, you can make an infusion using 1 cupful of Mullein leaves heated simmered in 4–5 cups of water. One cupful of this infusion can be given twice daily. It is a useful herb to give to your horse after an infection of the respiratory tract, as it will support and return strength to the lungs.

Mullein is a useful addition in a blend of herbs being used to rehabilitate an abused horse, as it strengthens the will to live and helps the horse regain his constitution.

NETTLE (*Urtica dioica*)

SPECIFIC INDICATION: IRRITATED SKIN CONDITIONS AND ECZEMA ASSOCIATED WITH NERVOUS CONDITIONS.

Nettles are useful as a general tonic to cleanse and feed the blood. The herb addresses blood disorders such as anaemia and itchy, irritating skin diseases. Because Nettles have an affinity with the blood the herb also improves circulation, so it is useful to treat horses suffering muscle wastage, arthritis and laminitis. A muscle or joint that has recently suffered an impact injury would benefit from a hot poultice made from Nettle leaves.

Your horse will not graze on the fresh plant because of the stinging spikes on the leaves, so pick them carefully and allow the leaves to wilt before offering them to your horse. If feeding them to your horse this way concerns you, dry the leaves (this softens the spikes) and cut them up before you add them to his feed. Alternatively, make an infusion from the fresh or dried plant to avoid your horse spiking his nose or tongue.

You can give your horse 1 cupful of wilted or dried and cut Nettles two or three times a day, or up to 3 cupfuls of the Nettle infusion daily.

Some horses may develop a rash when given Nettles. Discontinue treatment if this occurs, as it can be uncomfortable for your horse.

PARSLEY (*Petroselinum crispum*)

SPECIFIC INDICATION: FLATULENT DYSPEPSIA WITH INTESTINAL COLIC.

Parsley is a digestive tonic. It can help tone the intestines, minimize flatulence and stimulate gastric function. Parsley cleanses the blood and supports the kidneys and urinary system, too. If your horse has intermittent urination, skin discolouration or flaking skin on his back, feeding him Parsley will help. Parsley can also help your horse's body remove toxins that cause pain in the joints, as happens with conditions such as arthritis and rheumatism. It is especially good for horses during an intensive training period.

Simply pick 2 or 3 handfuls of the fresh herb and feed it to your horse each day.

Parsley is a good long-term supplement for a horse that is anaemic or debilitated after effort or illness. One cupful of the dried herb given twice daily in feed is a sufficient dose.

Do not give Parsley to a pregnant mare. The plant is especially dangerous if it has gone to seed, as the seed has abortive properties. Once the mare has dropped her foal, however, Parsley can help support the uterus and encourage lactation.

PASSION FLOWER (*Passiflora incarnata*)

SPECIFIC INDICATION: THE NERVOUS MARE WHO HOLDS HER MUSCLES TIGHT. ANY NERVOUS HORSE WILL BENEFIT FROM THIS HERB.

Passion flower is a nervine and antispasmodic. It can help a restless and irritable horse by relaxing muscles that may be in pain due to habitual tension. It is a very useful herb for the horse that never relaxes or is generally tense with human interaction.

Passion flower is hypnotic in its action, so do not exceed ½ a cupful of the dried cut leaves, stems and flowers, or 2 teaspoonfuls of the powdered herb daily. This herb may be used indefinitely, but do not exceed the recommended daily dose.

PAU D'ARCO (*Tabebuia heptaphylla*)

SPECIFIC INDICATION: ANY SYSTEMIC DISORDER OR GENERAL ILLNESS.

Pau d'arco strengthens a horse's immune system, increasing resistance to disease, and offers support to your horse if he needs help to fight viral infections. This herb is a blood cleanser, so it is useful with allergies, arthritis, skin diseases or any disorder that suppresses your horse's immune system.

Small doses of between 1 teaspoonful and 1 tablespoonful of the powdered herb given daily are suitable if your horse needs long-term support from this herb. In a situation where your horse needs intensive support, you can give the dose twice daily, but return to the original dose after 7 days. An infusion will help to re-establish the intestinal flora in your horse's gut and treat bacterial infections.

PEPPERMINT (*Mentha piperita*)

SPECIFIC INDICATION: FLATULENT DIGESTIVE PAIN.

Peppermint can be used to encourage fussy eaters or for those horses prone to colic, as it relaxes the muscles of the intestinal walls and relieves gas pains. Peppermint can be fed to horses that do not travel easily, to help dispel nervousness and relieve motion sickness. It is also useful in alleviating colds and general fevers and can be added to a rheumatism blend. Peppermint is pleasant to eat and helps to hide the taste of less pleasant herbs. The tea may also be poured on insect bites that have become swollen and hot.

This herb can be added to your horse's feed liberally: 1–2 cups of the dried, cut herb daily or as needed.

RASPBERRY (*Rubus idaeus*)

SPECIFIC INDICATION: FOR THE HEALTH OF A MARE'S UTERUS AND ANY CONDITIONS THAT REQUIRE AN ASTRINGENT.

Raspberry gives tone to the uterus, so it is beneficial for a mare that is having difficulty falling pregnant. Once the mare is pregnant, however, stop administering the herb as a precaution. Recommence using the herb in the last 3 months of her term by supplementing her feed with up to 1 cupful of the dried and cut or fresh Raspberry leaf daily. Two to three weeks before the expected date of foaling, increase the dose to 1 cupful twice daily. After she has given birth, continue with this dose for 1 month, to assist the recovery of the uterus and encourage milk production. After this time, either stop giving the mare the herb or reduce the dose to 1 cupful daily for as long as you consider necessary.

Raspberry also addresses diarrhoea and upper respiratory tract discomfort or inflammation. To treat these conditions, add 1–2 cupfuls of an infusion made from 1 cup of dried leaf to three parts water to your horse's feed.

ROSEHIPS (*Rosa canina*)

SPECIFIC INDICATION: DIETARY SUPPLEMENT AS A NATURAL SOURCE OF VITAMIN C, TOGETHER WITH SMALL AMOUNTS OF A AND B VITAMINS.

Rosehips provide an easily assimilated form of vitamin C and are particularly useful during the unstable seasons of autumn and spring. The tea can be used in autumn to tone your horse's immune system before the winter chills set in, especially if your horse has a performance schedule to meet and is stabled in a facility.

Rosehips stimulate and strengthen your horse's immune system, helping him cope better with stress. Rosehips have an astringent action, so the tea can be used to address gut disturbance, diarrhoea and excess mucous in the respiratory tract. It is a good secondary herb to use when your horse is suffering a mild infection. Rosehips also help address poor hoof and coat condition.

Add Rosehips to your horse's feed as a strong infusion, (1 cupful given twice daily), or as a commercially prepared syrup (1 tablespoonful given twice daily).

SAGE (*Salvia officinalis*)
SPECIFIC INDICATION: INFECTIONS OF WOUNDS AND THE MOUTH.

Sage is a useful herb for a horse recovering from respiratory infections, infected wounds, digestive complaints, or any debilitating state that needs support. Sage can be given in your horse's feed as a dried, cut herb, but do not exceed the dose of ½ a cupful daily. The safest way to use Sage with your horse is to make an infusion of 1 teaspoonful of the dried, powdered herb to 2 cups of water. This infusion can then be added to feed or used as a mouthwash (administer with a plastic 'squirty' sauce bottle). You can also use this infusion to clean out open wounds on a daily basis.

This herb has a very strong astringent action. Always use Sage in small quantities and never administer it for more than 2 months continuously. Avoid using Sage with pregnant mares.

SLIPPERY ELM (*Ulmus rubra*)
SPECIFIC INDICATION: TOO MUCH MUCOUS IN THE BOWEL OR RESPIRATORY TRACT.

The most common use of this herb is as a demulcent to soothe the lining of the digestive tract and regulate intestinal flora. Slippery elm bark will help treat scouring and act on wet respiratory diseases where there is excess mucous. The older or debilitated horse will benefit from the bark's nutritional value.

Slippery elm is best given moist so the whole intestinal tract benefits. Mix 2 tablespoonfuls of the powdered bark with enough honey to form a paste and dose orally using a needleless syringe. Alternatively, use a blender to mix 2 tablespoonfuls of the powdered bark with 1 cup of warm water, then add the mixture to your horse's feed.

Slippery elm can be used in a poultice to soothe wounds and draw out toxins from infected sores. As it is becoming so expensive to obtain, however, other herbs such as Cleavers can make an excellent substitute.

One caution you should be aware of is that Slippery elm is so mucilaginous that it may interfere with the absorption of other medicine administered at the same time.

ST MARY'S THISTLE (*Silybum marianum*)

SPECIFIC INDICATION: ANY CONDITION REQUIRING LIVER SUPPORT; AFTER INTRODUCED CHEMICALS OR CHEMICAL POLLUTION HAS COMPROMISED THE LIVER.

In the southern hemisphere the common name for this herb is St Mary's thistle, but in the northern hemisphere it is often referred to as milk thistle. Always check the botanical name to ensure you have the correct plant.

This herb will support your horse's liver function. It is useful if your horse is recovering from an illness where it was necessary to give high or ongoing doses of antibiotics or other pharmaceutical drugs. St Mary's thistle gives support to a horse that has been neglected or abused, a racehorse just off the track, a show horse that may have been given drugs to improve performance, or a horse that has been debilitated by a heavy worm infestation. The herb is also of benefit to the horse that has experienced an adverse reaction to a worming formulation or vaccination.

One tablespoonful of seed given morning and night in your horse's feed is a sufficient dose. The seeds can be ground to a powder for easier assimilation. This herb is suitable for long-term treatment and in fact needs to be taken for a minimum of 2–3 months to achieve the desired benefits.

VALERIAN (*Valeriana officinalis*)

SPECIFIC INDICATIONS: CONDITIONS REQUIRING RELAXING.

Valerian counteracts most diseases of the nervous system. It is a nervine, and when used over a period of time it can treat excitability, nervousness and hysterical behaviour in your horse. This herb is on the banned list of nearly every equestrian competition association, so avoid using it if you are competing at a level where your horse may be tested.

Valerian is useful for treating bruising and helps the horse suffering from a cough, by relieving the spasm. As an ongoing treatment for rheumatism, administer up to 2 tablespoonfuls twice daily. At this dose the herb has a gentle action, and it may take up to 6 weeks for you to see the full benefits of the herb at work. This dose is also suitable for the horse recovering from a colic episode.

Valerian can cause headaches and hyperactivity in your horse if it is introduced at too high a dose initially. Begin with 1–2 tablespoonfuls twice daily and only increase the dose to 3 tablespoonfuls if necessary. Monitor your horse's stools; if they become loose, decrease your dose again. Valerian is antispasmodic and analgesic, so a high dose of up to 4 tablespoonfuls of the powdered herb over a 24-hour period will address intense muscular pain. After 3 days you can bring the dose down to 1–2 tablespoonfuls, depending on the individual horse.

Consult a professional before using Valerian on a pregnant mare.

WHITE WILLOW (*Salix alba*)

SPECIAL INDICATION: RHEUMATOID ARTHRITIS AND OTHER SYSTEMIC CONNECTIVE TISSUE DISORDERS.

The medicinally potent part of this herb is the bark. Willow bark is a bitter digestive herb, and is very useful for addressing pain in your horse's body. If you are treating a chronic, ongoing pain such as that caused by arthritis, you can give your horse 2 teaspoonfuls of the powdered bark daily. If your horse is in a lot of pain following an injury, or suffering a fever due to infection, use up to 3 teaspoonfuls of the powdered bark two or three times a day. Willow bark is useful if your horse is stressed by fever, as it helps lower the temperature and relieves pain by depressing the central nervous system.

The tannins contained in this herb can tone irritated membranes and reduce bleeding. Willow bark is useful for treating horses that have bled on the track and are being rehabilitated; however, do not use it on a racehorse still in work, as the major constituent, salicin, converts to salicylic acid in the body and will test positive at a prohibited level.

WILD YAM (*Dioscerea villosa*)

SPECIFIC INDICATION: BILIOUS COLIC AND ACUTE PHASE RHEUMATISM.

Wild yam is a mild diaphoretic that can help the body deal with the active toxins associated with rheumatism and other diseases such as arthritis, which require increased warmth and circulation to help the body correct the imbalances. It is a mild peripheral vasodilator, so it is of help to the extremities. You can give Wild yam to a horse that has arthritis or bony changes in the fetlock, and it will have an action on that distant part of the limb.

Wild yam is also anti-inflammatory, and its action is believed to imitate that of steroids. Consider using this herb if you have a horse that has been on a long-term steroid prescription, as it will help his body readjust. Wild yam is also an excellent herb to use to help your horse recover from a bout of colic. It stimulates the liver to release bile, making the movement of feed easier, and it also addresses visceral tension so the colon can relax and recover from the tension and stress it has experienced.

The medicinally potent part of Wild yam is the rhizome, so this herb is best used in a powdered form. One tablespoonful added to feed morning and night, is enough to achieve results.

WOOD BETONY (*Betonica officinalis*)

SPECIFIC INDICATION: ANY COMPLAINT OF THE HEAD REGION THAT REQUIRES TONING AND CALMING.

Wood betony is useful for treating unusual behaviour caused by stress. It has a slightly relaxing action on your horse, and is helpful if there is tension held in the head or poll. Wood betony will help your horse if he head-tosses or suffers sinus infections. It has an astringent action and will help treat runny eyes and noses as well as neuralgia and facial pain.

This herb is also useful for a horse that is debilitated and hangs his head low when stabled. It will also address debility from poor digestion. It is a bitter stimulant, however, so keep your dose to no more than ½ a cupful of the dried cut herb twice daily.

Wood betony can also assist the horse that drifts away when in pain, and displays a dull look in his eye. It is an excellent support herb for Eyebright. Wood betony is not a herb to be fed on its own, but should be used to enhance the action of other herbs such as Ginkgo or Hawthorn berry.

YELLOW DOCK (*Rumex crispus*)

SPECIFIC INDICATION: SKIN DISEASE ESPECIALLY PSORIASIS WITH CONSTIPATION.

Yellow dock is an alterative that is useful for addressing chronic skin conditions. It is a mild laxative and encourages the gentle evacuation of the bowel, cleansing your horse from within.

This herb is a good male tonic, useful for treating stallions that have lost their spark. When combined with other herbs such as Dong quai, Licorice and St Mary's thistle, it will act as a tonic to balance him after a heavy season of serving. It is also a good herb to give a horse that needs his health rebalanced after long-term use of steroids or pharmaceuticals, as it helps the liver cleanse itself from these substances. You can give your horse 1 tablespoonful of the powdered root morning and night; however, if his bowels become too loose, reduce the dose to just an evening tablespoonful or discontinue altogether.

Yellow dock is useful as a poultice if you have a horse that has been 'blistered' or 'fired' on the front of his shins. This practice, which is carried out with the misperceived intention of strengthening the legs of a horse prone to shin soreness, is now illegal in most countries. If you have a horse that has been blistered and discarded, however, Comfrey and Yellow dock poultices daily will help restore some health to his shins.

A last note on using herbs with your horse

Using herbs with horses can be a rewarding experience. You may choose to use herbs for a short period (for example, to help overcome a training issue that stems from nervousness), or for a long-term chronic illness requiring ongoing support. It is a useful therapy if you are not sure whether you are achieving the right results or if you want to be able to monitor your horse's progress, as you can pause and gently resume treatment in most situations.

Please note: where I have suggested adding herbs or teas to your horse's drinking water, always make sure that there is an alternative water source available in case your horse decides he does not want to drink the treated water.

MASSAGE

MASSAGING YOUR HORSE

Being able to give your horse a 'good' massage depends on many things. It helps if you have technical knowledge of how your horse's muscles function, what a healthy muscle feels like, and what you can do to help your horse achieve homeostasis in his body. Practising the various massage strokes will also help you perfect your style.

Approach your horse with an open heart—massage is not a way to force your will upon him; it is a tool to help remove obstacles in his body so that he can move more efficiently and improve his performance in whatever discipline you are working him. Intention is a vital key in healing. Your horse is sensitive to your intentions, and can read subtle signals such as your body language and sometimes even your mind.

Massaging your horse is also a way to develop the bond between you on another level. Do you have trouble catching your horse? Does your horse resist your commands? Once your horse experiences the benefits of massage you will find he expresses a happier disposition and associates you with pleasure more than discomfort when he is in work.

There are commonsense guidelines that you should adhere to when you massage your horse. Firstly, never massage a horse while he is suffering from an acute condition such as fever or shock. If your horse has a fever, his body will be busy fighting an infection—massage would stimulate your horse's metabolism and could possibly trigger a healing crisis, where the symptoms appear to intensify. This can be scary for both the horse and the observer. If a horse has gone into shock for any reason, his blood pressure will be low. Massage lowers the blood pressure further still and, in this situation, could place the horse's vital signs within a life-threatening parameter. Massage is not an appropriate treatment for the horse that has been diagnosed with cancer. It is believed that massage could accelerate the spread of cancerous cells throughout the horse's body by speeding up the metabolism. If you are a therapist who has been asked to treat a horse in this situation, do not allow yourself to be placed in a position where it could be construed that you are attempting to treat a medical condition that you are not qualified to deal with. Philosophically, this is a very grey area—so if you are asked to massage a terminally ill horse to bring it some measure of comfort and relief, your role should be to administer palliative care only. Make sure that your intentions and limitations are clearly understood from the outset. Do not leave yourself open to ill-founded claims of litigation from a grief-stricken owner or a veterinary regulator.

When massaging a horse always be respectful of the horse's personal space and whatever pain he or she may be experiencing. This involves moving in gently and carefully, and never rushing your massage. You can keep to a routine, but never rush to complete it if you have not allowed enough time to do the massage thoroughly. Most massages can be completed within an hour; however, a first massage for a horse with specific problems may extend to an hour and a half. If your horse becomes agitated or bored easily, keep the duration of the massage to an hour or less.

If you are ever asked to massage someone's horse, be careful of passing judgement on the owner's care of the horse. Everyone trains and treats his or her horses slightly differently. Remember—this is the owner's way and probably the best he or she is capable of at this point in time. You can offer suggestions, but you should never be judgemental of the owner. Be mindful of your thoughts—they do have substance, and if you allow any negative thoughts towards the owner or horse to manifest, this will inhibit the effect of your massage. It is another matter if you feel that there is cruelty involved, however. If this is the case, discuss your concerns with the owner, then if the treatment you consider to be cruel continues, report it to the authorities and have the conviction to follow through on your actions. You will find this is extremely rare—if someone has called upon you to help with a horse, it is most likely that he or she will work with you to correct anything that has been done out of ignorance.

When massaging any horse, you are working on many seen and unseen levels, and you need to protect yourself on these same levels. Those of us whose nature is attracted to helping people often do so without a second thought (turning to the healing professions is an expression of this). On a subtle level we may inadvertently take on negative aspects of the physical and emotional imbalances of the horse in our own subtle bodies. This does not help the patient or the practitioner, as the horse will not have addressed and healed the situation and your own energy field will be burdened with your horse's problems. It is vitally important that you protect yourself from taking on your horse's 'stuff'. You can take steps towards this by visualizing yourself wearing a green cape or being surrounded by a pink bubble. The Lord's Prayer is one of the most powerful forms of protection you can call upon, or you can simply ask for protection in a way that fits in with your own belief system.

It is extremely important that you maintain focus while carrying out a massage. When massaging humans you can sometimes get away with daydreaming about your coming evening or the groceries you need to buy that week. However, horses are far more perceptive to your thoughts. Horses will often sense when you have mentally left the massage and may decide that you should come back to present time. A horse may move away from you until you focus again, or even use a quick kick or nip or carefully placed hoof to bring your mind back to the job.

Keep a sense of awareness about you as you massage your horse. Remain awake to your horse's body language—you will find that the horse 'talks' to you with his body, indicating the degree of pressure he prefers and which of your movements helps him most. He will also react swiftly if you hit a sore spot too quickly, or he feels he has to protect himself from your advancing hands. Also be aware of your environment, so that if anything goes wrong and the horse reacts in a way that places you in danger, you can get out of the way immediately. Never stand on a mounting block or milk crate while you work on your horse, as you cannot move quickly and safely if the horse suddenly moves, and it is difficult to sense the horse's movements when you are not connected to the ground with him.

WHY MASSAGE?

Sixty per cent of your horse's body weight is muscle. This often goes ignored. When a muscle fibre contracts under stress created by work or by emotion, it can get stuck in this point of contraction. It may stay stuck, then suggest to surrounding muscle fibres that they join in and contract as well. The muscle's fibres begin to group together until they form a muscle spasm, which in turn restricts the blood flow to that muscle and impedes the messages from the nerves. This restriction causes pain and discomfort and limits the range of movement of that muscle. It can then affect the surrounding or attached muscles as well. Often the only way to get the muscle fibres to relax and release the spasm is to manually suggest this to the muscle through the use of various massage techniques.

Muscle spasms usually result in unnecessary stress being placed on opposing muscles and joints. If this is not treated it can throw the horse out of balance, and other parts of the horse's body begin to compensate. This can lead to further damage, as those other parts of the horse's body become restricted and painful due to the additional strain. It is extremely important that you massage the whole horse so that any muscular problems are identified and addressed, and to ensure that the problem you think needs to be treated is not masking a bigger, underlying problem.

Most horses respond to one massage, sometimes two, and rarely need a third one unless they are being treated for chronic soreness or rehabilitation. If I am asked to massage a horse for a third time, because the horse does not appear to be improving, it usually means there is another contributing factor that has not been identified and will require a veterinary surgeon's diagnosis. The horse may have arthritis in his joints which is affecting his load-bearing action; he may have a tendon that needs treating; he may need his teeth fixed or a different approach in his shoeing; or he may have an internal problem requiring tests to determine his condition. Always ask a veterinary surgeon to examine your horse to rule out any other serious underlying problem.

After a muscular problem has been addressed by massage, the cause of the problem must be eliminated or it may recur. For example, if your horse got a sore shoulder because his suspensory ligament was weakening, this ligament needs to be given time to heal. If the ligament continues to cause the shoulder to carry more of the weight in work, then the shoulder will tighten up again. As another example, if your horse's biceps are tight because the hoof angle is not correct for the sort of work the horse has to perform, they will stay tight until this is redressed, despite any number of massages he receives. If your horse's jaw is always tight and he is relentlessly pulling on the reins, have his teeth checked or his jaw will always be tight, you will have trouble progressing with any training, and your massages will not have any lasting positive effect. After any underlying factors have been corrected, you can use massage to maintain your horse's muscle health and prevent injury. Healthy muscles are better able to cope with stress and the increasing demands of training.

Another benefit of massage is that it triggers the release of endorphins. This can help with nervous and uptight horses. Be patient as you work with your horse. If he reacts adversely to your touch, ease off on the pressure or modify your strokes, but do not break your contact with him. Demonstrate that every time you touch him it does not hurt, and you will slowly win his trust. As your horse grows accustomed to being massaged, you will find him easier to handle. Eventually he will come to you when he needs or desires a massage.

One of my favourite dressage horses had been a moderately successful racehorse at a moderate level. He had been retired after he fell and tore the muscles in his rump and blew a tendon. This area in his rump was often prone to flaring up; if it got to the point where he thought it should be massaged, he would manoeuvre his rump into everyone's face until I was called to relieve his tension.

Many behavioural problems are caused by pain. It is dangerous to blame your horse's poor performance on a stubborn or resistant attitude. Ask yourself why the horse is being stroppy or resistant to your commands. Often a horse is not refusing to do what you ask; he is simply telling you he just can't do it.

The way you and your horse's bodies work together when riding can be a useful indicator of when your horse needs a massage. Several of my regular clients know when their horse needs a massage, as their own symptoms mirror those of their horse. If their own lower back aches after riding, their horse's back seems to be sore too, or their shoulder has become sore after their horse has been pulling against them due to his own sore shoulder. Any pain experienced by you as the rider can be a good indicator that the horse is not moving at an optimum range.

STYLES OF MASSAGE

Massage is the manipulation of soft tissue to benefit the well-being of the horse. There are many styles of massage and all have useful applications for your horse. If you have learned massage in a clinical environment, you can use these same techniques with your horse. One difference between massaging horses and humans is that you don't need to apply oil when massaging a horse, because his coat acts as a lubricant for your fingers.

Let whatever knowledge you have of massage be a foundation and allow it to grow with further study and the expression of your own creativity. If all you know is Swedish or remedial massage, don't be discouraged, as it can achieve dramatic results with a horse—remember, it is all in your intention. It is easy to get caught up on one style of massage and think it is the only way, but you are only limited by your own mind as to what you can do with a horse. If you have no massage experience at all, start by having a professional massage carried out on your own body, as this will help give you an understanding of what feels good and why. Then learn your techniques, adopt the philosophy that sits with you best, and explore every horse as it presents itself. No course will teach you everything you need to know, but each horse you massage will teach you something new. As most gifted horsepeople will tell you, it's impossible to know everything about horses. Horses are a precious gift that can open so many doors to learning about every aspect of our own lives and theirs.

Myofascial Release

The body's myofascial system is one of support, protection, biomechanical linkage and movement. It is one of the foundations of your horse's form and function. The fascia tissue is a tough connective tissue that spreads throughout the body in a three-dimensional web from head to hoof without interruption. The fascia surrounds every muscle, bone, nerve, blood vessel and organ, all the way down to the cellular level.

The tightening of the fascial system is a protective mechanism that occurs in response to trauma. This trauma may come from an acute injury such as tendon strain, chronic compensatory muscular work or repetitive injury from poor training techniques. The fascia loses its pliability, becomes restricted and is a source of tension for the rest of the body. This loss of pliability is often further exacerbated by an inflammatory response. In this case, the fascia's gel-like state solidifies, the collagen becomes dense and fibrous and the elastin loses its resilience. These myofascial restrictions slowly affect the quality and quantity of motion available to the horse. Over time this can lead to poor muscular biomechanics, altered structural alignment and decreased strength and endurance.

Myofascial release is a hands-on technique that facilitates a stretch into the restricted soft tissues. A sustained pressure is applied into the tissue barrier for 90–120 seconds before the first release is felt. Follow the release into the new tissue barrier, and repeat the sustained pressure and release. After a few releases, the tissue will become soft and pliable. Restoring the length and health of the myofascial tissues in this way will ease the pressure being placed on pain-sensitive tissue like nerves and blood vessels, and restore alignment and mobility to the joints. By elongating the fascia you will restore efficiency within the neuromuscular elements and proper mechanical length of the connective tissues, thereby restoring your horse's natural abilities of coordination, flexibility, strength and power.

Lymphatic Drainage

The lymphatic system is one of your horse's first lines of defence against disease. It carries all the toxins back to the venous system where they can be removed by elimination organs. The lymphatic system is located just under the surface of the skin and has a network similar to the circulatory system. Like the circulatory system, it, too, requires movement in order to function. Horses that are stalled often suffer with puffy legs, a sign that stagnant lymph needed to be encouraged to move through your horse's system. This explains why the puffiness decreases when you exercise your horse.

Lymphatic 'pumping' techniques should only be used with the lightest of pressure (usually the amount of pressure you could bear on your own closed eyelid is sufficient).

When using lymphatic massage techniques to treat your horse's legs, use the webbing between the thumb and forefinger of you hand and place it around the area that is swollen. Lightly work along the limb towards the heart using a minimal amount of pressure, but do not allow your hand to lift away from the skin. It must stay in contact for the length of the movement. As you move along your horse's leg, squeeze very lightly at 3—5-cm (½-inch) intervals. Again, do not do this forcefully, as you are only trying to stimulate the lymphatic vessels.

If your horse's legs are too sensitive to be touched safely this way, use a finger pump method instead. To do this, carefully place your fingertips on the area where the horse is swollen. Using only the degree of pressure that you could bear on your own closed eyelid; do not let your fingertips leave the skin while you move each one in a little circle at the same time. As soon as you complete the circle, flick or spring your fingertips away from the surface of the skin. Repeat this randomly all over the swollen area to 'spring' the lymphatic vessels into action.

When treating larger areas such as a haematoma or an injury resulting in swelling, lightly place your thumbs or fingertips in the centre of the swelling and draw them outwards until you pass the edge of the swelling. Continue to do this following a pattern like the spokes on a bicycle wheel. If there is heat in the swelling, start on the edges circling the area of the swelling and move outwards, then gradually begin your strokes a little further towards the centre. This is the only situation where you may massage an inflamed area, and the only suitable method for doing so, as soon as the horse will allow it.

If your horse is recovering from a reaction to vaccinations or an illness where he has been prescribed many pharmaceutical drugs, use these lymphatic drainage techniques all over his body to help eliminate any toxins created from his situation. This will help get his body back to a healthy state.

MASSAGE STROKES

Effleurage

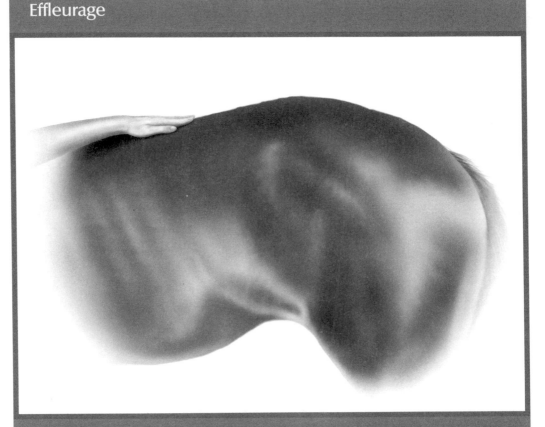

This technique simply involves stroking in a sweeping, flowing movement. It is a very reassuring stroke for your horse and different levels of pressure can be used to achieve different results The light pressure warms up the tissue and prepares the muscle for heavier strokes. If you begin with a stroke that is too heavy you may trigger a muscle spasm or find the muscle will not respond. Keep your pressure steady and mould your hand to your horse while following the natural fall of his coat. Remember to utilize your body weight to apply the pressure—if you force the pressure with the strength of your arm alone, you may again meet with resistance.

This technique is very effective along your horse's back where you can work on the Latissimus dorsi and Longissimus dorsi muscles.

Compression

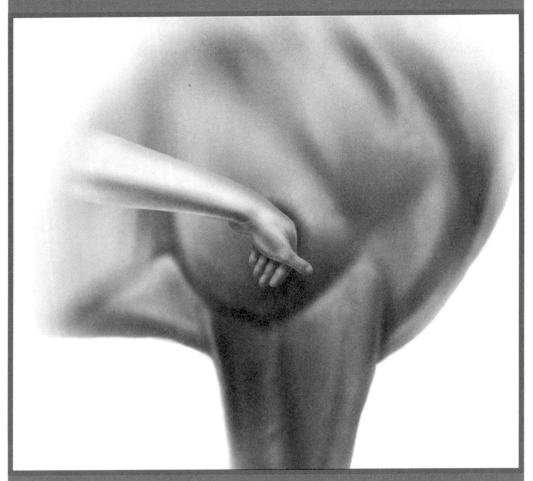

This stroke is similar to the movement of opening a jar—push down and twist at the same time. When you have completed one twist, move on to the next part of the muscle. Either use the flat area of your fingers between the base and middle knuckles (as shown) or use the palm of your hand. Keep your elbow close to your body so your hand maintains even pressure. Compression helps to open up the muscle fibres so the blood supply can flow more freely, carrying more oxygen and nutrients to the muscle and removing metabolic wastes.

The long, thick muscle groups such as the triceps and gluteals respond well to this technique.

Cross-fibre friction

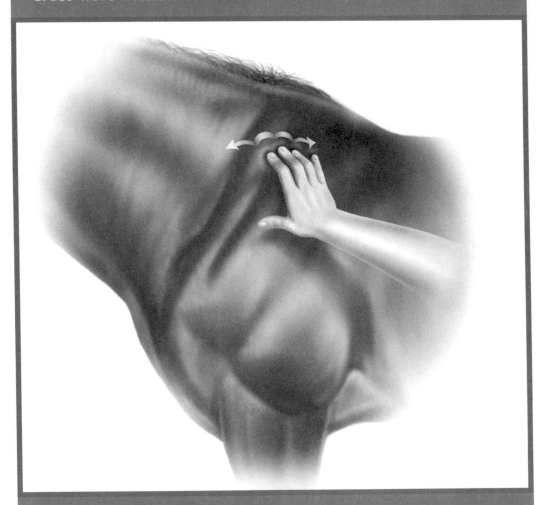

This technique requires knowledge of the positioning of your horse's muscles. Place your fingertips or thumb at right angles to the muscle fibres and move back and forth over them using digital pressure. This technique helps to break up adhesions in muscle fibres that contribute to spasms. Be careful not to do this technique too quickly or to go in too deeply to begin with, or you may cause your horse pain.

This is an effective technique to use on the muscles of the neck including the rhomboids and complexus.

Deep digital pressure

If you have palpated an area (see page 78) and found tension, you can use deep digital pressure to explore and release this area. The term 'digital' refers to either a finger or thumb. Simply place the pad of your finger or thumb on the spasm or tightness and gently increase the pressure. Use your body rather than pushing your hands in—this way you will be able to obtain an even pressure and your horse will accept you going in deeply. If you go too fast or deep too quickly your horse will move away or warn you off with his body language. Do not use this technique directly over bony landmarks such as vertebrae.

Percussion

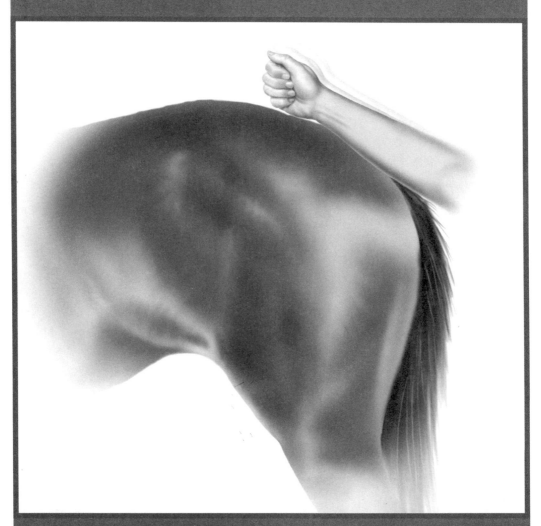

Percussion is sometimes referred to as 'pounding'. Using your fingertips, the side of your hand (hacking) or a loose fist, aim for a steady, rhythmic action. The key to this stroke is having a loose wrist and elbow with a relaxed hand. This technique cannot be forced, or it will jar the horse. Percussion triggers the release of endorphins so you can work more deeply into a sore area. It should only be employed on soft tissue such as the shoulder Cranial pectoral (subclavius) or the hind area along the gluteals.

Palpation

Palpation is a fancy word to describe a technique that really means 'to feel' or 'to touch'. This method of massage can be used all over your horse and will become your way of asking the muscles how they feel and whether they need you to explore them further. Your hands will become more sensitive to listening as you practice your massage skills and 'feeling' a horse this way will be able to tell you a story about the horse you are working on.

This technique can be used on any muscle to help you decide which other techniques may be the most appropriate for that part of your horse at that particular time.

Jostling

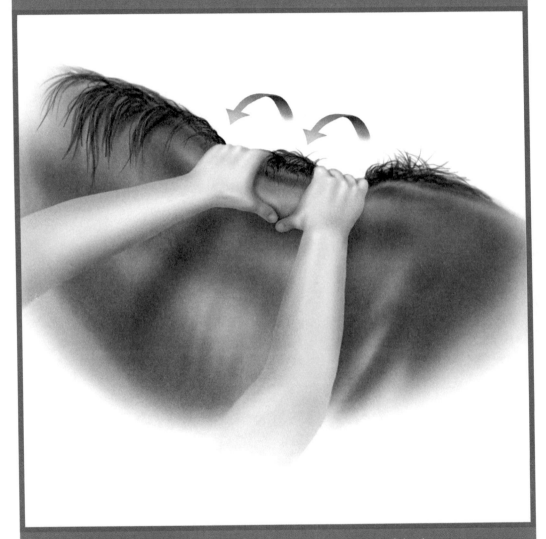

This technique involves cupping your hands over the crest of the horse, placing your thumbs at right angles, then rolling the crest towards your thumbs. This has to be done with light pressure at first otherwise the horse will resist the movement, and your objective is to release tension, not to create it. This technique can be used to release the Nuchal ligament and Trapezius muscle (cervical portion).

Sweating

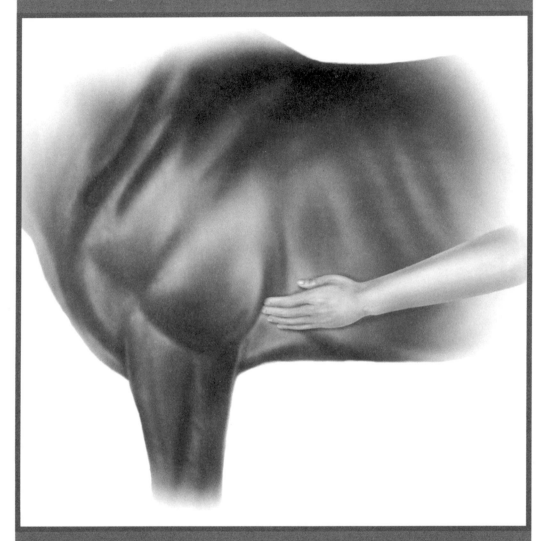

Sweating is a simple technique that can calm a sensitive area and allow you to work on it using other massage techniques. Place the palm of your hand over the area where you wish to ease discomfort, until your hands begin to sweat (hence the term 'sweating'). This is a very effective technique to use across the loins (Thoracolumbar fascia) and in the girth line area (Posterior pectoral muscle).

MUSCLES OF THE HORSE

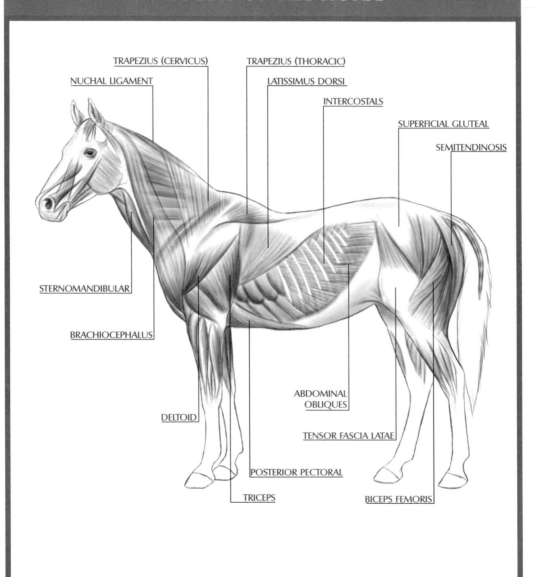

TRAPEZIUS (CERVICUS)

TRAPEZIUS (THORACIC)

NUCHAL LIGAMENT

LATISSIMUS DORSI

INTERCOSTALS

SUPERFICIAL GLUTEAL

SEMITENDINOSIS

STERNOMANDIBULAR

BRACHIOCEPHALUS

ABDOMINAL OBLIQUES

DELTOID

TENSOR FASCIA LATAE

POSTERIOR PECTORAL

TRICEPS

BICEPS FEMORIS

Some muscles mentioned in this chapter are not shown in this illustration—these are the deeper muscles such as the Longissimus dorsi, the Cranial deep pectoral and the quadriceps which lie below the layer shown above.

AREAS TO ADDRESS

In order to work most of your horse's body, here is a basic pattern to follow when giving your horse a massage.

The poll

Most horses have tightness in this area due to the weight of the head coming off the neck at an awkward angle, causing muscular stress. The act of riding asks your horse to carry his head in an unnatural position to maintain balance and this is further exaggerated when you ask your horse to go on the bit in a collected frame. The collected work in carriage driving, where the horse has to hold his head in a way that helps balance the weight of a cart also tightens this area.

The Nuchal ligament is the major ligament supporting the head. It passes centrally along the top line from the wither and attaches to the Nuchal crest (the bump between the ears). Major and minor muscle groups sit on top of the Wing of Atlas and to either side of the Nuchal ligament and above the first cervical vertebrae (Atlas) located directly behind the skull. This combination of bone and tissue is responsible for supporting and extending the head, so pay particularly close attention to this area if you showjump your horse.

Deep digital pressure and compression are effective techniques to use in this area.

The second region of concern in the poll area is located between the Wing of Atlas and the Ramus of the Mandible at the back of the jaw. This area can tighten-up for many reasons but it commonly occurs after a horse pulls back while tethered or when tied-up. If this area is tight or movement of this junction is restricted, your horse may be experiencing 'nagging' discomfort or pain. Always check the muscles in this area if your horse has had a sudden

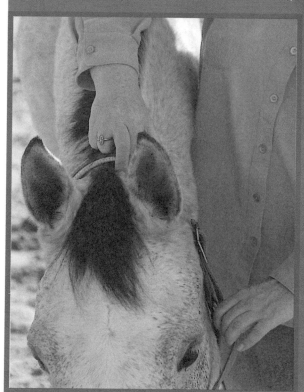

change in behaviour—consider the way your own behaviour changes when you have a headache! If your horse still seems to have a problem in this area after you have massaged it, consider contacting your horse's dentist.

The attachments on the Temporal Mandibular Joint (TMJ)

The Temporal Mandibular Joint is a hinge joint located between the mandible and skull. If your horse resists going on the bit or pulls against you, it could be a sign of tightness and restricted movement in this area. Once again, your horse may just be saying 'I can't', not 'I won't'. Tightness in this area is also an indication that there could be underlying teeth or sinus problems. Uneven teeth can restrict the range of movement of this hinge by causing the muscles on the side of the facial crest to tighten.

If you find that your horse is tight in this area, smell his breath. If it is a bit stinky and smells like stale food or if you then notice him chewing to one side, contact your horse's dentist. After dental problems have been ruled out, the best way to treat any tightness you find in this area is with direct thumb or finger pressure followed by cross-fibre friction.

Above the eyes (The Coronoid Process)

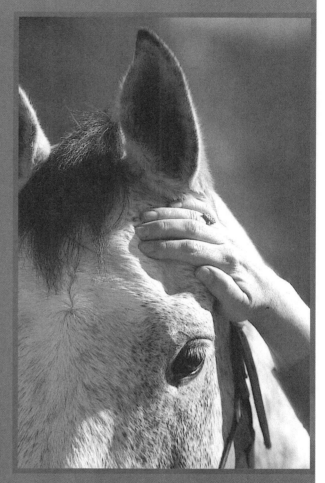

Another region directly related to the Temporal Mandibular Joint is the Coronoid Process. It runs upwards from the TMJ and passes through the Temporal fossa, the concave depression above your horse's eye. This region can develop a tightness that often coincides with restricted movement in the TMJ area. When this happens a horse may frequently half close its eyes against the pain. Another sign of tightness in this area is any difference in the sizes of the bulge of muscle above the eyes. If one is larger than the other, your horse is using this side of his mouth more than the other when eating. In this case you need to contact your horse's dentist. After dental problems have been treated or ruled out, you can use gentle circular fingertip compression to help address tightness in this area of the auriculars and temporalis muscles.

The neck

The cervical vertebra begin directly behind the skull and travel through the lower portion of the neck into the chest. This means the rhomboids, the Serratus ventralis cervicus muscles and the previously mentioned Nuchal ligament may all become very tight due to the stress of supporting your horse's neck. Your horse uses this group of muscles to extend and elevate the head. If your horse's flexion seems restricted also check the tension in the Brachiocephalic muscle which covers the entire length of the neck and influences sideways flexion and shoulder movement.

Jostling is recommended for releasing tension in the crest of a horse. Be aware that dietary factors and the sex of your horse can affect the crest, so bear these factors in mind before deciding if the neck is excessively tight. Use compression and percussion techniques for those muscles that are not directly over the vertebra, as these techniques can bruise the soft tissue that lies over the bony vertebral landmarks.

The cervical spine

Palpate the tissue surrounding the transverse processes of the cervical vertebrae (these are easily felt). Check that there is a smooth tone flowing from one vertebra to the next. Watch how your horse moves and check that he is even and balanced—if this area is sore, it is likely to affect his balance. Any sideways rotation of the cervical vertebrae at the point where it enters the chest (C6 and C7) can cause a horse to stand unevenly in front.

The Sternomandibular muscle, located below the cervical vertebra, along the base of the neck can be checked and treated by holding the muscle while applying a gentle squeeze and lift technique simultaneously. Loosening this tissue will help the horse flex his neck.

The shoulder

A sling of muscles supports the large area of the shoulder and as such, they can become quite tight. The Cranial deep pectoral runs down and in front of the scapula (shoulder blade) and can be released using a gentle lifting technique, which allows you to address the underlying tissue. The muscles here should be smooth and soft enough for you to be able to gently lift the scapula without causing the horse any stress. If they are tight or in spasm you will need to apply myofascial release first then cross-fibre friction to obtain enough elasticity to apply this lift.

The Supraspinatus, Infraspinatus and deltoids lie laterally along the scapula and can be addressed with light to medium compressions. These muscles run parallel to one another so just follow the fibre direction of these muscles. You can also check and attend to the triceps by following along the muscle fibres located between the scapula and elbow joint using fist compression.

If your horse's shoulder seems tight, don't forget to assess and compare both shoulders. Is one shoulder bearing more load that the other? Is one of the forelegs suffering stress? Check your horse's tendons and look for any signs of stress such as splints. Just behind the point of the shoulder is a small muscle called the Teres minor—in eighty-five per cent of cases, tightness here indicates an abnormality occurring around or below the knee.

When riding your horse tightness in either shoulder will show up when you change rein as this usually affects the horse's flexion and forward movement. At some time in your horse's life he will tighten up here, especially if he works heavily on the forehand and doesn't employ his hindquarters enough.

Top of the foreleg

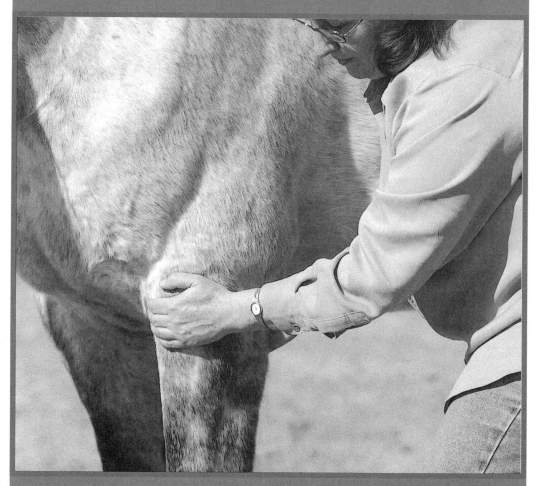

The top of your horse's foreleg may become tight if his hoof is not shaped to suit his build or workload. Work your way down each leg and wherever there is tissue to hold, apply a gentle squeeze and lift. Tendons can be difficult to check and are best left to your veterinary surgeon, though you can compare your horse's legs for variations in thickness, tightness or swellings. Racehorses with hooves trimmed to a long toe and low heel usually become tight at the top of the foreleg. If you are not getting the extension you desire from your horse's front legs when riding, check the muscles in the top of the forelegs from every angle and monitor your horse's tendons carefully.

The elbow

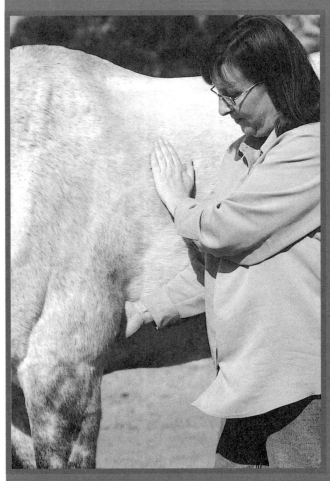

The area to the inside of your horse's elbow will tighten if he has been galloping and extending as far as he can. The triceps have a strong tendon attachment here that tightens under such stress. You can slip your hand in behind the elbow next to the girth area and relieve this tightness with myofascial release and by gently stretching the affected tissue.

Eventers are prone to this sort of tightness, but any horse that has slipped and pushed his foreleg out to balance himself, may have a weakness here. If you suspect your horse is not reaching as far as he can with his front action, always check this area. Often when a horse is being 'girthy' and badly behaved when you girth him up, he is simply trying to protect this area behind the elbow.

The girth

'Girthiness' can involve a number of muscles. 'Sweating' the girth line area first will help you to explore it before applying digital pressure. The Posterior pectoral runs along the girth region to a point midway under the belly. After you have sweated this area your horse will not object as strongly to a light to medium compression massage to release this muscle.

One of the major back muscles, the Latissimus dorsi, is located here under the girth area and attaches to the medial aspect of the humerus, in front of the elbow joint, and fans out up across the back. If your horse is girthy, always check the tightness of his back muscles as well as the girth area.

The belly

Soreness in your horse's back may be caused by poor posture and your horse not using his tummy muscles. Tickling the belly along the midline will encourage your horse to tuck up his tummy and elongate his back muscles to help him develop a stronger top line. If done regularly (once or twice a week initially) these belly lifts will help improve poor posture.

The wither

If a tight shoulder has been left untreated, the top of the wither will also be tight. First check the fit of your saddle and make sure it is not pinching your horse's back in the area where the front of the saddle sits. An incorrectly fitting saddle will cause tension in the muscles located directly behind the wither including the Spinalis dorsi and the area behind the scapula, the Serratus ventralis thoracis. Light to medium compression following the line of fibres in these muscles will help to relieve tension here.

Cross-fibre friction is a very useful technique to use along and into the groove at the top of the scapula near the withers where the rhomboids and the Trapezius attach, and tightness can occur. If your horse does not have elasticity in these muscles and their attachments he will have difficulty achieving a swinging shoulder movement.

After using cross-fibre friction to release the tightness in the wither, you can then modify the belly lift technique by placing pressure on the belly directly under the wither, to help open up the scapula.

The back

Check your horse's back for tension by using finger pressure on one side of the spine at a time, about 3cm (1inch) from the spinal processes, working from the wither to the sacrum. Ideally, repeat this three or four times as you assess the Longissimus dorsi and Latissimus dorsi along the top of the back. If you find that your horse dips as you work along this area, try to determine if it's a normal reaction. Some horses dip naturally when any pressure is applied here, so don't always presume this response is a sign of soreness. Light to firm compression working from the sacrum back towards the wither can be applied along these long back muscles, following the natural direction of the muscle fibres.

Long firm effleurage is one of the best ways to warm up your horse's back muscles before saddling up.

If your horse has poorly developed muscles along the back and he likes his treats, you can play the carrot game with him. Holding a carrot in your hand, get him to follow your hand as you move it down between his legs, never above his knees and preferably towards his fetlocks. If you can, get him to keep his head down there for a few seconds or longer so he stretches his back muscles, then repeat a few times.

The barrel

Your horse's barrel refers to the area outlined by his ribs. The beginning of the ribs can be felt directly behind the scapula, below the Longissimus dorsi. This area is known as the shelf of ribs. Check the intercostal muscles between each rib in the shelf of ribs to assess their relationship to the spine and the potential tension that may exist at a deeper level.

To do this, hold your thumb pointing downwards, and slowly run your thumb down each intercostal space. You should be able to feel the 'valleys' between the ribs, and this will help you assess the tightness of the intercostal muscles between each rib. Any tightness should be treated with cross-fibre friction, but remember your horse can be sensitive in this area.

The loins

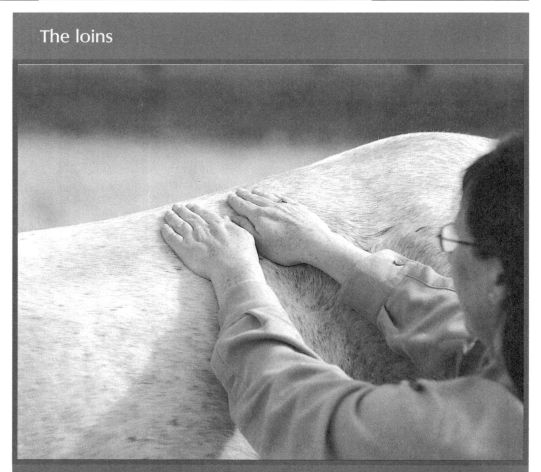

The loins are located over the lumbar region of the back. This is a very sensitive area, and you should never use percussion techniques here. The loins are often affected by poor saddle fit, and any swelling in this area may indicate that your horse is not eliminating toxins efficiently. Sweating this area can be very calming to your horse. Simply place your palms over your horse's loins and rest them there for about 20 seconds, or until your hands begin to sweat.

Following this treatment, the myofascial release technique can be used in this area, particularly if the horse has 'blown up' over the loins after strenuous work. The muscle beneath the palms may appear to ripple as the myofascia releases. When you see this happen, apply slightly more pressure until it relaxes once again. Try to hold this for approximately 2 minutes or more. This technique can help to release the toxins that build up in large muscle groups.

Point of hip

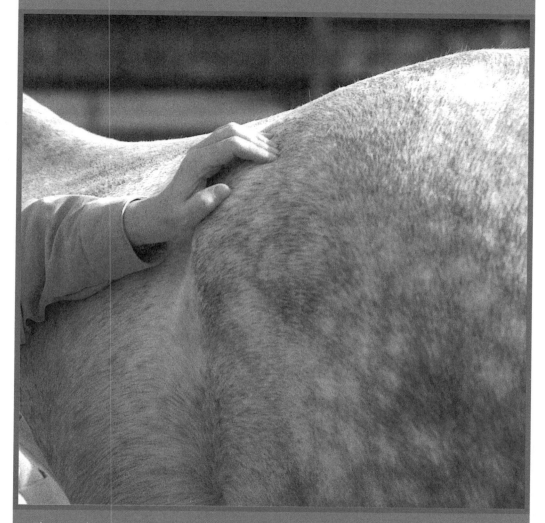

The attachments around the point of hip can become very tight if the horse has a sore back or problems with its hind leg action. In this area the attachments of the gluteals, Illiacus, Tensor fascia latea and the internal oblique muscles can be felt as strong tendons.

The point of hip should be sweated first to warm the area, then myofascial release, deep finger pressure and cross-fibre friction can be used to ease any tight areas your horse may have.

The rump

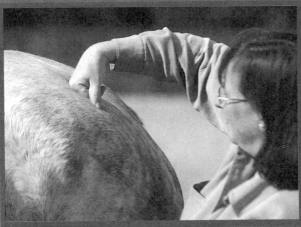

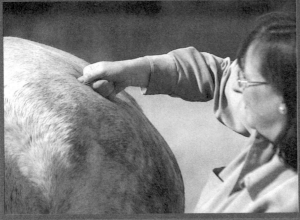

The rump is the powerhouse of your horse's drive. This area may tighten up if the attached hind leg has had to push through tightness in the shoulder diagonally opposite, or if his hind feet are not correctly shod.

A huge group of muscles collectively known as the gluteals are located here. Fist or palm compression can be very effective in releasing tight spasms in this area. You can also pound this area to send a tremor through the muscles and relax and release the deeper tissue.

This area is prone to accumulating lactic acid after strenuous work, and will go rock hard if your horse has 'tied-up' (the common term for a condition veterinary surgeons refer to as exertional rhabdomyosis). A mare may also show a similar heaviness over the rump and loins if her body is having difficulties dealing with the extra hormones in her body, so do not confuse this with tying-up. A vet should be consulted when a horse is suspected of tying-up. Never massage a horse in the acute stages of tying-up as this will exacerbate the condition.

The thigh

The four muscles in this region are collectively called the quadriceps. Significant nerves that govern this muscle group originate in the loins and any tightness in that region may also affect the action of your horse's hind legs. Many problems in the stifle area involve the quadricep muscles because they attach to the patella which in turn acts upon the stifle. If the horse goes down on its fetlocks during hard work, or if the hind leg is asked to extend past its normal stride when the diagonal shoulder is already sore or tight, your horse may be tight in these muscles as a result. If you find any tightness here it is worth checking the whole area extending from the loins to the hocks. To do this, use the compression technique and allow your pressure to range from light to firm. You can also cover the hamstrings (as shown).

Your horse's thigh muscles will tighten up if the angle of the hind leg hoof is too low and flat. If you find tightness in this area, consider whether a visit from the farrier may be a necessary part of your treatment too.

Inside of hind leg and the hamstrings

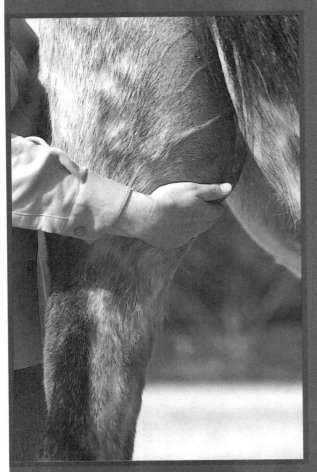

Use percussion, sweating or even myofascial release if you find any tightness in the hamstrings or the inside leg. Feel down the inside of the leg and reach around to feel the bulging Gracillus muscle and all accompanying muscle tissue on the inside of the leg. The hamstrings originate at the back of the sacrum and extend down the back of the hind legs. They comprise the Biceps femoris, Semitendinosus and the Semimembranosus. This group of muscles is largely responsible for flexing the stifle and extending the hock to give your horse locomotion. (The tone and size of your horse's hamstrings will tell you how much your horse is using his hindquarters.) Compression is very effective in releasing the hamstring muscles, along with deep finger pressure and cross-fibre friction where tight spots are located. Horses that compete in sports such as reining, campdrafting or polo, which require the hocks to slide under the horse's body, can be prone to developing fibrotic myopathy (scarring in muscle tissue). It is important to remember all these muscles when addressing hind-end muscular problems.

The stifle

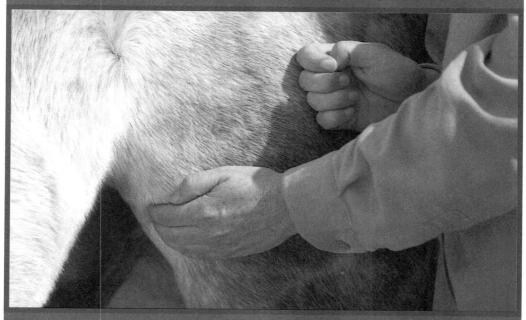

The stifle is a complicated joint comprising of three bones, femur, tibia and patella with many muscles attaching via tendons and ligaments. This is a dangerous area to work on—only attempt it if you are confident that you know the horse well.

Providing that you feel safe in doing so, feel all around the patella and check all the attachments. Always brace your other hand against the horse's thigh. This will give you some warning if he attempts to kick you away, as you will feel the muscle tighten first. The stifle is a complicated joint and many things can go wrong with its function (ie. an upward fixation of the patella commonly known as a locked stifle). When something is wrong in this area these attachments can feel like taut guitar strings.

To complete the massage, sweep your horse from head to tail using a smooth effleurage stroke. This will 'connect' all the areas you have worked and give your horse a sense of completion and connection to each part of his body.

AROMATHERAPY

SCENTED HORSES

Aromatherapy is based on the therapeutic use of essential oils extracted from plants. These essential oils may come from the flowers, leaves, bark or fruit of a plant and are products of the plant's metabolic processes. Essential oils have a strong scent that may vary from floral to herbal or earthy tones.

Aromatherapists do not condone or recommend any internal administration of essential oils. If ingested, essential oils must be processed directly by the liver, and this may prove fatal if the administered dose is above the therapeutic dose. Just a few drops of some essential oils may be enough to turn a therapeutic agent into a poison. Do not underestimate the strength of essential oils—the therapeutic action of some of those available is up to seventy times stronger than the fresh herb or source plant.

The safest ways to use aromatherapy with your horse are external massage and inhalation. In fact most treatments end up being a combination of both. When inhaled, essential oils address your horse's emotional states and stored memories, along with triggering an effect that eventually involves the endocrine system.

A scent is made up of minute aromatic molecules of different shapes. When detected by the tiny hairs in the nasal cavity, these molecules set off a chain reaction via the olfactory system. The tiny hairs (cilia) pick up the differently shaped molecules then transmit a signal in the form of electrical impulses along the nerve fibres to the olfactory bulb. The stimuli are processed here, and your horse then responds to these messages which are passed from the olfactory system to the limbic system, the area of the brain where emotions and memories are stored and the flight or fight response is triggered. In this way, aromatherapy has an impact on your horse's state of mind and can cause a cascade of internal responses. The limbic system and the hypothalamus gland instruct the release of neurochemicals throughout the body. They include endorphins and encephalin which reduce pain; serotonin which relaxes and calms; and noradrenaline which stimulates and enlivens. The hypothalamus gland is responsible for keeping a balance of this release and stimulating the correct release of these neurochemicals for this physical response.

After the messages have been picked up by the limbic system, the aroma molecules are transferred from the lungs to the bloodstream and consequently to every organ in the body. In this way, a physical response to aromatherapy is also achieved through olfaction. The simple action of inhaling an essential oil can begin a whole process that can have a physical effect throughout your horse's body.

Essential oils contain constituents small enough to enter a horse's body via the hair follicle and sweat glands when the oil is applied externally. The constituents then enter the bloodstream and have a physical effect on body tissues, working in a similar way to nicotine or hormone replacement therapy patches on humans. For example, camphor, which is a constituent of Rosemary, attaches itself to the haeme part of the blood and is circulated throughout the body in this way.

Essential oils should be simply applied with a cold-pressed vegetable oil or Aloe vera gel containing a 2.5 per cent dilution of essential oils. This is also the safest method, as the essential oils are absorbed through the skin into the bloodstream, circulated throughout the body and then excreted by the urinary system. A physical application also invites your horse to inhale the essential oils over their evaporation time. If a vegetable oil base is used, the essential oils may have an extended evaporation rate of up to 12 hours.

By staying within this safe, recommended range of dilution you will avoid irritating your horse's skin. Always keep in mind that your horse's skin is much more sensitive skin than yours. Pause and ask yourself if you would apply this massage oil to your own body. If not, do not even consider placing it anywhere near your horse's skin.

A 2.5 per cent dilution is usually excreted out of your horse's body within a week, though heavier resin-based essential oils may take longer. The constituents begin to be detectable in your horse's urine after approximately 4 hours. Depending on the essential oil you have used, the constituents could be out of your horse's system quickly or, if a fat soluble constituent is present, could take longer to leave the body. This is an important consideration if your horse is competing in a competition or race where he may be swabbed. Some associations have warned competitors that essential oils such as Eucalyptus and Peppermint are forbidden substances, and state that these essential oils are only examples (see page 24). Please take care if you are governed by such restrictions and list all essential oils on any required medication reports.

There is one important difference between the way aromatherapy blends should be used on your horse and the way they may be used on you. When you are given an aromatherapy treatment, the oils will be rubbed all over your body. When treating your horse, however, you only need to apply the essential oils (in their vegetable oil or Aloe vera gel carrier) to the area where you have determined the 'ouch' is. This is because it is difficult to remove vegetable oil from your horse's coat—using it on a small area will not diminish the treatment's effectiveness.

Quality is essential

Aromatherapy has become a commercial success for many businesses throughout the world. This has led to many aromatic products becoming available. Some of these products may be synthetic fragrances or just based on essential oils and 'extended' by some medium. The information in this chapter is based on years of experience using quality essential oils. If you deliberately choose or unknowingly use an inferior product, you may not achieve the result you desire, plus using synthetic fragrant oils on your horse will irritate broken or sensitive skin.

When you become experienced at selecting essential oils, your nose will be one of your best guides in assessing the true quality of an oil. Synthetic fragrances are high in alcohol content, which has a distinctive smell. You can also do several easy tests to determine if you have purchased a fragrant or essential oil that has been extended in some way. One test simply involves a glass of water. Essential oils are not water-soluble, so when you place a drop into water it should remain intact as a droplet for a reasonable period of time, sometimes as long as 10 seconds. If the droplet quickly dissolves into the water, it means that alcohol is present. If a milky, opaque film appears, it means that detergents or emulsifiers are present. Alcohol, detergents and emulsifiers are all adulterates which are not present in pure essential oils.

Another undesirable extension often used is vegetable or mineral oil. Unless they are derived from a resin base essential oils are watery to the touch, and adding a vegetable or mineral oil to the essential oil will make it feel greasy. A simple test for the presence of vegetable or mineral oil is to place a few drops of the essential oil onto white paper. A pure essential oil does not leave a grease mark or residue on the paper as it evaporates—if it does, the essential oil has almost certainly been extended with a vegetable or mineral oil.

Price is another useful indicator of the quality of an essential oil. The source of each essential oil must be painstakingly collected and processed to ensure the maximum yield. With delicate flowers such as jasmine and rose this is a labour-intensive exercise, which makes these essential oils much more expensive than the easily harvested and distilled oils such as Eucalyptus. If all the essential oils in a range you are considering are marked at the same price, many of the products may be synthetic fragrant oils.

The botanical source of your essential oil is very important. For example, there are two common oils labelled Sandalwood available; the Sandalwood referred to in most texts and in this book is obtained from the plant *Santalum album*. It has all the properties described and is relatively expensive. However, another plant commonly called sandalwood is *Amyris balsamifera*, which does not have the qualities described, is not as pleasant to the nose and is approximately a third of the cost.

A few cautions

Do not administer essential oils internally on your horse or yourself. Inhalation or topical applications combined with massage therapy are the safest ways for your horse to utilize essential oils. Only professionals should administer essential oils internally.

Keep essential oils away from the eye area. If you inadvertently irritate your eyes or your horse's eyes with essential oils, you can dilute the irritating oil with the plain base oil or milk to relieve the irritation. Do not use water to do this as it will spread the essential oil over a larger surface area and increase the irritability of the essential oil to the affected tissue. Veterinary advice should be sought for any irritation to your horse's eyes, and medical attention for irritation to your own.

It is always wise to use a base carrier oil or Aloe vera gel to apply essential oils to your horse's skin and to only use oils in a safe dilution. The use of undiluted essential oils may cause irritation, and the amount of essential oil used could be more costly than necessary. Always remember that your horse's skin is more sensitive than yours so if you would not put it on yourself, never put it on your horse.

Essential oils do not always have the same properties and actions as the original herb from which it was extracted. Sage, for example, is a powerful astringent when used in the form of a herbal extract or tea. This quality is attributed to the water-soluble tannins the herb contains. These tannins are not present in Sage essential oil, however, so it does not have an astringent action.

Avoid using essential oils on your horse close to competition dates if your chosen discipline is governed by an association that lists prohibited substances. Essential oils are absorbed into the bloodstream via the hair follicle and begin to be excreted out of the system within 4 hours, but some traces may remain in your horse's body for over a week. It is the owner's or rider's responsibility to ensure his or her horse is free of prohibited substances—so if you intend to use herbal preparations, check to see if a withholding period is necessary. To further complicate matters, the rules that determine which substances or levels of substances are illegal are always changing. Eucalyptus and Peppermint are two essential oils that are often mentioned, and care should be taken to avoid any essential oils containing camphor, menthol, phenol or thymol. Camphor is a ketone and, as such, it can build up in the body with constant use. Essential oils such as Rosemary, Marjoram and Cedarwood contain camphor and therefore should be avoided if you do not wish to be penalized.

While a mare is in foal it is wise to avoid the use of any essential oils with emmenagogic or diuretic properties—these oils could have an action on a pregnancy that is unlikely to go full-term. Ketone and phenol constituents have been attributed with an emmenagogic action. Some essential oils that contain these constituents and should be avoided with a pregnant mare are Ylang ylang, Thyme, Marjoram, Fennel, Cinnamon and Basil.

Among professionals there is much debate about whether these essential oils could cause a mare to slip a foal. There is little information available concerning the use of essential oils on pregnant women and even less on the use of essential oils with pregnant mares. Rely on your own common sense and avoid using oils during the first 3 months of pregnancy. Do not apply essential oils to the skin of a mare during the later stages of her pregancy, as the hormonal changes in her body will heighten her skin sensitivity and increase the likelihood of your oils causing irritation.

Avoid using any of the citrus oils on a horse that will be exposed to the sun within 4 hours after application. Most citrus oils are photosensitive and a reaction may occur. The sun will irritate the skin where the oil has been applied and your horse may then rub this area excessively. Bergamot, with its constituent begaptene, is the essential oil most likely to trigger a sensitivity, though some suppliers do have access to a begaptene-free variety.

If your horse is being treated with strong pharmaceutical drugs, avoid using any essential oils that are known to have a strong detoxifying action, as the drug needs to stay in your horse's system long enough for it to act. Grapefruit, Juniper and Lemon essential oils are all high in constituents that trigger the removal of toxins in the body, and so are best avoided in this situation.

You will find that there are many references available on aromatherapy. Information about how each essential oil should be used often varies from one author to another. If you are ever faced with contradictory information and are unsure about using an essential oil, seek the opinion of a qualified aromatherapist. My rule of thumb is 'If in doubt, don't'. Observe all these cautions, but have fun with aromatherapy. It is an activity that you and your horse can enjoy together.

THE SYNERGY OF ESSENTIAL OILS— PREPARE YOURSELF

When using aromatherapy with horses, you can either use one essential oil at a time or blend several essential oils together. Magic results can be created when more than one essential oil is used in combination. One essential oil used alone will have a result, but the combination of two essential oils will more than double that result. This enhanced 'energy' is what we aim to capture when combining essential oils.

The first thing to consider when blending essential oils—before you even select any oils—is intent. When you are making a blend of essential oils for your horse, your intention is intrinsically important; you must be focused and come from a quiet place within. If, for example, you are thinking about what groceries to buy or the argument that you had earlier in the day, that will be the energy you transmit to the oils as they blend together. Attempt to quiet your mind and come from your heart, and you will ensure a harmonious blend.

Now that you have prepared yourself for the task, here are three ways to blend essential oils for your horse. These different methods are only given as guidelines, and opinions about which is the best method are subjective—but each way is valid, so choose the one that works best for you.

Using notes

One way to approach blending essential oils is by isolating their 'notes'. The note of an essential oil is used in the perfumery industry to give an indication of the rate of evaporation. Perfumeries designate a top, middle or base note to an aroma. Top notes evaporate quickly. They create the first impression of your aromatherapy blend and often evaporate within 20 minutes. Middle notes evaporate within an hour and provide the body of your blend. Base notes are heavier essential oils and can take hours to evaporate. They are often added to a blend so that it stays on the skin and is appreciated longer. If you choose this method of blending, it is desirable to have at least one oil from each of these categories of notes. If you have a top, middle and base note represented you can rely on the blend to be well rounded.

Strength of odour

The second way to go about blending essential oils is by odour intensity. Some essential oils have a strong odour, and if you blend them with an essential oil with a weak odour, it will overpower the scent of the weaker essential oil. With this method each essential oil is given a number signifying the odour intensity of that oil compared to other essential oils. In the simplest method of doing this, the stronger essential oils are rated a 1, mid-range essential oils a 2, and weaker essential oils a 3.

Some systems get more complicated and broaden the range to a scale of 1–10 or 1–20, or give the essential oil an odour strength percentage. All are valid, just see what method suits you and your horse best.

These numbers then translate directly into a ratio for you to use when balancing your blend. For example, Basil has an odour intensity rating of 1, Lavender a 2 and Bergamot a 3. To get a balanced blend of these oils where none of them overpowers the scent as a whole, you would simply blend them in a ratio of 1:2:3, that is, 1 drop of Basil to 2 drops of Lavender and 3 drops of Bergamot. (This blend of oils is also balanced from a perfumer's perspective as Basil is a base note, Lavender is a middle note and Bergamot is a top note, thus giving you a representation of each rate of evaporation.) This chart gives you a guide to the notes and odour intensities of some of the most useful essential oils.

Blending Chart

ESSENTIAL OIL	BLENDING INDICATOR	NOTE
Basil	1	base
Bergamot	3	top
Carrot Seed	1	middle
Cardamom	2	middle
Cedarwood	2	base
Chamomile	1	base
Clary Sage	3	middle
Cypress	2	top
Eucalyptus	1	middle
Fennel	1	base
Frankincense	2	middle
Geranium	2	base
Ginger	1	middle
Grapefruit	3	top
Juniper	2	middle
Lavender	2	middle
Lemon	2	top
Lemongrass	1	base
Mandarin	2	top

ESSENTIAL OIL	BLENDING INDICATOR	NOTE
Marjoram	1	base
Myrrh	1	base
Orange	3	top
Palmarosa	2	base
Patchouli	1	base
Pepper	2	middle
Peppermint	1	top
Rosemary	1	middle
Tea Tree	1	middle/top
Vetiver	1	base
Yarrow	1	base
Ylang Ylang	1	base

Ask your horse

The third way to choose essential oils is to ask your horse. Narrow down a likely selection of essential oils and offer each to your horse, one at a time. Waft the uncapped bottle under his nose then slowly draw the bottle away. If the horse follows the bottle or shows interest with the Flehman response (lifting his nose and curling his top lip back to trap the scent inside his nasal cavity to obtain the maximum benefit from the scent), add this essential oil to his aromatherapy blend. If he shows no interest or even turns his head away, don't add this oil to his blend. If he shows a moderate interest in the oil, add 1–2 drops of this oil to the blend to give it a more balanced odour arrangement.

Balance the proportional amounts of the oils in the blend according to the enthusiasm of your horse's response. The larger portion of your blend should be made up of those oils in which your horse shows huge interest. The most positive response is the Flehman response, but you will get varying responses depending on your horse's age and needs. Your horse may follow the bottle as you draw it away, or even try to place his lip over the top of the bottle. Once you have found the oils that interest your horse the most, you need to prepare the blend.

I find the best results come from combining three or four essential oils. If you use more than six essential oils at once, the blend becomes too complicated to be appreciated and is less effective in treating the issues you have identified.

What to use as a carrier

When you have decided which essential oils you need to use with your horse, and in what proportions, you need to decide which carrier you will use. The carrier medium needs to hold the essential oils to the skin and slow down their evaporation, so that the constituents have time to find their way into the bloodstream via the hair follicle.

Cold-pressed vegetable oils are the most commonly recommended carriers for essential oils. One benefit of using cold-pressed vegetable oils is that they hold to the skin for 12 hours (but consequently are harder to wash off). Some professionals also select particular oils for certain conditions (for example, olive oil is very warming, so it is useful when treating conditions like arthritis). The most important factor when using cold-pressed vegetable oils is that they are what they say they are. Do not skimp on quality and buy your oil off the supermarket shelf. Vegetable oils sold for human consumption are often over-processed and have a pH balance that may cause blistering on your horse's skin. Many of these oils are rancid before you buy them. Never use a vegetable oil that feels sticky to the touch.

Aloe vera gel is soothing to the skin and useful for treating sensitive skin conditions, even when used on its own. It is also useful in situations where it is not suitable to apply a vegetable oil, or the blend has to be washed off easily before a competition. Ideally it is best to leave a blend of essential oils on the skin for up to 12 hours, but this is not always practical.

Mineral clays are also useful as a carrier and can have a healing ability even when used on their own. They are sold in a powdered form in various colours. You can add essential oil concentrations of up to 10 per cent when using powdered mineral clays as a carrier. Use a kitchen blender to mix the essential oils with the clay. If you wish to make a poultice, follow these steps but add a little water to the mixture.

Water can be used as a carrier, but because essential oils are not water-soluble you will need to add a detergent or alcohol to help disperse the droplets. Some situations in which water makes a suitable carrier are in a spray mister for cleansing the air in your horse's stable, and when making a compress. For the latter, add between 3–10 drops of the desired essential oils to the top of a bowl of warm water, then use a large piece of gauze to lift them off and apply the compress to the area you need to address.

Making a blend

It is best to add each essential oil to the carrier as it is selected. Because horses have a well-developed sense of smell, the blend of essential oils does not need to be very concentrated. A 2.5 per cent dilution of essential oils in cold-pressed vegetable oil or Aloe vera gel will give you the desired result—any stronger than this and you may be wasting money.

As a general rule, simply add 1 drop of essential oil for every millilitre of vegetable base oil or Aloe vera gel. If you are blending the oils in a bottle, simply rock the bottle to blend the essential oils. If blending the oils in a bowl, swirl your fingers through the blend.

Ask your horse again

When you have prepared the blend, ask your horse for his approval. Then you can decide how to apply the oils. If you have identified an area of sore muscles you can apply the blend to this area, but again, it is best to be guided by your horse. He may offer you his poll, neck, chest or loins, particularly if old memories or emotional issues need to be addressed.

THE ESSENTIAL OILS

There are over two hundred essential oils commercially available to use with horses. Of these, I have listed the ones that I have found to be safe and have regularly been 'selected' by horses themselves. Once you have gained confidence using these essential oils, you may wish to explore some of the oils not included in this book.

BASIL (*Ocimum basilicum*)

> Basil essential oil helps to release most muscle spasms. When used in a post-event massage, it minimizes the amount of uric acid in the blood and any other toxic waste that builds up during exercise. Basil is a warming winter oil, feeding the muscle fibres and stimulating blood flow to restricted areas. It is an expectorant, removing mucous from a clogged respiratory system when rubbed into the chest and inhaled. Basil rubbed onto your horse's abdomen may help to relieve the pain and symptoms of colic while you wait for a veterinary surgeon to arrive. Do not put yourself in danger if your horse is too restless and distressed for you to apply the oil safely, though.

During training and competition, Basil is an excellent essential oil to use to relieve nervousness and to help both you and your horse focus your minds on the task being performed. Basil is amphoteric in its action on the nervous system; that is, it will either stimulate or sedate depending on what the organism feels it requires.

Basil may irritate the skin if used in high doses. Note that it is an emmenagogue, so do not use it with a pregnant mare.

BERGAMOT (*Citrus bergamia*)

Bergamot essential oil is useful for treating any skin complaint, but particularly folliculitis, flaking skin and wounds. Lice infections respond to Bergamot, while the inflicted bites appreciate Bergamot's soothing action. Bergamot aids the healing of any wounds to the skin and will reduce the amount of scar tissue formed.

This essential oil is one to carry to competitions where anxiety levels are high and the 'butterflies in the tummy' become overpowering. By placing a few drops on the palm of your hand, rubbing your palms together and inhaling deeply, both you and your horse will dispel these feelings. Bergamot also has a stimulating effect on appetite. It is useful to have this aroma floating around your stable if your horse has gone off his food due to stress.

Be cautious when applying Bergamot to a grey horse or to sensitive skin areas that will be exposed to the sun. Bergamot is photosensitive and may stain a grey horse's coat or cause pigmentation changes.

CARDAMOM (*Elettaria cardamom*)

Cardamom essential oil is useful for treating digestive problems of a nervous origin. It encourages the flow of saliva and stimulates the loss of appetite. It is warming when the body feels cold and is useful in easing coughs and respiratory complaints. It is also useful in a body rub for horses during the cold winter months, as it strengthens and clears the respiratory tract. Cardamom is highly antiviral, and is second only to Eucalyptus in this respect.

Cardamom is useful for any horse that goes off his food at a competition or after a race. It is also a reputed aphrodisiac, so you can use it to help prepare your mare for serving to a stallion. Cardamom is a great essential oil to use during long competitions where you or your horse may suffer mental fatigue, weakness or confusion. Do not use it before or during an official competition where your horse may be swabbed, though.

Never mix Cardamom in water to apply it to your horse—always use a good quality carrier oil or Aloe vera gel. Cardamom irritates sensitive skins more than most other essential oils, so always stay within the recommended strengths.

CARROT SEED (*Daucus carota*)

Carrot seed is a good essential oil for your horse's all-round health and well-being. It strengthens the mucous membranes, so is helpful in treating respiratory conditions. Carrot seed is useful for regenerating the skin after wounds or skin diseases, and its antiseptic action will address minor infections. It has a toning, hormone-like action that will encourage conception and assist the infertile mare.

Carrot seed is very calming. If your horse is attracted to the scent it may be an indication that his stress levels are draining his biochemical needs, and his diet may be insufficient for his physical workload.

CEDARWOOD (*Cedrus atlantica*)

Cedarwood essential oil addresses sores that are slow to heal. If your horse suffers chronically from saddle sores or folliculitis, a direct application of Cedarwood in clay or base carrier oil will help to clear away any scabs or pus. Use compresses impregnated with Cedarwood to treat larger wounds. Cedarwood addresses dry, flaky skin and encourages regrowth of coat on areas that have been rug-rubbed. It also adds shine to the coat.

Cedarwood has a tonic effect on the kidneys, so it is useful in event preparation and post-event massage. If your horse pulls up stiff and tense, or has difficulty in urinating due to nerves after competitions, rub him down with Cedarwood or place a few drops of the essential oil on a firm brush and groom his coat. Cedarwood dries out excess phlegm and runny noses and removes excessive mucous from the respiratory tract when inhaled.

Cedarwood calms nervous tension and anxiety while also repelling insects, so it is a soothing oil to use during fly-ridden competitions.

CHAMOMILE (*Anthemis noblis*)

The strong analgesic properties of Chamomile essential oil relieve dull muscular aches and stubborn spasms. It also relieves overworked and inflamed muscles. Chamomile can address inflamed wounds and is particularly effective when used as a wash when cleaning and dressing such wounds. It is also useful in the local treatment of cuts and sores. Dry, flaking skin responds well to Chamomile. When using Chamomile to treat chronic skin conditions, use Jojoba oil as the base carrier oil as it moisturizes the skin deeply.

Chamomile is a useful essential oil for difficult horses. If your horse is having a temper tantrum, Chamomile's calming properties will ease unruly behaviour. Chamomile is a good oil for you to use if you are frustrated with your horse's training progress, as it promotes peace, eases worries and removes agitation.

If your mare becomes unmanageable when she cycles, include Chamomile in her daily care for a few days before this time. It is calming and regulates the hormonal activity in the body via the limbic system.

CLARY SAGE (*Salvia sclarea*)

Clary sage essential oil is for stress spasms that have been exacerbated by the anxiety of being asked to perform while in pain. This is the best oil to use when your horse seems to be saying 'I won't', but is really saying 'I can't'. If you try and push your horse into a movement that is uncomfortable or painful, the increased anxiety will cause his muscle to become more afflicted.

This oil has a strong cell regenerative power where hair loss is involved. It is also useful on puffy joints caused by long periods of standing, or as a preventative if your horse must stand for long periods of time, (for example, before a long journey in his box). Any swelling in the kidney area caused by strenuous work or sluggish kidney function can also be addressed by massaging a blend containing Clary sage into that area.

Clary sage calms underlying tension and soothes anxiety. It is useful when both the horse and rider are feeling the stress of competition and need settling without losing their competitive edge and focus. It has a grounding effect on racing minds and panicky states and keeps the whole team from losing inspiration during the day if a result comes in below expectations.

This essential oil is useful for a mare that is having trouble conceiving or is nervous when being matched to a stallion. It is an essential oil that many professionals avoid using during pregnancy, so avoid any physical applications of the oil after a mare has conceived.

CYPRESS (*Cupressus sempervirens*)

Cypress essential oil eases muscular cramps and rheumatism in older horses. Its styptic action can help to arrest bleeding when placed on a dressing and used with a pressure bandage, and make it effective in treating weeping wounds in a compress. Cypress is reputed to have a diuretic action on your horse's kidneys and will help if your horse is slow to urinate after a competition or ride. If there are any signs of puffiness in this zone, massage the lower back region with Cypress in a base carrier oil. The effect that Cypress has on the hypothalamus gland may also help to restore regular ovarian function in mares having difficulty in conceiving.

Do not apply Cypress essential oil undiluted, as its strong drying action may remove moisture too quickly.

Many horses take on the negative emotions or psychic state of people around them. Cypress will cleanse away this psychic debris. It can be useful on a recently purchased a horse whose erratic behaviour may be due to the imbalances of the previous owner.

EUCALYPTUS (*Eucalyptus globulus*)

Eucalyptus is the body rub oil. It eases muscular aches and pains caused by overexertion and relieves rheumatic pain and neuralgia. The antiviral action of Eucalyptus addresses respiratory infections by soothing inflammation and easing excess mucous. If an infection has caused a fever, eucalyptus used in a compress can lower the raised temperature.

Eucalyptus also heals sores prone to pus formation and, as it addresses any bacterial imbalance, it stops repeated infections from forming under new tissue. It aids concentration and will help a city-stabled horse connect with a sense of nature.

Eucalyptus is irritating to sensitive skins, so take care with its application and only use it in dilution.

FENNEL (*Foeniculum vulgare*)

Fennel essential oil strengthens your horse. It can be used as an inhalation or rubbed into the abdomen in a suspected case of colic, but always consult your veterinary surgeon first in this situation. Fennel is useful if your horse has difficulty eliminating toxins when stiff from exercise or competition. It is best applied to the body in a light, sweeping massage to stimulate the lymphatic and circulatory flow.

Fennel is a useful essential oil to use in any recovery period after an illness. It has an affinity with the liver and spleen and helps your horse's immune system regain strength.

Fennel's action via the limbic system can help to regulate the hormones of mares that behave unreasonably when they cycle, and can be used to encourage a sexual response from a mare. This is useful with maiden mares, who are sometimes reluctant to become mothers. Fennel also stimulates milk production (but do not apply it directly to the udder).

Because of Fennel's affinity with female hormones, I find it useful for mares and women during competitions as it gives courage and strength to both horse and rider. It maintains a healthy sense of caution if there is a chance the rider and horse may suddenly become reckless. Fennel eases any overexcitedness and restlessness caused by pre-competition jitters. You can use it yourself if your tummy needs settling—a few inhalations of this essential oil, and you will be able to face the most adversarial dressage test.

FRANKINCENSE (*Boswellia carteri*)

Frankincense eases shortness of breath and has a pronounced effect on mucous membranes and any respiratory problems. Rejuvenating in its action, it is useful in a massage blend for a horse recuperating from an operation or serious injury. Frankincense is an excellent tonic for an ageing horse that has lost the sheen in his eyes, and can be used as a daily pick-me-up.

Frankincense is good for cleaning old wounds that are stubborn to heal. Add a few drops to a bucket of water and wash the wound before applying your usual medication and bandaging. Do not apply it to or near the eyes, however.

Frankincense is contraindicated during pregnancy—do not use it on a pregnant mare.

Frankincense has the ability to dispel fear and anxiety. It is the 'rescue remedy' of the essential oils and is vital when you and your horse are recovering from the scare of a fall. Frankincense will help with any apprehension you experience when competing at grounds that are unfamiliar to you or your horse.

GERANIUM (*Pelargonium graveolens*)

Geranium essential oil is a gentle analgesic. It eases pain and gives you access to muscles that were previously too sore to massage, and comforts inflamed muscles when used in a topical application. (Take care not to work inflamed muscle problems too deeply, however, as you may increase the inflammation.) Geranium has diuretic properties and is useful when general elimination is poor. It has a tonic action on the liver and kidneys and, when combined with massage, helps to clear the body of toxins. It is a good essential oil to use after a competition, when your horse is sore from not being able to eliminate the build-up of lactic acid. Geranium's affinity with the lymphatic system helps your horse regain a balanced system.

It also balances the hormones and emotions. If you have a horse that suffers from erratic mood swings, regular inhalations of Geranium essential oil will help address this. Wear it as a perfume if you are competing on a mare in season.

Geranium is also good when you are training your horse to do something that requires a negotiation between the two of you. This essential oil clears the air for any negotiation, whether it is between you and your horse, you and your coach, or you and an official. The scent of Geranium always creates harmony.

GINGER (*Zingiber officinale*)

Ginger is a great essential oil to use in winter. Be careful when applying it to sensitive skins, as it is a strong rubefacient. Ginger will make up for any malady caused by cold or dampness. It stimulates circulation to cold joints and is analgesic, relieving arthritic and rheumatic pain, muscle spasms and sprains. Ginger will be helpful in treating any stiff movement in your horse. It is also useful for clearing bruising and treating any respiratory disorders where excess moisture or mucous is apparent.

Ginger essential oil is an appetite stimulant and will relieve travel sickness. If your horse goes off his food after a competition or after being transported by box, include Ginger in his massage treatment. Inhaling Ginger will raise the spirits if you or your horse are feeling discouraged by the cold.

GRAPEFRUIT (*Citrus paradisi*)

Grapefruit is a gentle and effective lymphatic stimulant. It nourishes cells while helping to eliminate toxins. Grapefruit is a tonic for the liver and is useful in helping the liver manufacture the white corpuscles necessary for fighting infections. This essential oil balances the kidneys and vascular system by having a cleansing effect on your horse. You can use Grapefruit if there is any sign of stiffness in your horse's movement after exercise. Grapefruit also stimulates the metabolism of cells in the skin, improving the tone of dull, lifeless skin caused by dehydration with poor circulation.

Grapefruit clears negativity and lifts resentment from the air. It is good to use when you feel that things are not going your way. It is also a useful way to begin apologizing to your horse if you have taken your frustration out on him. Hurtful words and abuse lodge in both human and horse energy fields. A few drops of Grapefruit on the hands and brushed through both your energy fields will clear the way for fresh communication without the hurt. Grapefruit is euphoric in its action, and can leave both you and your horse feeling quite intoxicated after its use.

Be careful not to expose your horse to strong sunlight within 4 hours of application, however, as Grapefruit is photosensitive and the skin may become irritated.

JUNIPER (*Juniperus communis*)

When applied with massage techniques, Juniper essential oil helps to clear toxins from your horse's system. When your horse goes back into work after a rest and stiffens up, Juniper helps to release any build-up of waste products produced by the cells. All aches and pains (including arthritis and stiffness) respond to Juniper. It purifies the blood and strengthens the myofascial tissue, helping it operate more efficiently and creating ease of movement.

Juniper works via the limbic system to help stimulate kidney function, so it is useful if your horse is not urinating regularly. If your horse's kidneys are not operating optimally, skin problems, aching limbs and swellings may result.

Drowsiness and lethargy after a competition may indicate your horse is not eliminating waste by-products very well. The overload of waste needs to be excreted by the urinary system, a process that can be stimulated by massage with Juniper. Juniper is a good day-after-competition pick-me-up oil. It can also help when you and your horse are suffering a lack of concentration. During competition Juniper is the anti-worry scent. It is useful in rehabilitating nervous horses after abuse or mishandling.

Juniper essential oil is so efficient in stimulating elimination that it should not be used on a pregnant mare. It should not be used if your horse is receiving antibiotics from your veterinary surgeon either, as it will remove the prescribed pharmaceuticals.

Other people's thoughts have an impact on our being. Juniper protects you from these thought projections. If you are at a competition and can't quite get it together, look for a possible cause—maybe another competitor is jealous of your achievements or someone you have an ongoing altercation with is upsetting you.

LAVENDER (*Lavandula officinalis*)

Always keep Lavender on hand as your first-aid kit in a bottle. Lavender is cell-regenerating and hastens the healing process by encouraging cell growth. You can apply Lavender to any cuts, rug-rubs or scarring. Lavender can be used to ease the heat out of almost any condition, particularly inflammatory conditions: gently apply Lavender oil in Aloe vera gel, then leave the area alone.

If your horse suffers from excessive abdominal gas, Lavender oil will help to dispel gas and ease muscle tightness.

Lavender sedates and soothes any wound or emotion. The scent gives a feeling of space and calms frazzled nerves. If you live in the city and have to rush to and from the stable each morning and night to attend to your horse, keep Lavender essential oil in your car. This will clear away your daily stresses, allowing you relate to your horse in a carefree way.

LEMON (*Citrus limonum*)

If your horse suffers from sores or skin maladies, Lemon essential oil will stimulate the body to excrete toxins and wastes via the skin. It is gently astringent and encourages the movement and release of excess toxins. Lemon is an age-old remedy for warts, though careful and daily application is required to achieve results. If applied after an event, Lemon will support the liver and kidneys as they struggle to decongest the cellular waste products accumulated through excessive work.

During the colder seasons, Lemon gently addresses runny, watery respiratory problems and boosts your horse's immune system. When treating older horses, Lemon can be included in a blend for rheumatic or arthritic pain. Adding Lemon to a massage blend will help your horse recover from dehydration.

Every instructor or coach should have Lemon on hand. It fortifies the mind, dries away tears and is refreshing if both parties get hot and bothered.

As with all citrus oils, Lemon can irritate sensitive skin. Lemon is one of the least photosensitive of the citrus oils, but are must be taken if your horse is to be exposed to sunlight after an application.

LEMONGRASS (*Cymbopogon citratus*)

Lemongrass essential oil is a remedy for aching muscles. It relieves pain and makes the muscles supple. Lemongrass is good to include in an after-sports blend to apply to hardened or damaged muscles, tendons and ligaments.

When combined with lymphatic drainage massage techniques, Lemongrass essential oil stimulates the removal of congestion if your horse has generated excessive toxins during heavy work. This oil will remove these toxins and restore tone to your horse's skin.

Lemongrass stimulates and revives the mind. It is useful if inhaled while you are studying dressage tests and attempting to imprint them in your mind. (If you use essential oils while studying tests or course layouts, a quick sniff of those oils before competing will help you recall the information more readily when it counts.) This is an essential oil that will help you and your horse complete that final event of the day.

Be cautious about applying Lemongrass to an area that is sensitive or has an open cut or wound, as it can be irritating when used in strong concentrations. Due to its strong detoxifying action, you should avoid using Lemongrass on your horse if your veterinary surgeon has already prescribed pharmaceutical drugs.

MANDARIN (*Citrus reticulata*)

Mandarin essential oil nourishes the peripheral circulation, feeding any extremity that suffers from poor circulation. It addresses muscle spasms in a 'happy' way, by lifting away any depression associated with pain. Mandarin's antispasmodic properties also have an action on the intestinal tract and will stimulate your horse's appetite if he is finding it difficult to adjust to any changes around him.

Mandarin can safely be used with pregnant mares. Though pregnancy is a natural state, a pregnant mare can get sore shoulders and a stiff back. Because Mandarin is gentle in its action, it is also recommended for recovery after foaling.

Mandarin is a 'happy' citrus oil that lifts away all feelings of irritability and sadness. It is good for riders suffering performance anxiety and will cheer-up and inspire the nervous rider. Mandarin is fresh and lively, and will calm young horses or lift older horses that have lost their childlike spark.

MARJORAM (*Oridanum majorana*)

Marjoram is a good essential oil to use in winter. It warms cold, aching joints, relieves muscle spasms and draws bruising to the surface. Marjoram also eases the aches and pains of arthritis and swollen joints in the older horse. It helps with any form of travel sickness, so it is useful for long-distance travel. This essential oil acts as a sedative, reduces any discomfort the horse may experience due to muscle spasms and has a beneficial effect on respiratory disorders. As it is soothing to the digestion, it is a good essential oil for your horse to inhale if he goes off his feed after being transported by box or competing. Do not use it prior to competing, however, as it is a strong sedative.

It is useful for horses that become agitated or restless at competitions or during lessons, and do not respond to gentler oils.

Marjoram has a reputation for dissipating sexual desire. It may be a useful essential oil if you are competing on a stallion and your poor boy is stabled next to the cutest mare at the competition.

MYRRH

Myrrh is a thick, resinous essential oil with a drying, antiseptic action that is useful for addressing deep-seated respiratory complaints when inhaled. It can also be used in a compress to address boils, chapped or weeping skin conditions, and fungal conditions like ringworm.

Myrrh is a very grounding essential oil. When wafted under your horse's nose after a period of weakness or close to the end of a hectic season, it will give him strength and encourage his appetite.

Myrrh has a very strong scent, so often less is better than more. Because Myrrh does not move through the body quickly, it is best suited to short-term use. It has a stimulating, toning action on the mare's reproductive system, so it is best to avoid using this oil on a pregnant mare.

ORANGE (*Citrus aurantium*)

Orange essential oil encourages the formation of collagen, a substance that is vital for the growth and repair of body tissues. Orange is excellent for treating old horses coming close to their life's end. It is useful with palliative care and for old horses suffering with sore muscles and rickety, arthritic bones.

Orange has a happy energy. It eases out the constriction of muscle spasm and is a gentle remover of toxins, especially if your horse is prone to congested skin after a competition. Include this oil in a post-event massage treat for your horse after he has been washed down.

Orange will revive you and your horse if you feel bored or your energy levels are dropping towards the end of a long day of competition. If you are feeling disgruntled with your results so far and you still have to perform later in the day or competition, Orange will bring you harmony and joy. It will cheer depression after a disappointing result, ease anxiety and dissipate sadness so that you and your horse can focus on your next training session or competition.

Caution: Orange is photosensitive. Avoid using it on any areas of white skin, as it may increase the likelihood of a reaction. You should also avoid using it on a grey horse, as it may stain the coat.

PALMAROSA (*Cymbopogon martini*)

Palmarosa essential oil is helpful when the body is overheated. It encourages cellular regeneration and aids hydration by encouraging the flow of fluids throughout your horse's body. Palmarosa has a beneficial effect on stiff joints and aching backs. Skin conditions also respond to Palmarosa. Sensitive skin conditions including folliculitis respond to gentle applications of Palmarosa in powdered clay. When diluted in Aloe vera gel, this oil stimulates the regrowth of your horse's coat after rug-rub or where there has been an injury.

Palmarosa tones the nervous system and brings balance to extreme situations. Use Palmarosa at competitions where emotions are high and outcomes vital. It is steadying for grooms when their employer is stressed and not considerate of their efforts.

PATCHOULI (*Pogostemon cablin*)

Patchouli is a tissue regenerator and aids in the healing of wounds. It has the unusual ability to address old scar tissue if applied regularly. Patchouli is useful when treating sores that contain heat; a compress impregnated with Patchouli will cool the wound and help heal the skin without drying it out too quickly. Fungal infections are also responsive to Patchouli.

Swelling and fluid retention can be reduced by the astringent properties of Patchouli. It helps the skin regain its elasticity and restores tone to loose skin. If your horse is not urinating at a competition because he is nervous, the diuretic properties of Patchouli, when massaged into the horse's back, will encourage him to urinate.

Patchouli is good to use on skittish horses that need to be calmed and given a sense of solid ground. It is also useful for the horse and rider that just can't get it together, as it connects the pair and plants all feet firmly on the ground. Patchouli helps the rider address self-doubts, too.

PEPPER (*Piper nigrum*)

Pepper essential oil gives tone to skeletal muscles and warms any winter chills. The action of this oil dilates local blood vessels and improves blood flow to the muscles, warming the muscles from the inside. With this improved circulation, the muscle is able to relax and resume its normal function. Pepper also expels toxins from your horse's body and relieves the ache of excessive exertion.

A horse with a constantly cold back will respond to a massage blend containing pepper. Pepper can be used to address stiff joints and restore smooth movement. Chronically arthritic joints respond well to Pepper, as its warming action helps with pain management when used over a long period of time. Because Pepper essential oil is detoxifying, avoid using it on your horse if your veterinary surgeon has prescribed pharmaceuticals that must stay in your horse's system.

If your horse has become moody and despondent, causing severe loss of appetite, the scent of Pepper will encourage your horse to eat by stimulating the flow of saliva, his appetite and digestion.

Pepper strengthens the nervous system and gives stamina when you and your horse are experiencing frustration. It warms the heart of those feeling indifferent.

PEPPERMINT (*Mentha piperita*)

Peppermint is a strong essential oil that should only be used for local applications, as it is too cooling to be applied in a full body rub. Peppermint is so effective it need only be added to a blend in a 1 per cent dilution. I never use Peppermint on a horse before I have gauged the horse's skin sensitivity, though, as it can burn sensitive skin. Peppermint has a cooling and analgesic action on heated local injuries. It is particularly useful for treating puffy tendons after a morning workout.

The cooling nature of Peppermint cools heated emotions, relieving anger and hysteria. It also drives away mental fatigue and depression.

A cup of Peppermint tea during long days of competition will lift a heavy load from the shoulders of competitors and support crews. Keep a bottle of Peppermint in your car for long trips to and from competitions, to keep you refreshed while driving and to relieve travel sickness.

Peppermint is a useful essential oil to use after any accident when you and your horse may be suffering from shock or nervous trembles. When inhaled, Peppermint will help you gather your thoughts. It is also useful for stabilizing your horse's appetite after a fright.

CAUTION: Peppermint should not be used if you or your horse are taking homeopathic remedies, as it can interfere with the vibratory effect of such treatments.

ROSEMARY (*Rosmarinus officinalis*)

Rosemary is the most stimulating essential oil available to you. It stimulates both the physical and mental bodies into action. Tired, overworked muscles benefit from Rosemary. It has a pain-relieving constituent that eases away most aches and pains without sedating your horse. Rosemary also aids with the relief of congestion and puffiness or swelling around joints. It can encourage hair growth and help restore health and vitality to a rubbed or dull coat.

Rosemary is useful for stimulating a horse that will not 'spark up' for a competition (unless your discipline is governed by prohibited substances rules), and to keep a horse alert for a long trip home after an exhausting competition. Rosemary energizes and activates a sloppy brain, quickly aiding access to the limbic system and memories. It is the best oil to have burning while studying a dressage test, and to inhale later when you have to recall each part of the test.

The stimulating effect of Rosemary is best avoided with horses or people prone to fits.

Due to its strong stimulative action, avoid using Rosemary on a pregnant mare.

TEA TREE (*Melaleuca alternifolia*)

Tea tree is one of the most useful essential oils to have in your stable. Be cautious when using it on a horse for the first time, though, as it may irritate sensitive skin.

The antibacterial and antiviral properties of Tea tree will address problems caused by bacterial or viral infection. Tea tree is antipruritic and will take the itch out of any condition. It is also anti-fungicidal and useful for treating ringworm and thrush. A few drops of Tea tree oil added to iodine spray will assist with the treatment of hoof thrush infections. Its strongly antiseptic properties will help your horse sweat away toxins and shorten the duration of an illness. As with many essential oils, Tea tree stimulates the manufacture of white corpuscles when infection is present. As a cleansing essential oil, it is helpful for treating wounds and can also be used to fortify your horse before he has surgery and to bring about a quicker recovery. Tea tree oil encourages healing with minimum scarring.

Tea tree should only be used in moderation, however, as some conditions can develop a resistance to Tea tree essential oil when it is given in repeated high doses.

The fresh scent of Tea tree can help you and your horse recover from a sudden shock.

VETIVER (*Vetiveria zizanoides*)

Vetiver is a thick, resinous essential oil. Though it can be used in moderation to treat aches and pains and is a good tonic for most body systems, its main use is on the emotional barometer.

Vetiver is useful for the horse that is debilitated and depressed. It also addresses almost every form of nervous tension. Your horse may be attracted to this essential oil between dressage tests if you are feeling nervous and he needs to ground himself in order to cope with your emotions. Vetiver also provides a protective shield from outside influences, so your horse can stay 'in the moment' throughout his performance.

Due to its resinous nature, I do not use Vetiver in a physical application. Inhalation is the most powerful application for this essential oil.

YARROW (*Achillea millefolium*)

Yarrow has anti-inflammatory properties due to its high azulene content. This oil has a broad healing action on skin imbalances, wounds, rheumatism, arthritic changes, winter ills, all forms of colic ranging from flatulent to spasmodic, and nerve pain. Yarrow is an after-care balm and it will encourage your horse's body to detoxify after an infection. It can help your horse's body regain equilibrium after a serious illness and stimulate the regrowth of his coat after injury. Yarrow can also encourage the appetite after a stressful incident.

The erratic moods of mares can be addressed with Yarrow. This essential oil has a very balancing and settling effect on a mare experiencing the rise and fall of hormones.

Avoid using Yarrow essential oil if your vet is treating your horse with pharmaceuticals, as it has a strong detoxifying action.

YLANG YLANG (*Cananga odorata*)

Ylang ylang is most commonly used as an aphrodisiac and can be used to prepare both mare and stallion before joining. It is also a useful essential oil for addressing irritated and oily skin conditions, but do not use it on any areas where you feel heat. When inhaled, it can help rebalance a stressed respiratory rhythm. As it has an affinity with the adrenal glands, Ylang ylang can be of particular help to the young male horse feeling drained and flat at the end of a competition season. The scent of this oil provides a safety blanket of reassurance that helps the younger horse feel appreciated when he first begins training and is asked to perform.

Ylang ylang needs only a hint of the fragrance to begin working—a strong dilution can cause headaches and nausea.

APPLYING ESSENTIAL OILS

You can offer your horse essential oils on a daily basis or make the process a weekly ritual. When treating respiratory tract infections or in times of distress, your horse may need to inhale essential oils at least three times a day. Essential oils can be used daily in dressings, in applications to localized muscle soreness, and on a brush in your horse's grooming session.

Do not assume that the essential oil or blend of essential oils that your horse needed yesterday or last week is the one he will need today. Your horse's physical symptoms, emotional states and outlook on life can change suddenly, and your selection of essential oils should remain flexible enough to meet these changes.

Always ask your horse which oils he needs. Using essential oils with your horse on a regular basis will help you understand your horse and help you relate to each other.

Remember there may be times when your horse simply needs the aroma of an essential oil, especially if he has an emotional issue. In this situation it is best to use only one essential oil and be guided by your horse's instructions. He may only want to inhale the scent from your warmed hands, or he may want you to wipe the essential oil, placed in a small amount of Aloe vera gel, on his poll.

HOMEOPATHY

HOMEOPATHIC REMEDIES

Homeopathy is based on the interesting idea that giving a horse a 'taste' of an illness that produces symptoms much like those already being experienced, can actually help him throw off the original illness. Homeopathic texts refer to this as 'similar treating similar'. This idea of treating a disease state with a dose of a similar disease in a highly diluted or potentized form (considered to be a 'minimum dose') was first developed by Samuel Hahnemann (1755–1843). Hahnemann found that by repeatedly diluting the crude material he had chosen and succussing (vigorously shaking) the material before making each dilution, he released what homeopaths refer to as the dynamis. The dynamis is the life force of the crude material. It is this life force that helps restore homeostasis in our horse's body when there is a situation that requires first-aid attention. If you were to use laboratory tests to try to identify what was within the remedy, the original material would not show up at all. In the preparation of homeopathic remedies, the herb or substance is diluted and succussed until all that remains of the substance is its vibration.

The philosophy of homeopathy is based on helping your horse maintain his vital force. In any living animal this vital force is the energy system that maintains a harmonious function within the body. When the horse's health is threatened by some other influence, this vital force attempts to restore balance. If it is unsuccessful and the balance remains disturbed, a disease state can occur. Your horse's physical and behavioural symptoms are expressions of the disease. These symptoms can give you clues about how the vital force of the horse has been disturbed and help you choose the best remedy to give to your horse. The vibrational interchange between the vital forces of the horse and the remedy stimulate the horse's immune response.

To determine which remedies would address certain disease states, the first homeopaths conducted carefully controlled systematic trials referred to as 'the testing of provings'. 'Proving' a remedy involved giving a number of healthy people a minute amount of a certain substance until symptoms developed that were different to their own state of health. Treatment was then discontinued and the symptoms usually wore off within a week. Each trial was documented and became part of what is referred to as Rubics in the homeopathic materia medica. Homeopaths believe that a substance that produces symptoms of sickness in a healthy body can potentially cure those symptoms when they are present in a sick body.

If you choose the correct homeopathic remedy, the remedy will only act on the diseased part you are targeting and have a benign action on healthy tissue. But if you choose and continue to use the wrong remedy you may 'prove' the remedy, that is, bring new symptoms typical of the illnesses associated with that remedy to your horse. If you do not exceed the doses recommended in this book, it is unlikely that the wrong choice of remedy will have an adverse affect on your horse.

CHOOSING A HOMEOPATHIC REMEDY

Choosing a remedy is a complex decision. Professionals begin by putting together a constitutional picture, assessing the horse and noting every possible detail concerning physical, mental and emotional symptoms, as well as unusual behaviour. Constructing a constitutional picture is a specialized area of practice that requires the skills of a professional, and therefore is not covered in this book. What is discussed in this chapter are those remedies that can be used by you when your horse is faced with a simple health challenge, or as first aid in an emergency while waiting for your veterinary surgeon to arrive.

The key to selecting the best remedy often lies in what appears to be a minor symptom. You may notice that your horse suddenly prefers to rest sitting or standing, or he wants you to fuss over him, or he appears to feel better if you apply cold or heat to an area. It is important to acknowledge anything that you or others notice about your horse when you are deciding which remedy to use. Look at your horse as fully as possible; remember you are treating the whole horse.

When you read through the list of first-aid remedies in this chapter, you will sometimes see that a disease state can be addressed by one of several different remedies. Examine your horse's symptoms as closely as you can to help you select the one correct remedy from those suggested. The classical homeopath chooses only one remedy at a time to avoid confusing the horse's body. Each remedy is peculiar to itself. If you introduce more than one remedy at a time, they may interfere with each other's actions—and if a successful result is obtained, you will not know which of the remedies gave you this result. (Experienced professionals may alternate remedies in certain cases, however.)

DECIDING ON THE SIZE OF THE DOSE

The sequential steps of dilution and succussion produce the two scales of potencies that you will use when treating your horse with this therapy. In an 'X' (decimal) potency remedy, the dilution factor is tenfold at each step with the consequent ten succussions after each dilution (i.e., 1 drop of substance to every 10 drops of alcohol base). In a 'C' (centesimal) potency remedy, the dilution factor is one hundredfold at each step with the consequent one hundred succussions after each dilution (i.e., 1 drop of substance to every 100 drops of alcohol base). A simple way to remember this is to take yourself back to school and your roman numerals: 'X' equals ten and 'C' equals one hundred. As ten is less than one hundred, it will also remind you that

X potencies are less potent than C potencies, which are more dynamic and have a wider action. C potencies contain less of the original substance's constituents but more of its concentrated vibration, and are therefore more dynamic on a physical, emotional, mental and spiritual level.

If all of the symptoms you observe are physical, keep the dose of your chosen remedy within the lower potencies. If the distinguishing symptoms are mental patterns, however, choose a higher potency dose such as 200C. Avoid using high potency doses with horses that you suspect have a weak vital force due to serious illness or age.

As a general rule, when selecting a homeopathic remedy it is best to address the symptoms with a low potency first. By starting with a low potency you reduce the risk of aggravating the horse's body. Aggravation occurs when you have chosen the correct remedy, but the potency you have selected is a little too strong. Don't be too concerned if you do see a mild aggravation (i.e., a slight worsening of symptoms); the remedy is having a stimulating effect on the immune response, and this is an indication that it is working. If a strong aggravation occurs soon after the dose has been given, the potency you have chosen is too strong or you may have used the wrong remedy. If you don't adjust your dose or remedy and the aggravation continues for more than 5 days, your horse may begin to 'prove' the remedy. At this point you must stop dosing the remedy altogether, and you may need to consult a professional who will help you antidote the remedy.

Very low potencies ranging from 1X or 6C work on a physical level, directly affecting your horse's cells and biochemical needs.

Low potencies such as 12X or 24C relate to specific tissues and organs, so the symptoms you are addressing are likely to be very specific. Low potency doses are safe for the owner who is just beginning to use homeopathic remedies or is unsure how to proceed. When in doubt, don't use a potency higher than 30C. A low potency dose is also a safe choice when there are only few characteristic symptoms, and the horse's condition does not appear to be complex. Use low potency doses when treating chronic conditions that have advanced to physical or structural changes, or when you suspect the horse's vital forces are low, as the higher potencies do have a definite action that could cause an imbalance in a very weak horse. It is also wise to begin with a low potency dose when the horse has had long-term pharmaceutical care, or the symptoms have been suppressed by cortisone treatments for a period of time.

Medium potencies such as 60X or 30C work on a slightly deeper level. These potencies tend to have an energetic affinity with entire body systems rather than one organ (for instance, the whole respiratory tract, not just the lungs).

Dose levels that should only be used by experienced practitioners

Doses ranging between 30C and 200C can be used by owners who are more experienced with homeopathic remedies. At this level there is flexibility to go from one scale of potencies to the other. In cases where two, three or four remedies seem equally indicated, select a medium potency dose of the most appropriate remedy. Certain situations may call for two remedies to be used in alternation; however, this requires the supervision of a professional, who will usually recommend known combinations. Where remedies must be alternated, potencies in this range give the best results.

Acute episodes or illnesses that may be a flare-up of a chronic condition also respond best to these potencies. A dose in this range would allow you to address localized symptoms. When these have been brought under control you can return to treating the horse at a constitutional level, as directed by a professional.

If you think you need to consider using a potency higher than 200C on your horse, consult a professional first. While a horse with strong vitality usually responds well to high potencies, the symptoms may not be clearly defined or they may have become confused. At this potency the remedy will have an effect on the horse's mental and emotional sphere and deeper personality structure, so it is essential that you seek professional advice.

High potency doses range from 200C to 1M (M represents the millesimal scale with a proportion of 1:1000, that is, one drop of substance to one thousand drops of alcohol base) and their action encompasses overall metabolic and control systems. These remedies influence whole body systems including the hormones and the nervous and immune systems, but should only be used under the advice and supervision of a professional.

Very high potency doses ranging from 10M to 50M and CM (CM represents the hundred-millesimal scale) and are strictly in the domain of the professional. These potencies address the deepest levels of biology, psychology, genetic predispositions, and even spiritual directions. Some countries now restrict access to these higher potencies to professionals only.

HOW TO ADMINISTER A HOMEOPATHIC REMEDY

Homeopathy has several methods of application. The easiest way to administer homeopathic remedies is to add 6–10 drops of the chosen liquid homeopathic remedy to a small syringe, fill the remainder with bottled water, then squeeze into your horse's mouth. If your horse has an aversion to this, you can use tablets and slip them behind his bottom lip, where they are absorbed by mucous membranes. (One tablet is the equivalent of 3–6 drops). Alternatively, add a powdered version to his feed or a bran mash. Remedies such as Arnica are suitable for external application and can be applied to the skin when diluted in a cream or lotion.

As soon as you observe a change or a definite improvement in your horse's condition, stop and wait before dosing again, if at all. You may also find that when you decide to dose again, there may be different symptoms, indicating that you need to re-evaluate and possibly change the remedy.

In general, a remedy only needs to be given until the body is stimulated to respond. It requires very careful observation to notice a subtle improvement, and a temporary worsening which indicates a mild aggravation caused by the remedy. Remember the role of a homeopathic remedy is to stimulate the horse's body to heal itself, and let nature do the rest.

In moderate acute cases it may be appropriate to dose every 4 hours until you have an improvement. In chronic cases, dose once or twice a day for no longer than 7 days. Sometimes with long-term treatments, you administer the dose once a week over several weeks. High potencies in chronic conditions do not need to be repeated until the first dose has finished working—which may be anything from weeks to months. Remember, higher potencies are the domain of professionals, and in these cases it takes their experience to recognize when remedies have ceased to act effectively.

What if it's not working?—the wrong dose or the wrong remedy?

In classical homeopathy only one remedy is given at a time, and if the need for a second remedy is required the practitioner waits for at least 20 minutes before administering it. If the remedy seems a perfect match for your horse's symptoms but you haven't observed any change after six doses, try a different potency. Always change the potency before you try changing to another remedy (it is usual to choose a higher potency, though a weaker one will occasionally be indicated for some remedies). If you decide to select a higher potency, increase the level of the dose gradually over several treatments.

If the body is still not in balance after the remedy has been given ample time to act (six doses for an acute condition, anywhere from 2–8 weeks for a chronic condition), decide whether to continue using the remedy at a higher dose or select a different remedy. A remedy can, however, act on other diseased areas of the horse, known or unknown, and raise the whole horse's health level to its optimum by addressing these other regions of ill health, particularly in constitutional prescribing when a professional is working with your horse.

If for some reason the horse gets worse and the reaction seems like more than a mild aggravation, you should antidote the remedy with a dose of homeopathic Camphor or offer him regular inhalations of strong essential oils such as Camphor, Eucalyptus and Peppermint. You should also contact a professional as soon as possible, as he or she may also have other suggestions to help you.

Dose levels for first-aid treatment

In first-aid situations you often have a choice of several suitable remedies. Usually one or two indicators will help you decide which is the most appropriate remedy. For example, both Belladonna and Bryonia can be used for painful symptoms; however, their specific indicators are quite distinct: Belladonna is specifically recommended for symptoms that came on quickly and aggressively, whereas Byronia is more effective in treating pain that came on slowly, making the patient most reluctant to move.

Most first-aid scenarios require a standard potency dose ranging between 3X and 200C. Remember, lower potency doses are effective in most situations where a physical cause or symptom is involved, while higher doses encompass the mental aspects of disease as well.

In an acute emergency situation a 30C potency dose given every 10–20 minutes or a 200C potency dose given every 30–60 minutes for 4 hours is recommended. In moderately acute situations give a 30C potency dose once every 1–2 hours for up to six doses, or a 200C dose every 6 hours for up to four doses. For mildly acute situations administer a 30C potency dose once daily for up to 3 days, or a 200C potency dose once daily for only 1–2 days. As soon as you see significant improvement give your doses less frequently, but do not continue treatment when you have reached the point where homeostasis has been restored. Never give more than twelve doses of any remedy without professional consultation.

There are of course first-aid situations where your horse is unconcious or choking, and it isn't possible to administer drops or tablets internally. In this case you can dab drops on his face, muzzle and around the ears while you wait for your vet.

Purchasing and storing homeopathic remedies

Many pharmacies and health food stores now carry a broad range of homeopathic remedies. Do not confuse them with herbal preparations. Labelling should include the wording 'Homeopathic Medicine' with the remedy name and the potency level of that remedy. It is not a good idea to make your own remedies, as specialist knowledge is required. It is also a time-consuming process, and you need a licence to obtain pure alcohol for the base of the remedy.

Store your homeopathic remedies away from direct sunlight and below 40°C (104°F). Do not place them near strong smelling substances such as camphor (mothballs, tiger balm or camphor wood furniture), disinfectants, toothpaste or essential oils (particularly Eucalyptus, Rosemary and Peppermint).

HOMEOPATHIC FIRST RESPONSE REMEDIES FOR HORSES:

ACONITE

Aconite is a remedy you will need if your horse suffers a sudden ailment, especially if it is the result of a violent, painful and frightening episode. You may notice that your horse is restless, head tossing and showing signs of extreme stress. You may also notice that his eyes are shining very brightly. Contact your veterinary surgeon, and use Aconite to help dispel the fear you and your horse are feeling. You can use Aconite for acute inflammatory complaints and in situations where distress has been triggered by exposure to cold, dry wind, shock or fear.

Aconite is also a remedy for fever caused by exposure to cold; the main indicator is a bounding pulse or a pulse with strong palpitations. Aconite can be useful for treating the early stages of uveitis, systemic infection and laminitis. It is specifically appropriate if fright, shock or emotional trauma occurred early in the development of symptoms.

The symptoms of the Aconite horse often deteriorate if the horse is exposed to dry, cold winds or extreme cold. This horse is often worse during the night, or if his stable is overheated and stuffy. It will help if you can make sure he has access to fresh air. He will begin to improve when he is able to sweat as a response to his affliction.

If the situation is a flare-up of a chronic situation, you may decide to alternate doses of Aconite with Belladona. Consider this combination where there is anxiety, and the symptoms of this chronic condition have returned suddenly, often violently.

THE REMEDY IS THE VIBRATION OF *ACONITE NAPELLUS*, A PLANT COMMONLY KNOWN AS MONKSHOOD OR WOLFSBANE.

APIS MEL

Apis Mel is the remedy of choice if your horse has oedematous swelling, weepy serous discharge, puffiness under the eyes, insect bites or stings, or if any allergic reaction has caused swelling anywhere in your horse. This can also include musculoskeletal inflammation where there is heat and swelling, for example joint and bursa (joint capsule) inflammation. Apis Mel is the appropriate remedy if your horse has any swelling that is hot or sensitive to touch, but is not showing signs of being thirsty. If the swelling is not hot, Ledum may be a better choice.

The Apis Mel horse appears worse when any form of heat, touch or pressure is applied to the injured area. The symptoms often worsen during the afternoon or after sleeping, so bear this in mind when observing your horse's reaction to a dose of the remedy.

This horse improves when given access to fresh, open air and his rugs are removed. Cold hosing may also help.

THE REMEDY IS THE VIBRATION OF APIS MELLIFICA (HONEYBEE POISON) OBTAINED FROM WHOLE, CRUSHED HONEYBEES.

ARNICA

Arnica is the remedy for any first-aid situation where trauma has been experienced. Even if you have no other homeopathic remedy in your tack room, this one will prove invaluable. Arnica helps the body reabsorb blood from bruised tissue while reducing blood loss caused by injury. It is useful for any horse prone to muscle soreness or cramping when given before and after exertion. It may also be given before and after surgery or after foaling.

Arnica is also indicated for the horse that is extremely restless and experiencing discomfort that is sensitive or sore to the touch. Keep Arnica on hand if your horse bruises easily or is prone to general stiffness and weariness when asked to work or compete. When your horse is most in need of this remedy, he may appear intolerant of your attempts to care for him, giving you signals that he would prefer to be left alone.

This horse appears to be worse at night, with exposure to cold damp conditions, when overexposed to heat or sunlight, after too much exercise or following a sudden increase in what is expected of him. This horse appears to improve when he can position himself with his head lower than his body.

THE REMEDY IS THE VIBRATION OF *ARNICA MONTANA*, A PLANT COMMONLY KNOWN AS LEOPARD'S BANE OR FALLKRAUT.

BELLADONNA

Belladonna is the remedy for sudden, acutely painful inflamed joints and any sudden fever. Belladonna states often reflect similar symptoms to Aconite states. These two remedies do work well together, and in some cases you may alternate the dose; however, there are important differences between the two remedies.

Belladonna is specifically useful for treating sudden, violent symptoms with throbbing and pulsating pains. Like the Aconite horse, you may notice that the Belladonna horse has very shiny eyes; however, the Belladonna horse will also have dilated pupils. The Belladonna horse distinguishes himself from the Aconite horse by displaying violent mental symptoms including striking, biting, kicking and extreme sensitivity to touch (especially anything jarring), light and noise. For example, Belladonna is more suitable for laminitis, where heat has come on suddenly with a bounding digital pulse.

The Belladonna horse worsens at 3pm, and symptoms will often be on the right side of the body. For example, if you find uveitis in only the right eye of your horse, Belladonna is a more appropriate remedy than Aconite. Belladonna is the more suitable remedy if the horse is worse when exposed to the glare of bright light, is uncomfortable being around running water or noise, or if his complaint worsens after being washed or clipped. This horse improves when his head is allowed to rest against something and finds comfort when lightly rugged and able to be close to you.

THE REMEDY IS THE VIBRATION OF *ATROPA BELLADONNA*, A PLANT COMMONLY KNOWN AS DEADLY NIGHTSHADE.

BRYONIA

Bryonia is the remedy for sore muscles or bones. It is particularly useful for a horse suffering with acute rheumatic symptoms or swollen, painful joints or limbs. Your horse needs this remedy if he suffers constipation when travelling away from home, or is developing a cold or flu with a slow onset of symptoms including a hard, painful cough. This horse will show a great thirst, and his mucous membranes will be dry.

The Bryonia horse worsens in the evenings, on rising in the morning, after eating, with warmth and even with the slightest movement. He will appear to improve with rest and when pressure is applied either as bandages or by lying on the painful areas.

THE REMEDY IS THE VIBRATION OF *BRYONIA ALBA*, A PLANT COMMONLY KNOWN AS WHITE BRYONY OR WILD HOP.

CALC FLUOR

Calc Fluor is a remedy for ailments caused by straining or overstretching. It is useful for treating general stiffness, swellings and hard nodes in ligaments, adhesions and scar tissue damage to muscles, tendons and connective tissue. It is also a useful remedy for horses with bony exostoses such as spurs, bone splints, ringbone and pedal osteitis. When given to a horse soon after surgery, Calc Fluor will reduce the likelihood of developing adhesions.

Calc Fluor can be of help to a horse with deteriorating teeth, mammary glands suffering mastitis, enlarged vascular vessels or recovering from X-ray burns. The Calc Fluor horse may crave salt.

A Calc Fluor condition will worsen when your horse rests. He will appear to be stiff when beginning to move or with changes of weather. He will improve with heat, massage or rubbing, warm applications of

wraps, bandages, liniments and poultices, and continued motion.
THE REMEDY IS THE VIBRATION OF THE ORIGINAL MATERIAL, FLUOR SPAR.

CALENDULA

Calendula is one of the best wound healers. In an emergency, do not use Calendula to treat deep or puncture wounds, as the healing ability of Calendula is so quick it may seal the wound with foreign matter still within. (Consider Hypericum for deeper wounds.) Calendula encourages granulation of damaged tissue and helps your horse heal without scarring. When your horse is healing from a wound or an operation, Calendula prevents accumulation of pus and aids healing. Calendula is excellent for relieving pain caused by wounds, lacerations or even torn muscles. It is useful when your horse appears to be exhausted by injury or pain.

A Calendula horse appears to be worse with damp, cloudy weather, during chill or when perfectly still, and appears to improve when walking about or lying down.
THE REMEDY IS THE VIBRATION OF *CALENDULA OFFICINALIS*, A PLANT COMMONLY KNOWN AS MARIGOLD.

CARBO VEG

Carbo Veg is the remedy for sudden states of collapse. It can be used in situations involving blood loss ranging from nosebleeds to post partum haemorrhage, especially when your horse is showing signs of shock from a lack of oxygen in the body. Other symptoms indicating that Carbo Veg is required include a blue tinge to the mucous membranes, wheezing or gasping for air and clammy skin. Carbo Veg is also useful when your horse suffers diarrhoea, bloating or flatulence associated with gastro-intestinal complaints.

The Carbo Veg horse reacts badly to extreme changes in temperature. He may also seem anxious and have a specific fear of the dark. His symptoms will appear worse in stuffy surrounds and humidity. He will improve when he breaks wind, sleeps and is exposed to fresh, cool, open air. If your horse is too stressed to take tablets, rub the fluid homeopathic remedy on his face or muzzle.
THE REMEDY IS THE VIBRATION OF VEGETABLE CHARCOAL

CHINA

China is a useful remedy to help your horse cope with loss of fluid and dehydration. It may be used in situations where your horse is cold and sweating profusely while in shock, haemorrhaging and is exhausted from frequent or continuous discharges, excessive urination, lactation or diarrhoea. It is also worth using if your horse is suffering a flu with intermittent or high, debilitating fever.

The China horse has good and bad days. He is supersensitive and may appear to be worse at the slightest touch, indifferent to his situation, depressed and taciturn. His symptoms will be worse if caught in a draft at night or after eating. This horse will improve when allowed to keep his head lowered towards the ground and when kept warm out in the fresh open air.

THE REMEDY IS THE VIBRATION OF THE BARK OF A PERUVIAN TREE COMMONLY KNOWN AS CHINCHONA.

COLCHICUM

Colchicum is a remedy for gaseous colic or bloat, particularly the kind your horse may experience after eating an excessive amount of clover. Your horse needs Colchicum if he has a disturbance of the digestive tract combined with an extreme disinclination to move, and appears sensitive to cold. He may also be oversensitive to odours and his gut distended with flatulence. Colchicum is also useful with horses that have arthritis in their joints and experience pain in the evenings, which only eases at daybreak. It can be applied to a horse that has rheumatic joints which are painful when flexed and is prone to swelling and coldness in the legs.

The Colchicum horse appears to be worse between sundown and sunrise, with any sort of motion or vibration, or when presented with the smell of food. This horse will appear better with warmth and rest, lying quietly after stools have been dropped. He will prefer open air while needing this remedy. The colic of a Colchicum horse often occurs in autumn, and is made worse by stretching.

THE REMEDY IS THE VIBRATION OF THE BULB PART OF *COLCHICUM AUTUMNALE*, A PLANT COMMONLY KNOWN AS MEADOW SAFFRON.

COLOCYNTHIS

Colocynthis is the remedy to select when your horse is suffering from colic with an unknown cause. This horse may be irritable, restless, inclined to lie down, and susceptible to sudden, violent cramping pains.

The Colocynthis horse worsens when he has feelings of anger and indignation. His twisting, contorting pains will be worse if he tries to rest, or if he feels cold and damp. This horse will appear to be better when doubled over with his head lowered to the ground, and when hard pressure is placed against his abdomen. Warmth, gentle motion and gentle massage will also help, and he will appear to improve if he can release gas or stools.

THE REMEDY IS THE VIBRATION OF THE FRUIT PULP OF *CITRULLUS COLOCYNTHIS*, A PLANT COMMONLY KNOWN AS BITTER APPLE.

ECHINACEA

Echinacea is the remedy to use when your horse has any tissue that is infected or toxic with septic involvement. This is a first-aid remedy for post-partum infections after a mare has given birth, infected bites or stings, snakebite, boils/ulcers, blood poisoning, infected wounds, gangrene, ulcerated sore throat, bedsores, piles, lymphatic inflammation, aching limbs and general lassitude.

If your horse is worn down by infection and is weak, tired and energy depleted, use this remedy in very low potency doses such as 3X or 6X daily for a period of 1–2 weeks, to stimulate the immune system. At this low potency the remedy still contains traces of the original plant matter, so its action is close to that of the herb with the added benefit of potentization.

THE REMEDY IS THE VIBRATION OF *ECHINACEA ANGUSTIFOLIA*, A PLANT COMMONLY KNOWN AS PURPLE CONE FLOWER.

EUPHRASIA

Euphrasia is the remedy for eye problems. It is of great help to the horse suffering with: conjunctivitis; teary, bloodshot, cloudy, swollen, itchy, diseased or injured eyes; red, swollen eyelids; photophobic and constant winking. Euphrasia will give uveitis that has been stubborn to respond to drug treatment an opportunity to heal. This remedy is also useful for the horse that suffers from hayfever. To bathe your horse's eyes, use 2–3 low potency (i.e., 3X or 6X) tablets dissolved in ½ a cup of tepid, distilled water or boiled rainwater.

The Euphrasia horse appears to be worse when in direct light, in the evening, and if there are southerly winds. This horse appears to be better in the dark and when out of the wind.

THE REMEDY IS THE VIBRATION OF *EUPHRASIA OFFICINALIS*, A PLANT COMMONLY KNOWN AS EYEBRIGHT.

HAMAMELIS

Hamamelis is the remedy to select for bleeding, particularly in the case of slow, dark venous blood that fails to clot. It is useful for treating long-lasting nosebleeds, a horse coughing blood and also a horse that is bleeding from injuries and appears to be weaker than would normally be associated with the amount of blood loss. Hamamelis can also be used to treat other blood-related disorders such as venous congestion, phlebitis, inflammation of the veins with accompanying leg pain, ulcers (both open and gastric), sore bruises and haemorrhoids.

This remedy is distinct from Carbo Veg, which is specific for more extreme symptoms and a horse in a state of collapse.

The Hamamelis horse is irritated by moist, warm air and by being touched. He will appear to be worse with motion and during the day, but will appear to be better when allowed to lie quietly.

THE REMEDY IS THE VIBRATION OF THE ROOT AND BARK OF *HAMAMELIS VIRGINIANA*, A PLANT COMMONLY KNOWN AS WITCH HAZEL.

HEPAR SULPH

Hepar Sulph is the primary remedy for treating abscesses, swollen glands and painful inflammatory conditions. It is useful for treating infected sinuses, infectious coughs and pus-filled discharges associated with strangles, cold sore and ulcers. This horse may be irritable, aggressive and aloof due to the intense pain of his symptoms.

The Hepar Sulph horse will appear to be worse in cold draughts, when touched, and if any part of his body is uncovered, but will appear to be better with damp weather and warmth.

Low potencies of 30C and under will promote the expulsion or discharge of pus. High potencies of 200C and above will promote resolution of the condition.

THE REMEDY IS THE VIBRATION OF THE WHITE INTERIOR PART OF OYSTER SHELLS BURNT WITH PURE FLOWERS OF SULPHUR.

HYPERICUM

Hypericum is the remedy to select for any nerve injury. This includes nerves that have been injured directly, neuralgia, pain in scar tissue, bites or stings and puncture wounds. Always have Hypericum in your first-aid kit for treating spinal injuries, crushed parts, deep lacerations and head injuries that lead to shock or convulsions. This remedy will address injured areas that have a rich nerve supply. These areas can be recognized when the horse seems to be exhibiting pain that is more severe than the extent of the injury merits. The horse may be depressed or drowsy following the accident or wound, and the symptoms will worsen when the affected area is touched. If you suspect the injury may lead to tetanus, give your horse Ledum followed by Hypericum as a preventative.

The Hypericum horse will appear to be worse when in damp, cold air, with movement, when touched and after urinating. This horse will appear better when allowed to stay still.

THE REMEDY IS THE VIBRATION OF *HYPERICUM PERFORATUM*, A PLANT COMMONLY KNOWN AS ST JOHN'S WORT.

LEDUM

Ledum is the remedy for puncture wounds. It is similar to Hypericum, yet addresses slightly different symptoms. The pains from Ledum wounds are sharp and stabbing and appear to shift about. A Ledum wound will often swell, and the skin wil tighten across it. Fluid retention is often associated with the injury. The skin may quickly turn septic and the affected areas become chilly, stiff and painful.

Ledum can also be used to address painful bruising, sprains and hard swellings. This horse will be withdrawn and irritable.

The Ledum horse will appear to be worse with warmth, at night, when walking and when wrapped up. He will seem to be better with rest, cool air and bathing, and when compresses or ice are applied to the region.

Ledum and Hypericum are often used together in alternate doses to treat any form of puncture wounds, including bites and stings, vaccination needles and puncture wounds from a nail. Used this way the remedies can also act as a deterrent to the tetanus bacteria. Dose your horse with Ledum 200C followed 20 minutes later by Hypericum 200C. Repeat, if you believe there is a danger that your horse may contract tetanus.

THE REMEDY IS THE VIBRATION OF THE LEAVES AND TWIGS OF *LEDUM PALUSTRE*, A PLANT COMMONLY KNOWN AS WILD ROSEMARY.

MILLEFOLIUM

Millefolium is the remedy for haemorrhage occurring after injury or overex-ertion. If your horse is bleeding profusely from the sinuses, respiratory tract, bowel, urinary tract or after foaling—and his blood is bright red—consider using Millefolium. It is a useful remedy for the horse that will not rest after surgery and has caused bleeding with painful haematomas or bleeding without signs of heat. Despite the severity of the symptoms, this horse will not appear to be distressed while you are waiting for your vet to arrive.

The Millefolium horse is worse after exertion or injury, in the evening after 4pm and during the night. His condition will appear to be better during the day.

THE REMEDY IS THE VIBRATION OF *ACHILLEA MILLEFOLIUM*, A PLANT COMMONLY KNOWN AS YARROW.

NUX VOMICA

Nux Vomica is the remedy to use when your horse has developed colic after ingesting bad food or water, overeating or as a reaction to a pharmaceutical drug. It can also be used if your horse has a bowel blockage and is ineffectually straining to pass stools. This horse will be irritable, depressed, intolerant of odours and will move away from you, trying to stay in his own space.

The Nux Vomica horse appears worse at 3 or 4am, with noise and when cold or uncovered. He will improve with rest, during damp, wet

weather, when pressure is applied and when allowed to lie on his side.
THE REMEDY IS THE VIBRATION OF THE POISONS STRICHNIA AND BRUCIA
OBTAINED FROM THE SEEDS OF THE POISON NUT *STRYCHNOS NUX VOMICA,*
ORIGINALLY FROM THE COROMANDEL COAST OF CHINA.

PHOSPHORUS

Phosphorus is a remedy to use following profuse bleeding, and may be used after surgery, nosebleeds and any other situation where your horse has lost more blood than could be expected. These symptoms of course require urgent veterinary attention first. Phosphorus is also a remedy for anaemia, wheezing, chest infections and colds that go quickly to the chest. When he needs this remedy, your horse will crave affection and assurances and have a strong desire for company. He will also show signs of anxiety, alternate between states of exhaustion and introversion, and tend to become overheated quickly when excited.

This horse appears to be worse when there is too much excitement, when left alone, in damp and cold conditions, in crowds and during thunderstorms, when he will exhibit fear and lie on his left side. He will appear to be better with massage, physical expressions of affection and comfort, sound sleep, warmth and by eating little but often.
THE REMEDY IS THE VIBRATION OF THE ELEMENT PHOSPHORUS.

PYROGEN

Pyrogen is a dynamic antiseptic for extreme septic states—hopefully you will not need to use it often. It may be used to address foul, offensive and purulent secretions, blood poisoning, a high fever, rapid pulse and sweating. Pyrogen can also be given to a mare suffering post-partum infections or discharges from the vulva. This remedy is useful with painful, burning abscesses, recurring abscesses and abscessed teeth, as well as extreme vaccination reactions such as inflamed site swelling, high fever or toxemia.

This horse will worsen in cold, damp stalls. He needs warmth, but he will not improve with external covers such as rugs. Administer tepid drinks, hot baths and any firm pressure contact. Allow your horse freedom to stretch, change position and walk.

THE REMEDY IS THE VIBRATION OF A PRODUCT DERIVED FROM THE DECOMPO-
SITION OF CHOPPED LEAN BEEF PLACED IN WATER IN THE SUN FOR 2–3 WEEKS.

RHUS TOX

Rhus Tox is the remedy to select for muscle and bone soreness. This
horse shifts and changes his position frequently. During exercise he is stiff
and sore when he begins to move, but improves with continued motion
while warming up. Rhus Tox is a good remedy to use with a horse that is
suffering the symptoms of arthritis, rheumatism or tendonitis.

The Rhus Tox horse is worse with damp weather, at night, when
beginning exercise and after experiencing a chill or being hot and sweaty.
This horse benefits from being outdoors. He will appear to be better with
continued motion and when he is allowed to stretch and walk. Although
this horse appears to improve with constant motion, he will quickly tire
and need to rest, which will then turn into restlessness.

THE REMEDY IS THE VIBRATION OF THE FRESH LEAVES OF *RHUS TOXICODENDRON*,
GATHERED AT SUNSET, JUST BEFORE FLOWERING COMMENCES. IT IS INTERESTING TO
NOTE THAT SUNSET IS ALSO THE BEST TIME TO ADMINISTER THE REMEDY. (THIS
PLANT IS COMMONLY KNOWN AS POISON OAK.)

RUTA GRAV

Ruta Grav is the remedy to select when connective tissue has been
damaged. This tissue includes cartilage, muscles, tendons and ligaments.
Ruta Grav can be used to address lameness following a sprain, damaged
tendon sheaths, cracking in joints, pain when bending joints, injuries from
overuse, bruised or broken bones, fractures and dislocations. The horse
may be sore, restless, aching and tire easily. He may also seem suspicious
or fretful. Another sign that your horse may benefit from Ruta Grav is an
increased thirst for cold water, drinking much and often.

The Ruta Grav horse is worse when the weather is cold, wet and
damp, and with movement of any kind (especially the exertion of
climbing up and down hills). This horse will be better with warmth
and when rubbed or scratched in the area that has been damaged.

THE REMEDY IS THE VIBRATION OF THE WHOLE, FRESH PLANT *RUTA GRAVEOLENS*,
COMMONLY KNOWN AS RUE.

SILICEA

Silicea is an abscess remedy, though it also has an affinity with bones, ligaments and most body tissues. Silicea can help bring an abscess to the surface and is useful if there is a foreign body (such as a splinter or a thorn) under the skin. Silicea improves hoof development and addresses fungal infections such as thrush.

Low potencies of 30C and under will promote the expulsion or discharge of pus, whereas higher potencies of 200C and above will promote resolution of the condition.

The Silicea horse appears to be worse when cold, uncovered, during the full moon, before a storm and when being groomed. This horse will appear to be better when given warmth, kept rugged, during hot, humid weather and while eating (but is often worse after having eaten).

THE REMEDY IS THE VIBRATION OF PURE FLINT (SILICON DIOXIDE).

SYMPHYTUM

Symphytum is the principle remedy for bone injuries. This includes fractures, stone bruises, torn ligaments or tendons, penetrating wounds to the bone, blows from blunt instruments, cartilage damage, slow repair of a broken bone, inflammation of the bone and phantom limb pain. Symphytum is also the first remedy to use for blunt trauma to the eye, where there is great pain in the eyeball.

The Symphytum horse is worse after the injury, being touched, motion, walking and pressure. This horse will appear to be better with warmth and rest.

THE REMEDY IS THE VIBRATION OF THE FRESH ROOT OF *SYMPHYTUM OFFICINALE*, COMMONLY KNOWN AS COMFREY, COLLECTED IN AUTUMN JUST BEFORE THE PLANT FLOWERS.

THUJA

Thuja is a remedy for warty growths and post-vaccination reactions, when the horse may develop urogenital problems, skin conditions, or spinal chord or neuralgic complaints. It is a useful remedy for addressing bleeding fungal growths, figworts, anal warts, sarcoids, spongy tumours and glandular enlargement. Thuja may also be helpful if your horse's hair grows slowly and splits, especially if the hair is dry and brittle or falling out after re-vaccination. These symptoms often occur predominantly on the left side. He may also have increased thirst, especially at night, and a complete loss of appetite.

Thuja is used more for chronic conditions than acute symptoms. A dose of Thuja is often used to help clear the effects of a reaction to a past vaccination. The Thuja horse can be mistrustful and fearful of new situations, and may avoid joining a herd.

The Thuja horse is worse with cold, damp, with urinating, chewing, bright light and stretching, at 3am and 3pm, after a morning feed and vaccination. He will often have periodic symptoms that reoccur weekly, monthly, annually or with the lunar cycles. The Thuja horse will be better with warmth, warm air or wind, free secretions, sneezing, motion, touch, rubbing and scratching.

THIS REMEDY IS THE VIBRATION OF *THUJA OCCIDENTALIS*, A CONIFER TREE COMMONLY KNOWN AS NORTHERN WHITE CEDAR.

BIOCHEMIC TISSUE SALTS

Dr Wilhelm Schuessler (1822–1898) developed a process based on twelve homeopathically treated mineral salts. He analyzed human ashes and discovered they were primarily made up of the twelve mineral salts listed below. He concluded that these minerals must play a vital role in both the physical integrity and proper functioning of the body. Schussler did not 'prove' tissue salts in the way described in the homeopathic chapter of this book. He believed that the salts were naturally present as constituents within most homeopathic remedies anyway—and because these remedies had already been proved, so were his salts. He did analyze individual organs and body parts to support his conclusions about the specific disease states addressed by each tissue salt. Any deficiency of a mineral showed as symptoms in the organs or body parts composed primarily of that tissue salt.

Mineral salts can be employed to treat an existing complaint. They can also be used as a preventative if your horse is going to be put under physical pressure, or if the respiratory illness season is approaching. The tissue salts require no breakdown by the digestive processes and are immediately assimilated by the body. The salts work on a molecular level and may address an imbalance that is impeding the nutritional process, so that the body can utilize the nutrients in food more efficiently.

Small amounts of salts are sufficient to trigger a healing response in horses, so they are homeopathically processed at a potency of 6X. I find the mineral salts that work best are the ones that dissolve as they stick onto your horses tongue when he licks your hand. The most common prescription is 3 tablets, twice daily, for up to 3 weeks, though you will usually see a result in 10 days. You then need to maintain the treatment by reducing the dose to 2 tablets once daily, for a further 1–3 months. In acute cases you can give half-hourly doses until you observe a change.

THE TISSUE SALTS
CALC FLUOR (*Calcium Fluoride*)

> Calc Fluor is often called the elasticity salt. It is important for tissue strength, and a deficiency of the salt can result in relaxed condition of any tissue. It is specifically useful for any condition involving a loss of integrity and strength of connective tissue, all weaknesses of bone, teeth, muscle and ligaments, and prolapsed organs. These conditions include windgalls, capped hocks and leg injuries sustained by young racehorses before their growth plates have had time to close.

CALC PHOS (*Calcium Phosphate*)

> Calc Phos is the cell builder. It is often referred to as the nutrition salt. It is specifically used for any condition where there is poor cell development, particularly in the bones, muscles and blood. It can be used to stimulate

a poor appetite in young horses, address signs of anaemia in the horse in heavy work and treat eyes that are photophobic or prone to inflammation and dryness.

A deficiency of this tissue salt is a sign that you need to assess the nutritive value of your horse's feed. Calc Phos can support your horse while you are adjusting his feed to suit different stages of performance or life.

CALC SULPH (*Calcium Sulphate*)

Calc Sulph is the blood purifier and suppuration remover. It is specifically used for unpleasant, even purulent, discharges from wounds that have surfaced after the pus has found a way to the surface. Skin eruptions that can or have lead to ulcers or abscesses, or become septic, indicate a need for this tissue salt. If your horse suffers from boils, fistulas, ulcers exposed to air, or has had a weeping, slow-to-heal wound for some time, this tissue salt may be useful. Calc Sulph is similar to Silica in action (see page 155), but don't use these two tissue salts at the same time, as they will counteract each other.

FERR PHOS (*Iron Phosphate*)

Ferr Phos is the inflammation remover and first-aid tissue salt. It can be used at the first stage of all inflammations and infections, for acute localized inflammations that have heat and pain, and for chronic conditions with signs of pallor, tiredness and weakness. You can also use this tissue salt with 'a bleeder' (a common condition in racehorses, where the horse bleeds from the respiratory tract after exertion) or in the first stages of any illness, where your horse might be feverish.

KALI MUR (*Potassium Chloride*)

Kali Mur is the congestion remover and is often used to condition the blood. A deficiency of Kali Mur is often presented in symptoms such as thick white discharges, glandular swellings or excess catarrh. It can be helpful with slow-to-heal injuries, wounds that could develop proud flesh and for treating any inflammation that is accompanied by swelling, pain, burns or bruising. Kali Mur can also be used if your horse's legs have become puffy and/or painful due to a grass allergy, or after a competition or a long journey in his box.

KALI PHOS (*Potassium Phosphate*)

Kali Phos is the nerve nutrient tissue salt. It is useful for the nervous horse that has lowered nervous energy. This salt will help the horse that shies frequently, is lethargic, depressed, irritable, nervous, easily spooked, lacking drive and motivation, hypersensitive to noise or easily fatigued. Kali Phos has a 'pick-me-up' effect while addressing the nervous system at a cellular level.

KALI SULPH (*Potassium Sulphate*)

This tissue salt is the cell oxygenator and is often referred to as the skin salt. A deficiency of this tissue salt can show up as chilliness or pain in the limbs or yellow-green discharges from mucous membranes. This salt will help your horse with any condition that requires oxygen on a cellular level. This includes purulent mucous and discharges, inflammation, fungal infections and dry, flaky skin. Other conditions that respond to this tissue salt are cold weather colic, rattling chest infections, vague shifting leg pains and crusty skin complaints.

MAG PHOS (*Magnesium Phosphate*)

Mag Phos is the neuromuscular coordinator and nerve relaxant. When there is a deficiency of Mag Phos in the body, nerve fibres may contract, causing muscle spasms or cramps. Mag Phos is useful for any conditions where a problem arises between muscles and nerves. This includes muscle spasms, neuralgia, anxieties with hyperexcitability, tension and depression. Mag Phos can help if your horse has spasmodic colic with pain occurring anywhere along the intestinal tract, diarrhoea, constipation from stress, muscle twitching or pain in the myofascial tissue.

NAT MUR (*Sodium Chloride*)

Nat Mur is often referred to as the water distributing tissue salt. Approximately two-thirds of your horse's body is water, and this salt works with the ebb and flow of the fluids in his body. Signs of a deficiency of this tissue salt include a watery discharge and sneezing, or dehydration with dry mucous membranes. Nat Mur can help to address muscle soreness and drowsiness due to muscle fatigue and relieve head colds where a watery discharge is present. It can also help with slow bowel function, thereby reducing the likelihood of food fermenting in a constipated gut.

NAT PHOS (*Sodium Phosphate*)

Nat Phos is the metabolic acid remover and is often referred to as the acid neutralizer. Any creamy golden-yellow exudations are symptomatic of a Nat Phos deficiency. This salt is useful in treating conditions that result from an incomplete breakdown and elimination of metabolic wastes such as lactic and uric acid within the tissue. Nat Phos is helpful with tying-up syndrome, arthritis and itchy skin conditions.

NAT SULPH (*Sodium Sulphate*)

Nat Sulph is the remover of problem fluid. It regulates the density of intercellular fluid and helps the liver and blood eliminate toxins, oedema and congestion of lymph. It can help the horse suffering from weepy skin conditions, swollen legs or 'heaves' with symptoms that worsen with a change in weather—or the mare with an infected discharge from her reproductive organs.

SILICA (*Silica*)

This tissue salt is the calcium reorganizer. It is specifically for conditions involving an abnormal calcification of bone, tendon, ligament or cartilage. Silica also facilitates the removal of foreign wastes from the body and can be used in place of Calc Sulph. Do not combine Silica with any of the Calc tissue salts, however, as they counteract each other's actions. Silica has a more specific action on the hoof, teeth and coat than Calc Sulph does, so use Silica rather than Calc Sulph if your horse suffers an abscess of the tooth or hoof.

BACH FLOWER REMEDIES

HEALING YOUR HORSE'S EMOTIONS

Flower essences are obtained by placing a flower or plant matter in water and allowing the spiritual vibration of that plant to be taken on by the water. Bach flower remedies are usually, but not always, obtained from the flower. Sometimes foliage or other live parts of a plant are used. None of the remedies are harmful or habit-forming in any way and, if you choose the wrong remedy, there is no effect. An added benefit of using Bach flower remedies with your horse is that they are only vibrational in their activity and contain no measurable substance—they cannot show up as a performance-enhancing substance in a swab test.

Bach flower remedies were developed by Dr Edward Bach in the 1930s. He was a medical doctor and practised successfully for over 20 years on London's Harley Street. He gave up his practice in order to devote himself to understanding the emotions that lay behind disease states, and began sourcing plants that contained the keys to helping the body release particular emotions, so the physical symptoms could be healed. In his medical practice Dr Bach had observed patterns in his patients that led him to look closely at the link between emotional states and disease. He isolated seven states (pride, cruelty, hate, self-love, ignorance, instability and greed) which lead on to an expression of seven emotions: fear, uncertainty, disinterest, loneliness, oversensitivity, despondency and overconcern. He theorized that when a person was acting out any of the negative emotions, his or her soul would create a disease state in the physical body to alert the person that he or she was not operating with the highest integrity. And when people missed those cues, they became ill.

After giving up his medical practice, Dr Bach spent many years in nature, simply sitting with flowers and feeling their qualities. When he felt he had begun to understand the emotions the plant could assist with, he placed the flower in water and allowed those energies to be transferred to the water. He then stored this and used it to assist his fellow man. His selection of thirty-eight essences addressed the emotional states that he saw were sabotaging people's health, including anxiety and apprehension, uncertainty and indecision, loneliness, lack of interest, oversensitivity, and despondency and despair.

I find horses readily accept the use of Bach flowers, and are sensitive to the change they feel as the remedy lifts away the negative emotion. Because Bach flowers work on the subtle world of emotions such as will, anger and fear, they help you and your horse to release negative emotions that can interfere with your riding relationship.

Bach flowers can be used with horses in several different ways—a few drops can be rubbed across your horse's body, or about 10 drops can be added to your horse's drinking water (regardless of whether this is a bucket, trough or automatic feeder) or sprinkled on your horse's feed. Remember this is not a physical dose—your aim is to introduce the vibration of the essence into the horse's energy field.

Bach flower remedies can be used individually or you can combine up to seven essences in one dose bottle. Using more than seven essences in one dose can be too confusing for your horse. Remember to keep the process simple; if you think your horse needs more than seven essences, choose the remedies that will address the most obvious traits first. As these peel away, you can introduce a different combination to your horse.

As Bach flowers relate to emotional states you may find a horse referred to as being an 'agrimony' or a 'vine' horse, for example. When you hear a horse described this way, it is because he is predominantly expressing the characteristics of this essence. After using Bach flowers for a sustained period of time, you will probably find that you are selecting one essence consistently. This essence denotes the horse's basic core pattern, while the other essences you select will address issues that arise from the environment or the owner. I encourage owners to use the same essence or combination of essences as their horses, as sometimes the emotions they notice in their horse are simply reflections of emotions they are not recognizing in their own lives. Seven drops can be placed directly under your tongue or taken in a glass of water, three times a day.

Dr Bach's Rescue Remedy (a combination of Rock Rose, Impatiens, Clematis, Star of Bethlehem and Cherry Plum flower essences) is a must at competitions and after any trauma a horse may experience. It can immediately restore calm to a distressed horse and dissolve any discordance between you and your horse.

AGRIMONY (*Agrimonia eupatoria*)

The Agrimony horse will continue to perform while suffering a pain or disease. When he can no longer hide the fact that he is sore, you will be surprised at how much pain he was in. When injured this horse will often continue as if nothing is wrong. This horse may always be friendly, but is in fact scouring due to the stress he is hiding.
This essence is useful for riders who have a happy face but are continually worrying underneath the surface. In this case, your horse may need Agrimony to be free of the emotions you are covering up.

ASPEN (*Populus tremula*)

The Aspen horse is nervous and anxious. He may shy at invisible objects in a familiar arena. He is often afraid of predators that are not there and may suddenly bolt for no known reason. Aspen should be used throughout this horse's training to constantly reassure him. When you are riding this horse, you will often sense that he has an air of anticipation or dread of what may happen.

This essence is useful for the competition rider whose mind is analyzing the test or course to the point of obsessiveness.

BEECH (*Fagus sylvatica*)

The Beech horse is often stand-offish. He will be less tolerant of your misgivings and become irritated quickly, especially if you are giving him confused messages with your aids. This horse will also refuse feed he dislikes, will not be a fast eater and may pick through what is offered. You cannot hide medication in his feed, as he will simply leave it to the side of his feed bin. This horse may have trouble accepting change, and any changes you make to his routine should be done carefully and introduced slowly.

This essence is for the rider who is overly critical of their own performance, their horse's performance or that of other competitors.

CENTAURY (*Centaurium umbellatum*)

The Centaury horse is easily dominated. A habitual giver, this horse tries hard to please his rider and will attempt everything asked of him, even if it is beyond his ability. Unfortunately, because of his nature, he is at the bottom of the ranking in a herd situation and may be attacked by aggressive horses. This remedy is necessary for any horse that has been abused or neglected.

This essence is for the docile, timid, quiet, submissive horse, and the student rider who is overly anxious to please the instructor during a lesson or at a pony club.

CERATO (*Ceratostigma wilmottiana*)

The Cerato horse needs constant reassurance. This horse may be unsure of his footing and often trip. His mind is always on you, seeking your approval and confirmation. If you lose your temper with this horse he will lose confidence in his ability, and it may take weeks to get back to the level of training you had achieved.

This essence is for the rider who lacks confidence and has doubts about their own ability.

CHERRY PLUM (*Prunus cerasifera*)

The Cherry plum horse is full of fear. This horse may lose control and explode, then be fearful of his own reaction. He may self-mutilate or behave aggressively to hide his fear. When this horse panics he is difficult to calm down, and can often injure himself in his frenzy to get away from whatever frightened him.

This essence is for the rider who won't attempt new challenges because they fear that things will go wrong and circumstances could get beyond their control. Cherry plum will help a rider gain control of this irrational fear.

CHESTNUT BUD (*Aesculus hippocastanum*)

The Chestnut bud horse often appears to have forgotten yesterday's lesson and continually repeat mistakes. He is the horse that you ride the day after a lesson only to find it's like beginning again, and he does not comprehend your instruction.

This essence is for the student rider who appears slow and inattentive and repeats the same mistake again and again.

CHICORY (*Cichorium intybus*)

The Chicory horse is possessive and often manipulative. This horse needs to exchange affections and will compete with other horses for your attention if you are at a livery stable. The Chicory horse will shun you if you send him out for a rest and will strongly object to any new friends in your life. It is best to ride this horse with your full attention, because if he gives you what you ask he will expect acknowledgement.

This essence is a must for the instructor trying to deal with a manipulative student who blames them when things go wrong and makes them feel guilty for the student's poor performance. It is also a good remedy for the bossy child who manipulates non-horsey parents with ridiculous demands.

CLEMATIS (*Clematis vitalba*)

The Clematis horse has a far away look in his eye and may suffer silly accidents due to lack of attention. It is often difficult to 'connect' with him, as he tends to escape into an inner world, especially when it all gets too difficult or when pressure is applied.

This is the essence for the daydreaming rider who has difficulty focusing on a test because they are dreaming of the day when they will be competing at the Olympics.

CRAB APPLE (*Malus pumila*)

The Crab apple horse exhibits signs of vanity and will always be alert to a camera in the vicinity. If you try to take a photo of this horse while he is at rest you will have no luck, for the instant you aim the camera he will hold his head up high and pose. This horse does not like being ridden during inclement weather, as he dislikes getting mud on his legs. You must groom this horse before saddling up, as he will be irritated and unable to relax into a ride if his appearance is not clean. This horse becomes depressed when suffering with a skin ailment or if left unwashed after exercise.

This essence is for the rider obsessed with detail and their own appearance, especially the fussy, finicky show hack rider who says 'I look awful' when they appear in perfect attire

ELM (*Ulmus procera*)

The Elm horse suffers a temporary loss of confidence when he feels overwhelmed. This usually happens when the horse has been schooled to a level at which he is about to compete for the first time. He knows that he can do what will be asked of him, but the pressure of the competition and the owner's expectations unbalance him.

This essence is for the rider or groom feeling overwhelmed by the responsibility of preparing for a competition, and for anyone who starts out enthusiastically, but soon tires and feels burdened.

GENTIAN (*Gentiana amarella*)

The Gentian horse is withdrawn and despondent after experiencing a setback. This horse may have slipped during a competition, or performed poorly when he was expected to succeed. The Gentian horse may become depressed when a stablemate is moved or he becomes ill. This essence is for chronic doubt and depression. It helps the rider who spreads dissension because they feel it is important their truth be known, even if that means writing anonymous letters to committees to undermine morale.

GORSE (*Ulex europoeus*)

The Gorse horse has given up and does not respond to any form of encouragement. Often a horse in transition between disciplines, this horse will make no effort to enjoy life and often keep to himself in a corner of a paddock. If this horse suffers an illness he will be very slow to recover, if at all. A common example is the failed racehorse, unable to recognize that life can be good as a dressage horse because he was not good enough in his former career.
This essence is for the rider who is slipping into hopelessness and despair, losing ambition and interest in their riding. You will often hear this rider utter 'what's the use?'

HEATHER (*Calluna vulgaris*)

The Heather horse is totally self-obsessed. He does not respond well to being left alone, and is typically the horse tied up to his box screaming for attention when his owner has been distracted with other duties. If this is the only horse in your paddock he will excessively crave attention whenever you go to feed, groom or ride him. This is also the paddock pony that hangs over the fence when school children walk past to get their pats and affections.
This essence is for the rider who is consumed with interest in themselves. They parade around and incessantly talk about their horse-related achievements while leaving a trail of drained listeners behind.

HOLLY (*Ilex aquifolium*)

The Holly horse seems to be full of hate and expresses strong negative emotions. This horse often has a golden heart under all this negative emotion, but all you may get to see is jealousy, suspicion, envy and spite.

This horse will not welcome a new horse to the herd and is often seen kicking out for no reason and for more than could be justified as showing one's dominance. If you own a Holly horse and show another horse affection, this horse may bite or kick you viciously without warning as a punishment. This horse holds onto thoughts, waits for opportunities for revenge and calculates acts of aggression. The Holly horse's feelings of hate usually stem from the way he has been treated in the past. This may be physical abuse or feelings of being betrayed by a human. Holly is a long-term remedy and will help the owner connect with the horse by slowly peeling away the layers protecting the true essence of this horse's nature.

This essence is for the rider who is overly sensitive to judges' reports and criticism from other riders. When there is a desire for revenge due to envy or jealousy, take Holly.

HONEYSUCKLE (*Lonicera caprifolium*)

The Honeysuckle horse is rarely in present time. He will hold onto memories of any past owners and, if he sees a previous owner on an outing, he will instantly recognize and make it known he still has an attachment to the past. A horse in a Honeysuckle state will often grieve the loss of a paddock mate for longer than usual, becoming withdrawn and losing weight.

This essence is for riders, grooms and horses when away on extended trips and feeling homesick and for riders who have lost a beloved horse and are learning to like a new one.

HORNBEAM (*Carpinus betulus*)

The Hornbeam horse suffers Monday morning-itis. He is slow and lethargic when first saddled, and you will often find him lying down on his stable floor when you arrive. Once you begin to work him the lethargy peels away and he has plenty of energy, though to begin with it feels like you are riding a horse with bricks tied to his feet.

This essence is for weariness, and temporary tiredness. Hornbeam will revitalise the 3-Day Eventer between disciplines. It is useful for the rider growing weary of their gruelling training schedule for an important competition.

IMPATIENS (*Impatiens glandulifera*)

The Impatiens horse is always in a hurry. This horse won't wait for you to feed him and will be grabbing at the feed before it is all in his feed bin. This horse will be difficult in the dressage arena as he is thinking ahead in the test and will often miss the cue to change direction. This horse will be irritable if kept waiting at the hitching rail while you gossip, but this fades quickly once his mind is stimulated.

This essence is for the impatient, impetuous rider that becomes irritable when offered assistance, while declaring he or she is bored with instruction.

LARCH (*Larix decidua*)

The Larch horse is often timid and in need of confidence. This horse believes that all new challenges are doomed to failure. He will find a new showjumping course impossible to complete clear—though he is capable of the task, he lacks the confidence to do it with ease. The Larch horse will compete with better results if he is able to observe several other competitors before his attempt. Larch is an excellent remedy for a horse that seems hesitant when offered a new feed supplement or moved to a different stabling facility.

This essence is for the rider lacking confidence and in fear of ridicule. This rider may brag about their successful friends to take the attention way from their low self-image.

MIMULUS (*Mimulus guttatus*)

The Mimulus horse displays fear or anxiety in certain situations where he must confront a known and familiar fear (for example, bicycles or a particular person or object in the stable—possibly the farrier or the box). This horse may be shy and timid with poor social skills. If this horse is aggressive, it will be a fear-based aggression in an attempt to keep the cause of the fright at a distance. For example, this horse may jump at unexpected noise or each time he passes the speakers in a freestyle dressage test. You may notice this horse pull his ears back to warn off strangers, or if his groom or handler has approached too quickly.

This essence is for both the rider and horse who fear an accident or crowds, and it is vital when recovering from a car accident.

MUSTARD (*Sinapis arvensis*)

The Mustard horse experiences sudden mood changes, turning gloomy and introspective for no apparent reason. Often this horse stands to the side with his head hung low. Get your veterinary surgeon to rule out illness. If the veterinary surgeon gives your horse a clean bill of health, you can use this essence to treat the sudden depression. This melancholy can disappear as quickly as it developed, but it can also recur just as suddenly.

This essence is for the melancholic rider who feels they are slipping into misery or sadness for no apparent reason.

OAK (*Quercus robur*)

The Oak horse has great endurance and just keeps going and going. This horse will steadily meet any challenges presented to him and will often go beyond what is expected. Unfortunately, this horse may keep going until he is physically forced to stop by injury. Because this horse seems invincible and never complains when placed under pressure, the owner is often surprised when this horse becomes ill.

This essence is for the compulsive rider who battles against all odds— plodding, struggling and becoming despondent due to lack of progress.

OLIVE (*Olea europoea*)

The Olive horse is exhausted after making any effort. This horse fatigues more easily than other horses asked to complete the same task, or after a major operation or long period of illness or recuperation. Most horses would benefit from this essence after long periods of stress.

This essence is for the rider feeling physically and emotionally exhausted after a competition, or in tears and collapsing after a major effort.

PINE (*Pinus sylvestris*)

The Pine horse blames himself when his rider gets angry. This horse is submissive and eager to please, but his overly keen attempts to please can be annoying. This horse will assume responsibility for an act even if he was not the perpetrator.

This essence is for the overly conscientious rider who sets high standards for themselves, and apologizes to everyone if they do not succeed.

RED CHESTNUT (*Aesculus carnea*)

The Red Chestnut horse is typically a broodmare who strikes out at handlers in an attempt to protect the foal by her side. They are also the horses that will stand between their owner and any perceived threat. This overly protective behaviour can be dangerous. The Red Chestnut horse is often a weaver, hanging over the stable door anxiously waiting for his owner to return.

This essence is for the overly concerned or protective mother or coach at competitions, whose attention is becoming intrusive and hindering the rider.

ROCK ROSE (*Helianthemum nummularium*)

The Rock Rose horse is frozen to the spot by panic or terror. When riding this horse you may feel the pounding of his heart rise between your legs, or observe fear-induced shivers when this horse is panicked. This horse will make desperate efforts to get away from the source of his fear, often rushing over anyone in his way.

This essence is for the rider who is a habitual panicker. It is always a good essence to have handy if you are involved in an emergency or have just observed an accident.

ROCK WATER

The Rock Water horse is rigid and inflexible. This horse follows directions and performs in a regimented manner. You must feed and ride this horse at the same time every day. If you ever deviate from this routine, he will become stiff and rigid in his neck.

This essence is for the rider who is uptight and rigid. These symptoms may mean the rider is striving for perfection with a sense of self-martyrdom.

SCLERANTHUS (*Scleranthus annus*)

The Scleranthus horse is indecisive. This horse hesitates at jumps as, he is unsure whether or not he should jump them. This indecisiveness may be the source of mood swings.

This essence is for the rider who is struggling to attain balance and poise due to uncertainty and indecision.

STAR OF BETHLEHEM (*Ornithogalum umbetelatum*)

The Star of Bethlehem horse has often experienced cruelty or harsh handling. This essence is primarily a shock remedy. The abuse may have been recent or have occurred many years ago. If it has been a long time since the horse was treated with kindness, it may take him a while to understand and accept your actions.

This essence is for the rider and horse that will shy easily. It clears away trauma and shock after any fright.

SWEET CHESTNUT (*Castanea sativa*)

The Sweet Chestnut horse is at the lowest depths of anguish. He may be deeply mourning the loss of a human or horse companion, or be suffering with a terminal illness. This horse will often withdraw into himself and not acknowledge any attempts to communicate.

This essence is for the rider suffering from a loss of face or feelings of not having achieved the desired result.

VERVAIN (*Verbena officinalis*)

The Vervain horse is overly enthusiastic and excitable. This horse rushes to the gate or stable door to greet anyone who passes his way. In lessons this horse tries to throw himself into tasks with gusto. Sometimes this may lead to this horse going sour and irritable.

This essence is for the forceful, dogmatic, overbearing rider who is argumentative with the instructor or their own horse.

VINE (*Vitis vinifera*)

The Vine horse is the dominant alpha horse. This horse insists on things being done his way and, in a paddock herd, will intimidate all the other horses. If the horse is not in a herd situation he will attempt to dominate his human, sometimes with force.

This essence is for the rider who rigidly demands unquestioning obedience from their horse, and sets impossible tasks.

WALNUT (*Juglans regia*)

The Walnut horse is slow to accept change. This horse finds anything that disrupts the status quo difficult. This includes moving stables or changing paddock mates, and changes in lifestyle such as occupation. Some horses find it difficult to move from dressage to showjumping, for example.

This essence is for the rider who blindly follows instructions and is led away from their goals by other people's strong opinions.

WATER VIOLET (*Hottonia palustris*)

The Water Violet horse prefers his own company, which means he is going against his herd instinct. This horse is aloof and will ignore anyone who arrives to ride him. He will not run away, but will make you come to him.

This essence is for the shy rider who never asks for help or the rider who avoids social contact because they like to suffer in silence.

WHITE CHESTNUT (*Aesculus hippocastanum*)

The White Chestnut horse is the internal worrier. This horse appears agitated, though more often he is distracted by his own thoughts. Asking for his attention may provoke his annoyance. This horse has difficulty concentrating on what you ask of him, as he is stuck in his own internal world.

This essence is for any rider the night before a competition, when obsessing and unable to think of anything else. White Chestnut allows the mind to switch off so the rider can sleep, and wake refreshed.

WILD OAT (*Bromus ramosus*)

The Wild Oats horse is frustrated in his retirement. This horse cannot handle being retired to a paddock with nothing to do in his old age. In addition to using this remedy, you need to find this horse something useful to do or he will develop antisocial behaviour—or even will himself to a quick death. A typical Wild Oats horse is one that has been a school horse for many years and is suddenly retired in a faraway paddock with no purpose. This horse would be happy at a Riding for the Disabled (RDA) or therapeutic riding centre.

This essence is for the very talented rider who is unable to decide on a focus for their riding career or a horse that constantly baulks at jumps due to a fear of commitment. It is also a useful essence for a horse and rider who feel their progress is blocked or that they need to find a new direction.

WILD ROSE (*Rosa canina*)

The Wild Rose horse has developed a total lack of interest in his surroundings. This horse is usually easy-going, but when he is confined or sick for an extended period, he will often fall into a state of apathy and it will be difficult to entice him back to his normally sunny disposition. This may also be the horse that has had a rapid succession of owners.

This essence is for the rider who waits for things to happen and relies too much on other people to help them. They cannot be bothered making an effort, and express a feeling of apathy.

WILLOW (*Salix vitellina*)

The Willow horse is a sulker. He simply goes into moods and refuses any attention. There may be no apparent reason for this mood swing, but the horse will attempt to create an atmosphere of blame, which he places upon the owner.

This essence is for the rider who feels a victim of fate and focuses on the negative by complaining and expressing self-pity.

RESCUE REMEDY

Rescue Remedy is a combination of Rock Rose, Star of Bethlehem, Impatiens, Cherry Plum and Clematis essences. You do not need your horse to 'fit' an essence profile for him to need Rescue Remedy. Dr Bach combined this group of essences so that they could deal with any stress that may be faced. This is primarily a shock remedy, but consider using it daily, for our horses are constantly being confronted with today's stresses. This is also a useful remedy to use before a competition, when a horse is reluctant to be transported by box, won't behave for a farrier or is nervous of a new situation.

This combination of essences is beneficial for the rider who is getting to know a new horse, or when he or she is returning to riding after a fall. A rider can often be absorbed with the above emotions, and it may take a wise instructor to observe the signs and administer the correct remedy to both horse and rider.

FAR-REACHING EFFECTS

There is a joy with Bach flower remedies. As they release the negative behaviour from our energy fields, layer by layer, we become aware of our own patterning and become responsible for our own behaviour around horses.

The principles discussed in regard to Bach flower remedies can be applied to the use of other flower essences. I prefer Dr Bach's selection, as it is a set I understand and have seen results with. However, there are many new essence ranges now available to the consumer, so there is no need to limit your selection. Commercially produced essences made from Australian bush flowers, Hawaiian native plants, shells, crystals and even planetary transitions can be found. The philosophies are similar, and if you can see a possible application with your horse, it may be worth using them. These manufacturers follow strict preparation methods to ensure a consistent vibration.

EMOTIONS AND THOUGHTS

VIBRATIONAL HEALING—WHAT'S IN THE AIR?

Most diseases stem from our thoughts and emotions. Everything in our lives, including possessions, incidents and the way we relate to other people, is a reflection of our inside self, of what we think and feel. Our thoughts, emotions and even our habits all have a lingering presence in the unseen subtle bodies, the thirty-three layers of personal energy that surround us, and attract experiences to us. When we have a thought or emotion it vibrates in our subtle bodies. If we don't take the time to understand why we are having these thoughts or experiencing these emotions, they eventually lodge in our physical body to draw our attention to them. By the time they present as symptoms in our physical body, they are so deeply entrenched in our way of being that we do not realize they are causing us harm.

Disease states often lurk in our subtle bodies, waiting for a certain time in our lives when we are more vulnerable and the corresponding physical area is weakened. Sometimes our soul uses the illness as an opportunity to learn more about ourselves. If we are successful in reflecting upon and realizing the possible root causes of the disease, we then heal from it. Many people change their life path after facing a serious illness.

MAYBE YOUR HORSE HAS YOUR DISEASE

Horses are acutely sensitive to emotional vibrations and have the amazing ability to reflect the issues we need to address in our own lives and bodies. Horses have served humans throughout history. They carried our soldiers to war, pulled our ploughs in the field and carried millions of us countless miles when travelling. Technological developments have made horses redundant in these roles and they are now used mainly for sport and recreation, but this history of loyal assistance is imprinted on a cellular level, deep within their genetic memory. This desire to help humankind means it is rare to find a horse that will not try, even when the task is physically impossible. This need to be of service resonates in their energy field and gives them innate sensitivity to the vibrations emanating from our environment and us, and the ability to reflect them back towards us. These vibrations may be emotions, thoughts, habits or an aspect in disharmony within our soul.

We are often more relaxed around our horses than we are with the people in our lives. When spending time with our horses, we let our public faces drop and connect with what lies beneath the surface of our characters. Sometimes this self we try to hide from ourselves and others is not so pleasant—it's difficult to acknowledge our own faults or let the rest of the world see them. Our horses, however, sense all our selves, even those we attempt to hide.

Horses sense and feel not only our disease states and the emotions we are holding within, but also those emotions being directed towards us from other people. The vibrations of these emotions permeate our horse's subtle bodies. Any emotions that are in discord with our development as spiritual beings then cause discomfort in our horse's body or disruption to his normal behaviour, as well as affecting our own bodies.

If your horse's coat is dull and lacks lustre, or if his feet are brittle, consider your own diet and whether your life has lost its lustre. If your horse is suffering from a respiratory complaint such as heaves, perhaps you or one of your children may have an undiagnosed condition such as asthma or a chronic lung problem. Is someone in your life suffocating you, or are you finding you cannot express yourself with confidence? Do you have sufficient freedom to explore the opportunities in your life?

When your horse suffers an injury or an illness, always treat the physical aspects first and seek veterinary advice and attention if necessary. After a veterinary surgeon has checked your horse and the physical symptoms are in hand, you can decide what other therapies should be included in your horse's treatment.

It is always a good idea to sit back and look at what is happening around you and your horse. Sometimes an accident is just an accident. But sometimes an accident may have happened because you were not concentrating on the task at hand, and your mind was drifting back and forth to someone or something causing disharmony in your life.

If your horse is suffering with a chronic health problem, you need to consider how much of this problem belongs to your horse and how much actually 'belongs' to you. Look beyond the physical symptoms and consider whether you could be the root cause of the problem, and therefore in a unique position to help your horse.

Simple, niggly disorders are often a reflection of the small annoyances in life. If these issues are not addressed, they can result in full-blown health problems. Skin eruptions and sinus problems are often clues that small adjustments are needed.

In most situations these symptoms are likely to be connected to the owner's emotions or someone he or she is closely associated with at the time. We weave an intricate emotional and mental web around ourselves and our lives. Our thoughts and emotions spiral around us like a windstorm creating havoc in our lives while we sit in the centre, in the eye of the storm, and perceive it to be calm and safe. A friend can often see something that is causing us harm in our lives, or something we are doing that is creating disease in our bodies. If your horse is continually being exiled to the sick paddock with any number of problems, take the time to discuss this with an honest and sensitive observer who may help you gain some insights.

There are occasions where an accident is purely an accident, but it's still important to consult your vet with any physical injury or disorder. Always value the opportunity to look within and learn something about yourself at these times.

OUR EMOTIONS

Our emotions have a 'charge'. They release this energy around our body where it is taken on by our horse. This is how our emotions affect our horses.

Anger

This is one of the most destructive emotions. Many of us sit on our anger and may think we are successfully controlling or suppressing it. If you could see your energy field when you are angry, you would see sharp sparks shooting out of your head.

Anger sparks and zaps everything around it. If you are not dealing with your anger appropriately, you may find your horse more and more resistant to your requests to hold his head in a collected frame. Your horse will drag and hang on the bit and often have a tight jaw. If this doesn't get your attention, he may then begin to toss his head.

It is difficult to deal with anger appropriately. When you feel angry, take a quiet moment to see if you can identify the source of this anger within yourself. Make sure you are not feeling angry on someone else's behalf, then find something of beauty in that moment and embrace it with joy. This may be something as simple as a flower or a look in your horse's eye—anything that makes you feel good and helps to dissipate the anger.

Jealousy

This emotion oozes, slimes and pours out of you and hangs as a menacing cloud. If your horse begins to find it difficult to bring his hind legs in under him and engage correctly, look at feelings of jealousy in your own life. You can also look to Bach flower remedies for help. If your horse is or becomes weak over the loins or dips away from your touch when you groom his back, check your feelings about others. You should also consider those around you who may be projecting jealous thoughts towards you.

If you can address your own ill feelings, other people's jealousies will have less effect on you (and in turn your horse). You and your horse can then focus on your goals, unaffected by these destructive emotions.

Jealousy is a lack of joy for others. To overcome the emotion, focus on feeling a genuine joy for other's success. Try visualizing the sun shining brilliantly into your heart so you can create a space for joy.

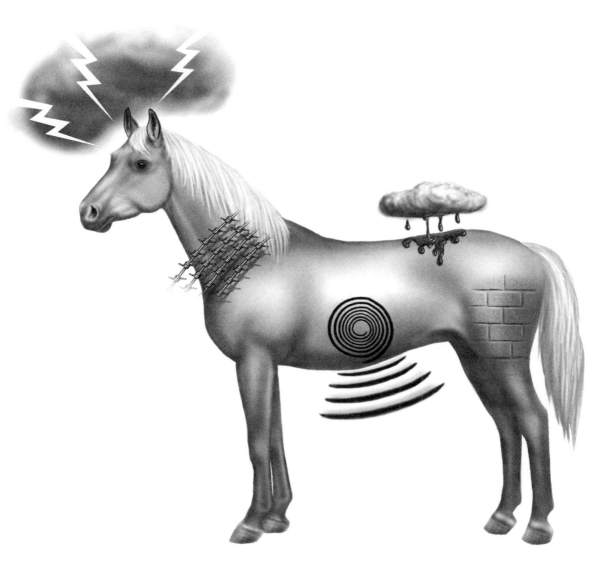

Martyrdom

If your horse becomes heavy on the forehand and develops muscle spasms in the front of the shoulder where his neck joins his body, it may be a sign that you are carrying around too much emotional baggage. Your horse is simply attempting to help you carry the load, but why should he?—especially if it is a load that you should not have taken on in the first place.

Address any areas in your life where you give too much of yourself, let yourself be abused or taken advantage of, or sacrifice what is special to you. Start appreciating your own special qualities—recognize their value and think twice about the people who are wasting them. You will find that when you begin to lift yourself above the role of a doormat, your horse's shoulders will be more responsive to your massages.

Fear and worry

These emotions vibrate so rapidly they can send tremors through your body. If left unchecked, your energy field will look like a kitchen blender on a high setting, spinning out of control. I have discussed essential oils, herbs and homeopathic remedies for the nervous horse in previous chapters, but all of these will fail if your energy field is rapidly vibrating with your worries while you are riding.

You need to release these fears and worries so that your horse does not have them bubbling up inside him. I have seen the soundest horse become very jittery with a nervous rider. If you are always a bundle of nerves before competing, your horse will associate your fears and worries with the expectation of a performance to come. He may begin to pre-empt you and become unmanageable under saddle.

If your horse does become unmanageable at competitions, begin by addressing your own nerves. Deal with any memories of bad experiences you may be locking onto and humbly take whatever herb or Bach flower you feel your horse may need; the remedy may actually benefit you more than it does your horse.

Impatience

It takes years to bring a horse up through the levels of your chosen discipline. It also takes years for the rider to be as skilled as he or she hopes to be. In this age, so many things around us offer instant gratification and happen so fast that we can become impatient with our horses and ourselves.

Impatience creates barriers between you and your horse and slows the progress towards your goals. It creates tightness and rigidity in the horse's hind legs, particularly in the area commonly referred to as the poverty line, which runs like a channel from the point of the buttock leading towards the hock. (When a horse loses condition this line becomes very distinct.) As a result, your horse may lose his fluidity of movement. When this happens, it is time to relax. Take the time to review how far you and your horse have come, take pride in what you have achieved together, then plan out where you will go next. Accept that your horse needs to learn at his own pace and is doing his best for you.

OUR THOUGHTS

Our habitual thoughts can become so solid that they take form in the physical body. Once you have a thought, you must make an action that brings that thought into being. Positive thoughts need to be followed through with positive steps so one can benefit. Negative thoughts need to be acknowledged, and then a conscious decision must be made about how to dispel the negativity that has been generated. If left unchecked these thoughts settle in the subtle bodies; if generated repeatedly, they will become so dense that they move beyond this point and begin to vibrate in the physical body, eventually manifesting as a physical complaint. Your horse will often compromise the health of his body in an attempt to alert you to your problem. If your horse suffers a recurring health problem, look inwards to see if you are not expressing a thought that keeps coming to you.

If you accept the concepts in this chapter, you will become aware of areas in your life that are not quite right. Take a quiet moment to reflect on your own thoughts and see if you can identify any thoughts that may have contributed to this. The first step is becoming aware, the second is making a conscious decision to change the thoughts and attitudes that brought you to this place.

Feet

Your horse's feet are his physical foundation, but they can also reflect the foundation of your own outlook on life. If your horse's hooves are brittle and cracking, it may be a sign that you need to stop thinking you do not have enough in life. Your horse's hooves may also become brittle when you are feeling vulnerable in major areas of your life, such as work or a relationship. If your horse is repeatedly getting abscesses in his feet, look at what is eating away at your feelings of security and the direction your future happens to be taking.

Teeth

Teeth can be a representation of how we take in the nourishment of life. If your horse grinds his teeth excessively, it could be a sign that you need to look at areas of your life that are not fulfilling. If your horse is suffering with recurring mouth ulcers, look to see if you are procrastinating about something or whether something in your life is stagnating.

You should also look at what is coming out of your mouth verbally—what you do and say may not be in harmony with what you want in life. Another possibility is that others are not hearing your words the way you would like.

Eyes

Our eyes can represent the way we see others and ourselves. If your horse's eyes are watering, it may be an indication that you are unable to express what you see with honesty. If his eyes are itching, you might not be noticing and acknowledging how well you are working together. If he has conjunctivitis, bottled-up emotions may be clouding the way you see things. An ulcer is a sign that something you often see happening is unacceptable and eating away at you.

Ears

Ears don't always like what they hear. They can have difficulty tolerating the things that other people say and difficulty tolerating people who won't stop and listen to what we want to say. If your horse gets ear mites or an ear infection, it could be a sign that you need to look at the way you want people to listen to you and accept what you have to say. You may need to open yourself up to receiving new information with more tolerance and patience.

Skin

The skin is a very receptive organ and one that reveals a lot about our daily environment. If your horse has an itch, there may be something irritating you almost daily in your life. Warts can indicate a build-up of long-held feelings of inadequacy or unworthiness. Proud flesh can be an indication that you are avoiding addressing a wound in your life. Dry, flaky skin is often a sign that things in your own life have clogged up due to a lack of self-acceptance.

Lungs

Our lungs are a reflection of how much we enjoy breathing in each day. If your horse develops heaves, consider whether you are enjoying life. Look at what you need to address in your life so that you gain a little joy. Devote some time to yourself and look at the way you accept the ebbs and flows of change. If your horse develops a flu, consider whether you have heeded some advice from others that does not sit well with you. Any underlying feelings of guilt about not speaking up and saying how things are for you often manifest in flu-like symptoms.

Muscles

When your horse's muscles go awry due to spasms or weakness, it can be a sign that you are feeling guilty about your own standard of performance or the restricted amount of time you can spend with your horse. If the horse's muscles become painful, it is usually a sign that the owner doesn't feel good enough and has begun to give him or herself a hard time. This often happens when a new owner tries to live up to the expectations of other riders at the livery stable—when really, there are no expectations.

Bones

Bones give structure to our bodies and can also be a reflection of the structure of our lives. If your horse has arthritis which flares up at competitions and affects his performance, it may be that you are being inflexible and not feeling in control of your life. Any damage to your horse's bones can mean that you are feeling resentment towards yourself or others. Each individual bone can represent different feelings, but generally, if a bone on the left side of your horse's body is causing problems, you need to address your own spiritual direction. If, however, a bone on the right side of the body is causing problems, you need to address your material life.

Joints

Free movement of joints indicates a flexible approach to the challenges of life. If your horse's joints become stiff or have problems with the attached tissue, look at ways in which you are being inflexible about yourself. Legs are often an indication of how happy you are with the direction of your life. If your horse's stifle or hock are sticking, you may need to look at what is stopping you from following your desired direction in life.

Gut

If your horse suffers digestive ailments such as colic, it can indicate you are holding back where you can help yourself or others to move forward freely. These ailments often occur when it is time to decide on a new phase in life, and you are resisting the changes that are presenting themselves. If your horse suffers from constipation, you may need to look at an area in your life where you have been resistant, mean-spirited or not open with your feelings and try to let go of this rigidity. If your horse is scouring, look at what you have given up recently when you wanted to pursue a goal or situation, and ask yourself whether fear is blocking you from accepting changes. Change is an inevitable part of life—if we can greet it with joy, it can bring wonderful experiences.

Saddle

Your saddle can indicate how you feel about your position in life. If you are having trouble getting a saddle to fit your horse, look at where you are in your life. It may be time to review where you are at work and ask your boss for a raise. It may simply be time to buy a new riding outfit so you feel you are looking the part in the dressage arena at your next competition. However, an ill-fitting saddle can also be an indication that you are living beyond your means and that it is time to draw up a new budget—probably so you can afford that new saddle.

AN OPPORTUNITY TO HEAL

Owners often blame themselves when they realize that something they were doing or were ignorant of was the cause of their horse's pain. There is no need to do this. What is important is that you come to a realization of how you may be contributing to your horse's ill-health—with that awareness you can make positive changes and stop the cycle. If your horse cannot be relieved of a vice or continually suffers a sore area, take the time to sit quietly and see what you might be able to improve or rectify in yourself.

One way to begin addressing your own health and emotional issues is to listen to the message of your horse's symptoms—whatever treatment he requires is likely to be exactly what you need, too. If your horse is always suffering a sore back and you are massaging it and not getting results, you need to look at your own back. When you have a professional give your horse a massage, book one for yourself as well. If you need to check the fit of your horse's saddle, check also that your riding clothes are comfortable and that you are happy with your appearance. If your horse needs Ruta grav in a homeopathic form to relax the muscles, maybe you also need to take it to help your muscles in your back relax. If your horse is recovering from a colic episode and you decide that the Bach flower remedy he needs is Agrimony, take a dose yourself, too. Look at what you may be hiding from the world and see if it is really something you need to hide. If you are concerned about your horse's infrequent bowel movements, consider how often you go to the toilet. If it's not at least once a day, and with ease, take the same herbs you have given your horse (but in smaller doses). A cup of herbal tea, taken with intention, can help you overcome these limitations on an energetic level.

As humans we are trained to hide our nerves, but they tremble under the surface of our bodies. Our horses are very attuned to these vibrations. There is no point administering huge doses of Rescue Remedy to a nervous horse if you are the nervous one and he is merely reflecting this back to you. You have to take the dose yourself and deal with your own nerves. When you are preparing for your competition, it helps to take the time to sit quietly and visualize your jump round or your dressage test going perfectly and calmly—you may find that you and your horse fulfill this image!

Interpreting disease states by reading the effects of your emotions and vibes in the symptoms of your horse is never clear-cut, as we are all individuals with our own paradigms and genetic inheritance. Each horse has his own idiosyncrasies and body issues, too. Horses and owners often possess similar qualities—that is, our horses are often a mirror image of our emotional selves. On a subtle level we may recognize these attributes when we select our horses; at other times it could be a simple coincidence. Either way, this philosophy is a handy tool that can provide one key to improving the quality of your horse's life and your own life, too.

Life should not be a struggle—if it is, you need to look at what you are doing and see what is creating the struggle. Often a shift in the way we perceive things in our lives is enough to take some of the effort out of our daily woes. Start taking responsibility for your actions, thoughts and emotions and watch the world around you become less chaotic and an easier place to be.

PUTTING IT ALL TOGETHER

COMBINING NATURAL THERAPIES

The most common mistake that people make when they use natural therapies is expecting that they can replace a pharmaceutical pill with a 'natural' pill and get the same results. This simplistic line of thinking is misguided. Pharmaceutical and natural medicines work in very different ways. You cannot, for example, simply take a horse off corticoid steroids and give him a herb with a similar action.

Using natural therapies is more about embracing a philosophy that looks at the bigger picture of your horse's health and well-being. This can be hard to accept if you are accustomed to popping pills for this and that. A natural approach gently addresses visible symptoms, but focuses on the bigger picture to try to get to the cause of the problem—thereby mending any other 'invisible' symptoms (that is, any developing symptoms related to the cause that have not yet presented themselves visibly) that only exist on a subclinical level.

A natural approach is not a substitute for modern medical attention; the two are complementary. When your horse is faced with an illness, a vet's diagnosis and advice is vitally important. This is most crucial when emergency treatment is needed, as natural therapies may take too long to have an effect. In these situations look to the veterinary approach first. After the acute symptoms have been brought under control, use natural therapies to help restore vitality and health to your horse. While there is no substitute for veterinary attention in an emergency, natural remedies have an invaluable and irreplaceable role in the long-term reversal of symptoms, in bringing about a full healing and actually strengthening the horse's own system to do the restorative work. If you want to use natural therapies concurrently with your veterinary surgeon's treatment, most natural therapies complement each other well and rarely conflict with your veterinary surgeon's treatment. It is always best, though, to advise your vet of what you intend to do before you do it.

When using natural therapies on a horse that is or has recently been ill or suffering a disease, you need to look at the symptoms first and then at the body system most affected. Your veterinary surgeon's diagnosis can be useful for this. Once you have identified this body system, you can look further and determine which organs your horse will rely on to get back to a state of wellness. You can then tailor your choice of natural therapies and applications to support these particular organs—in this way, addressing your horse's whole body.

The previous chapters of this book discuss the tools available for working with horses using a natural health approach. This chapter will give you an understanding of how and where each therapy can fit into the jigsaw puzzle of your horse's whole health and well-being, and show you how to apply these therapies practically. As I discuss the common scenarios, I list some of the most appropriate therapies and remedies you can use in these situations. You do not have to use every homeopathic remedy, herb or essential oil listed for any one entry. If you have the recommended homeopathic remedy but do not have the herbs, just use whatever you have. If, for example, your horse is slow to respond to the recommended herbs, try using the essential oils I have suggested. The key to all of this is to keep whatever you use simple. You may also adapt my suggestions to suit the specific conditions and symptoms of your own horse. One of the great things about natural therapies is that they allow you a flexible approach; pharmaceuticals often do not. Unfortunately, it is not possible to describe every type of situation your horse may encounter. As you read each section of the book, however, you should be able to get an idea of how you can draw on the ideas I have compiled for many common complaints and address your own situation.

As you learn more about natural therapies and become more confident in your understanding of them, you will discover that what has been provided in this is book is merely a foundation. There are many more herbs, homeopathic remedies, essential oils, other flower essences, massage techniques and other tangents to discover if you are interested in understanding your horse on a deeper dimension. This book is your introduction to exploring your horse's world, naturally.

SKIN PROBLEMS

Your horse's skin is easily visible, so you will usually notice a blemish or any loss of condition in your horse's coat. Some skin problems are contagious and need to be carefully managed to avoid infecting any other horses on the property. Isolate the horse and don't share any tack, rugs or grooming equipment. It is best that contagious skin diseases are managed by a vet. Other skin problems are a sign of a bigger, underlying systemic problem (that is, any illness or weakening of other body systems). Natural therapies are particularly useful when treating these problems.

The skin is the largest elimination system in the body. When it appears to be affected by ill-health, the naturopathic approach is to consider which other elimination organs in your horse's body are not performing at an optimum level, thus burdening the skin. To address skin disorders on a deeper, systemic level, you need to give your horse a combination of herbs that assist the waste-elimination functions of the liver, bowel, lungs and kidneys. When all of these organs are functioning at their optimum level, the horse's body will eliminate waste more effectively, and fewer elimination demands will be placed on the skin. Your aim is to feed the skin to nourish it and help restore vitality. You may need to sustain this treatment for up to 3 months to give the herbs a chance to be assimilated into the horse's body and take effect, and to allow your horse to regain some stability.

A sensible blend of herbs for treating problem skin is a mixture of equal parts of Burdock, Yellow dock, St Mary's thistle, Cleavers and Nettle. (As the medicinal part of Burdock is the root, you will need to use this herb in a powdered form. You will find it easier if all the herbs are powdered for this formulation.) With a powdered formulation such as this one, you can give 2 tablespoonfuls in the morning and night feed. If there is an infection present, add Echinacea to the blend. (Only include Echinacea for a short time as it will not be effective after 3 weeks. See page 47.) If the horse has previously been on repeated doses of steroids to treat skin problems in the past, include one quarter-part Licorice in the mixture.

If you are unable to obtain the powdered herbs but have access to fresh or dried Cleavers or Nettles, you can add these to your horse's feed by the cupful (on their own or combined) or make an infusion from the dried cut herb. One to two cupfuls of the fresh herbs, chopped and added to feed, is sufficient—though be sure to wilt the Nettles first, to soften the prickles. A safer method is to make a brew of these herbs and add up to 3 cups of the infusion to you horse's feed each day.

Chronic skin problems such as Sweet Itch need long-term support, and often there is no complete cure. In this situation your treatment should aim to make the horse as comfortable as possible. Depending on your horse's level of sensitivity, you can also address the problem with homeopathic remedies such as Rhus Tox, Apis Mel, Calendula, Ledum and Hypericum. These remedies address the acute stages of a chronic skin disorder, but you will still need to consult a professional to prescribe a constitutional programme for greater success. A professional may include highly potent remedies not included in this book such as Sulphur and Arsenicum, which must be used with great care to avoid possible aggravation. As skin conditions can be such deep-seated physical afflictions, you may want to support your horse through the vulnerable seasons with tissues salts such as Nat Mur, Kali Sulph and Calc Fluor. The insects often associated with dermal hypersensitivity are more prevalent in spring and summer, while the wetter seasons favour fungal conditions and rain scald. You can also address the symptoms with topical washes such as Chamomile tea or with an Aloe vera gel carrying Tea tree or Lavender essential oils in a 2.5 per cent dilution.

The first Bach flower remedy to consider when treating any skin disorder is Crab apple. Crab apple addresses most of the emotions that commonly contribute to skin irritations. Most skin disorders are a sign of an irritation in life that you or your horse may be suppressing or not expressing to the people who make a difference. There is more truth than you may realize in the saying 'it gets under my skin'.

SADDLE SORES AND GIRTH GALLS

As the name suggests, these sores are caused by a rubbing saddle, blanket or girth. To avoid this painful condition, check the fit of your saddle to make sure it is packed evenly and keep your saddlecloth clean (but avoid using powdered washing detergents, as the residue may cause irritation that can develop into a sore). Petroleum jelly can be used on the areas behind the point of elbow and in front of where the girth sits, to reduce chafing. Girth galls most often occur in front of the girth.

The early signs of saddle sores are a soreness that is tender to the touch and white patches where circulation has been suppressed by uneven pressure. These early signs must not be ignored. They are an indication that your horse is in pain, and it is best to avoid riding altogether. After the skin breaks and the sores develop, it may take up to 10 days for them to heal.

To help the sores heal, add a fresh Comfrey leaf to your horse's morning and evening feeds. A paste of the fresh leaves combined with Aloe vera gel can be applied externally. The homeopathic remedy Arnica, at a 30C dose given once daily for 3 days, is also appropriate if bruising is present. To help take the 'ouch' out of the sore, a 30C dose of Calendula can be given once daily (but not within 30 minutes of a feed and at a different time of day to the Arnica dose) for 5 days. If there is no bruising present, use Calendula only. Alternatively, support your horse with 2 tablets of Nat Mur or Calc Sulph tissue salts until the sores heal, then 2 tablets, two to three times a day for a further week to help the area strengthen.

Topically apply Aloe vera gel carrying a 2.5 per cent dilution of Lavender essential oil. Don't apply this at the same time of day that you give your horse homeopathic remedies or tissue salts, however, as this topical treatment could antidote them.

NETTLE RASH OR HIVES

This condition can occur anywhere on the horse's body and is usually an allergic reaction triggered by nettles, an insect bite, something in your horse's diet or even a reaction to drugs such as antibiotics. The reaction causes the development of raised patches where fluid accumulates under the skin. These swellings are usually itchy and irritating and, if allowed to develop untreated, may ooze serum.

In severe cases call your veterinary surgeon, as your horse will need a pharmaceutical to address the immediate symptoms and bring the condition under control. Whether your horse has a severe or mild case, it is important that you simplify his feed until the condition is resolved. A hay and chaff diet might be best, as animal proteins in concentrate feeds and fresh grass proteins can produce an allergic reaction.

While deciding what course of action to take, Bach flowers such as Agrimony, Cherry plum or Crab apple can be given to your horse internally or simply wiped across the affected area.

The first homeopathic remedy to consider is Apis Mel. If the symptoms are mild, give your horse a 30C potency dose twice daily for 5 days. If the symptoms are severe, give your horse a single 200C potency and call out your veterinary surgeon.

If your horse suffers this problem regularly, you should support his general internal health with herbs. A simple formula of herbs that can help do this contains equal parts of Burdock, Yellow dock, St Mary's thistle, Cleavers and Dandelion. The medicinal qualities of the herbs Burdock, Dandelion and Yellow dock are obtained from the root part of the plants, and therefore need to be used in a powdered form. It is best to use the herbs in the same powdered form when making the blend. Give your horse 2 tablespoonfuls of the formula, mixed in with feed, morning and night for a month. After this time, you can halve the dose to 1 tablespoonful mixed in feed morning and night, or 2 tablespoonfuls mixed into night feed only for a further 2 months.

Nat Mur is a tissue salt that will help your horse if there is an itch present with the condition. Two tablets given three times a day for 10 days, then 2 tablets given once a day for about a month, will help strengthen your horse's body and reduce the likelihood or severity of another reaction.

A compress of Lavender and Tea tree essential oils can help to make your horse more comfortable, but do not administer a compress within 30 minutes of giving your horse homeopathic remedies.

WARTS

Warts often occur in young horses and usually disappear without treatment. Warts are rarely painful, but can be a nuisance if they appear in an area where they may be rubbed by tack or rugs. You can apply a neat application of either Lemon or Tea tree essential oil to the warts.

Thuja is the first homeopathic remedy to consider when addressing this condition, especially if the warts bleed when knocked. Give your horse a daily dose of Thuja at 30C potency until you notice a change, but not for longer than 7–10 days. If your horse has a number of small warts, use Calc-carb at a potency of 200C once a week for 3–4 weeks. If your horse has itchy warts, try Kali-carb given at a potency of 30C every second day for 10 days. (Calc-carb and Kali-carb are usually only used by experienced practitioners and, therefore, are not discussed in detail in this book. Do not use these homeopathic remedies together—choose the one remedy that best matches your horse's symptoms.)

RINGWORM

Ringworm is one of the most common fungal infections affecting horses. It is caused by a fungus and may be transferred from horse to human and from human to horse, so take careful precautions when treating a horse with ringworm. The lesions are variable in appearance. In the early stages, you may notice tufts of hair standing on end. Usually these tufts fall out and the skin below it forms a scab exuding serum. When this dries the skin becomes dry and scaly. In some cases the hair in the raised tufts simply breaks off, and the lesions are dry and scaly from the start.

The tissue salt Kali Sulph can be given twice daily. Two tablets each dose will help support your horse's immune system and resist further infection, which is important as the area affected can spread and become quite extensive if left untreated. Your horse will also need the support of herbs. A mixture of equal parts Echinacea, Cleavers, Yellow dock and Burdock will support your horse and encourage hair growth.

Topically you can cover the ringworm in Aloe vera gel containing a 2.5 per cent dilution of Tea tree essential oil (one of the most anti-fungal essential oils). If the infection is slow to respond, add Geranium essential oil to the blend.

The Bach flowers Crab apple, Mimulus, Aspen and Holly can help your horse with any underlying emotional issues associated with his condition. Select one of these remedies and either add it to your horse's feed, wipe it across the coat, or include it in the topical application by adding 6 drops of your chosen remedy to Aloe vera gel or Tea tree oil.

Homeopathically, Thuja is a useful remedy for addressing ringworm. A 6C potency dose can be given twice daily until you observe a change. If you horse does not respond, seek the advice of a professional.

MANGE

Mange is caused by an infestation of parasites (usually mites). They are very small, which makes it difficult for them to be seen by the naked eye. The first visible signs are areas of irritated skin which become thick and wrinkled, followed by patchy hair loss. If left untreated, a crusty surface will form on the uncovered skin. There are several types of mange, each caused by a different mite or parasite, and all of them are contagious. If you suspect your horse has mange, seek a veterinary surgeon's diagnosis immediately. If the diagnosis is positive, isolate your horse and disinfect the stable, rugs, tack and grooming equipment.

The best homeopathic remedy to begin with is Sulphur. Start with a low potency such as 6C, given twice daily until you observe a change in condition. If the condition worsens, cease using the remedy altogether. If the condition shows improvement, however, change to a 200C potency dose given once a week until the condition clears.

Bach flower remedies Crab apple, Aspen and Gorse can help address the irritating emotions that may have left your horse vulnerable to an attack by these parasites. You can give one of these to your horse internally by adding 10 drops to his feed or drinking water, or by adding it to a topical application.

You can make an infused oil of Garlic for the topical treatment of mange. The sulfur content of Garlic is lethal to mange mites and creates an environment that is inhospitable to opportunistic secondary bacteria. Simply crush 6 cloves of Garlic, place in a small jar, cover with a good quality cold-pressed vegetable oil, seal and leave overnight. Rub this infused oil into the infected area.

When the condition begins to improve and heal, change the topical application to Aloe vera gel carrying a 2.5 per cent blend of Bergamot, Lavender, Chamomile and Tea tree essential oils. This will hasten the healing process. You can also continue adding the chosen Bach flower remedy to this topical application.

Finally, you can give your horse the support of herbs. One tablespoonful of powdered Burdock root given daily in feed will aid the regrowth of your horse's coat. A blend of two parts each of Echinacea and Nettle with one part each of Burdock root and Bladderwrack would help your horse regain a healthy coat and avoid any infection while he is recovering.

RESPIRATORY COMPLAINTS

Your horse's lungs govern your horse's quality of life. Whether your horse can give you the performance you desire and maintain a healthy routine depends a great deal on how much oxygen he can get into his lungs. The function of the lungs can be affected by illnesses such as a simple head cold or more chronic diseases such as heaves (similar to asthma in humans).

The primary medicinal herbs to use if your horse has respiratory complaints are Echinacea, Ginger and Garlic. Echinacea will give your horse's body a short-term boost and fight off immediate infections. Garlic is a useful long-term maintenance and preventative herb, and is particularly good for warding off winter ills. Ginger will warm your horse's body against chills and, when added to a blend of herbs, is a catalyst to trigger these other herbs into action. You can also use a blend of herbs such as Eyebright, Hawthorn berry, Mullein, Peppermint and Sage in equal parts, adding one of the primary herbs depending on the stage of the illness. Give your horse 1 cupful of the blend in feed, once or twice a day. If your horse is distressed by his symptoms, as is often the case with heaves, consider adding a herb with a nervine action such as Passion flower to the blend, to help with the stressful effects of the symptoms.

Try to minimize the irritation to your horse's airway. Essential oils can be helpful for this. Make up spray misters that can be used around the stable block throughout the day. A blend of Eucalyptus, Frankincense and Lemon makes a revitalizing, cleansing spray. This also restricts the movement of airborne viruses, so any infection is less likely to spread to other horses.

When your horse feels the effects of a change in the weather, tissue salts can be used to address the symptoms very quickly. Begin with Ferr Phos—but if this is not effective, use Mag Phos instead to address deeper symptoms.

When a horse is suffering with recurring respiratory complaints, I often find that the owner or a child of that owner is having trouble taking in fresh ideas in life or is feeling restricted and suffocated by current situations. It may be that there are money worries, or that a lack of funds is restricting their freedom to explore new offers. Alternatively, they may feel stuck in a restrictive relationship. It can also stem from fear of a new situation to which someone is being forced to adjust—for example, changing schools or moving into a brand-new area. Bach flowers are extremely effective in these situations and can be helpful for horses, owners, parents and children.

COLDS

Your horse can suffer a common cold just like you do, and experience quite similar symptoms. These include sneezing, a discharge from the nostrils, watery eyes, and being slightly feverish and off his feed. If you suspect your horse has a cold, contact your veterinary surgeon to check that there is not a serious outbreak of a contagious infection in the area. You can give your horse 2 cloves of Garlic and 1 cupful of Echinacea a day, in feed, for a week or so. Your horse is most likely to catch cold when in heavy work.

If you notice the cold in its early stages of development, three or four doses of the tissue salt Ferr Phos, given to your horse at intervals throughout the day, will stop the cold developing any further and help your horse's body overcome any infection the symptoms have caused. If the symptoms have already taken firm hold, Mag Phos is a more suitable tissue salt remedy.

If your horse has a cold, isolate his drinking water from that of any other horses. Place your horse in a well-ventilated stall, keep him warm with a blanket rug and ensure he has a plentiful supply of fresh water (change his drinking water frequently). Offer Eucalyptus essential oil for your horse to inhale, or a blend of Eucalyptus and Lavender essential oils if the horse is stressed.

A cold is often a warning that too much is happening at once. It is nature's way of suggesting that you or your horse may be doing too much and worrying about too many things. Slow down and use the time to think about some of these issues. The homeopathic remedies Euphrasia and Echinacea can be of assistance, while Bach flower remedies such as Chicory and White Chestnut often help with these inconvenient complaints.

COUGHS

A cough is a normal defence mechanism of the respiratory system. It can be a simple physical reaction to dust, mucous, cold air or inflammation. If it persists, it may be the symptom of a bigger health problem, and a virus, bacteria, parasite, disease state or the environment may be the underlying cause. A cough is a common symptom of so many different illnesses. If your horse has a persistent cough, contact your veterinary surgeon. Sometimes a cough may be nothing more than a mild reaction to a different bedding or food catching in neglected back teeth, but it is always wise to rule out anything nastier. Make sure you can provide your vet with plenty of details that could help with his or her diagnosis. For example: when the coughing began; whether it is a chronic cough or has come on quickly; whether the cough is wet, dry, harsh or soft; whether there is any discharge present; and any recent changes in your horse's appetite and general health, including temperature and respiration rate. Your veterinary surgeon may also find it useful to know your horse's age, as this has some bearing on the likelihood of possible disease states. It is also worth noting whether your horse has recently been in contact with other horses at a competition or training day.

When you have isolated the cause of your horse's cough, you may choose your remedies to match your horse's symptoms more specifically than the following ones I have chosen. However, these combinations are useful in treating most coughs and may also be varied to fit your horse's condition.

The homeopathic remedies Bryonia, Belladonna and Phosphorus can address most coughs. You can use any one of these homeopathic remedies in a potency ranging from 6C to 200C depending on the severity of the cough. Give a 6C potency dose for a light, irritating cough, and upward towards 200C depending on the degree of developing and accumulated mucous. The Bach flower remedies Chicory, Crab apple and Gorse can help deal with any of the emotional irritations around you that have made your horse susceptible to these physical irritants.

When your horse initially begins to cough, give him 2 tablets of Ferr Phos tissue salts three times a day for 10 days. If, in that time, the cough still does not improve, change to Mag Phos or Kali Sulph tissue salts depending on his symptoms. Mag Phos is the best remedy for addressing loud, spasmodic coughs with no phlegm; Kali Sulph for rattling coughs with a slimy or watery yellow discharge; Nat Mur for a cough with clear, watery phlegm; and Calc Sulph for coughs with blood-streaked phlegm. If your horse has developed a chronic cough, the tissue salt Silica may be the best choice—again an intense administration of 2 tablets, two to three times a day for 10 days, but you can continue giving 2 tablets daily for 2–3 months.

Herbs that will support your horse when he has a cough are Echinacea, Mullein, Pau d'arco, Fenugreek and Garlic. Add 1 cup of a blend of Echinacea, Mullein and Fenugreek as cut, dried herbs to your horse's morning and evening feed. One to two teaspoonfuls of powdered Pau d'arco may be added at the same time.

You can also make an inhalation of essential oils for your horse. Place boiling water into a bowl or bucket and place this inside a chaff bag. Select essential oils such as Lemon, Eucalyptus, Cardamom, Peppermint, Cedarwood, Frankincense, Sandalwood or Lavender, and add no more than 10 drops of essential oil to the boiling water. Let your horse inhale the essential oils from the steam rising through the top of the bag. Don't close the top of the bag around his nose, and don't offer the inhalation for more than 10 minutes at a time.

HEAVES

Heaves is similar to the condition we as humans call asthma. This condition is caused by a sensitivity to fungal spores and dust particles, which makes your horse's breathing sound 'broken' and laboured. Your treatment of these symptoms must be guided by your veterinary surgeon, whose diagnosis at an early stage can help keep this disease manageable. Note that natural therapies can only offer palliative care to a horse with heaves and help this horse lead a more comfortable lifestyle.

It is important to reduce the amount of dust to which your horse is exposed. You can pour a herbal tea made from Chamomile, Mullein and Comfrey over your horse's hay. However, some horses need to be taken off hay completely, in which case you can pour this brew over your horse's hard feed instead. If you don't wish to make a tea, add the herbs in a cut form (like potpourri), not as a powder.

You can offer your horse Cedarwood, Lavender and Frankincense essential oils individually. Then apply a 2.5 per cent dilution of the essential oil or oils he chooses in Aloe vera gel as a chest rub when the symptoms are annoying him. Make a mixture of your horse's favourite essential oils in water with a small amount of mild detergent as a demulcent, and spray his stable each night before he enters it.

A twice daily application of Nat Sulph tissue salts can be given when the symptoms are expressing themselves aggressively. Later this can be reduced to a daily dose in the ongoing management of the symptoms. If your horse becomes distressed when experiencing breathing difficulties, and appears to be looking for air, Carbo Veg can bring effective homeopathic relief. In acute situations a 200C dose of this remedy can be given while you wait for the veterinary surgeon to arrive.

The Bach flower remedy Mustard can help with the deeper, more restrictive emotions that often accompany this condition.

TUMMY UPSETS

Your horse's digestive system is very different to yours. The way that a horse's small and large intestines loop up inside each other makes them prone to 'clogging up'. Often this is caused by a backlog of food, a twist in the intestines or a build-up of gas. This is never comfortable and, most times, is painful for your horse. Pain in the abdominal area can affect any part of the intestine from the stomach to the rectum. What can happen as a result of this pain may place your horse's life at risk. Horses often respond to this pain by pinning their ears back, looking at their flanks or violently biting the painful area. They will also paw the ground, roll and kick aggressively at their abdomen. Rolling can be dangerous for a horse in this situation, as the violent, twisting action can convolute the intestine further or even cause a bowel section to wrap around itself, resulting in a blockage that could prove to be fatal. Symptoms such as these are not to be ignored. Do not panic. Call your veterinary surgeon immediately, describe your horse's symptoms as accurately as you can and get his or her advice.

Some natural health practitioners recommend feeding yoghurt to a horse with a troubled digestive system, to re-establish the bowel bacteria. In my opinion this is unwise. After being weaned, a horse's gut is intolerant to milk products. Milk products could even cause a colic episode if your horse is particularly sensitive.

Horses were never meant to drink other mammal's milk. Goat's milk is for baby goats, cow's milk is for calves and neither are for horses, so please avoid them. If you suspect that your horse has depleted levels of healthy bowel bacteria, probiotics (a live, microbial feed supplement) designed to balance the gut bacteria of your horse are commercially available. These probiotics are produced in a lab environment from a blend of different strains of bacteria, in a formulation created specifically for horses.

Horses thrive on routine when it comes to meal times. Your horse is likely to become stressed if you are late in giving a feed, especially if he is stabled throughout most of the day. Try not to make radical changes to your horse's diet, as the normal bacterium in your horse's gut produces more gas when adjusting to a different feed. If you must make changes to your horse's diet, introduce the changes gradually, over 1 week. Ensure that any hard feed you are giving your horse matches his current workload. Always check the quality of any hay before you feed it to your horse and never feed out mouldy or dusty hay. Movement helps your horse maintain a healthy gut. Horses that are turned out for more than 12 hours a day are less prone to colic. If your horse has to be stabled all the time, take extra care with his feed. Avoid riding your horse within an hour before or after feeding, as his body will have difficulty coping with the digestive load and the exertion.

Water is another important factor. If your horse does not drink enough water, the movement of food through the digestive system slows down, increasing the risk of impaction in the bowels. It is important that your horse does not get dehydrated during hot weather or while travelling. Many horses don't drink enough when away from home, particularly if travel is involved. A cupful of apple juice added to your horse's drinking water will make it more appealing. Remember to stop and break your trip, and monitor your horse's water intake. If your horse is feeling stressed, do not presume he is drinking the amount required. In the wild, horses tend to drink at dusk and dawn, but stabled horses need to drink more often due to their dry feed diet. A stabled horse should normally drink between 20–40 litres of water every day, depending on his size, workload, feed and climatic conditions. You should also take care if your horse is in a particularly cold climate where his drinking water may become icy or freeze over, as very cold water or a lack of water could contribute to a colic episode.

If your horse suddenly goes off his feed, check his manure. It pays to get familiar with your horse's stools and learn to recognize what is normal for your horse. You will then be more aware of any change in consistency, odour or regularity. You should also try to get familiar with the sounds of his gut, as silence or excessive noise can also be an indicator that something is wrong. If your horse becomes a fussy eater and seems to have low energy reserves after a digestive health incident, consider using the homeopathic remedy, China. If your horse is just being picky with his food, Nux Vomica is the most appropriate homeopathic remedy.

Intestinal worms can irritate your horse's gut, so it is important that you follow a worming regimen with your horse. If more than one horse is kept on the property, ensure that all horses are being treated with the same programme to reduce the likelihood of re-infestation. Many herbs and practices can keep worm infestations to a minimum, but pharmaceuticals are certainly the most effective approach. Ask for an annual feacal egg count test on your horse's stools so you know how effective your worming programme has been. If you want to reduce your reliance on pharmaceutical worming preparations, ask a professional to design a regimen to suit your horse. He or she may suggest something like the remedy Cina and Granatum repeated in very low potency doses for 10–14 days, then one dose of Calc Carb 200C given as a post-worming treatment to help maintain an internal environment that is less hospitable for worms. It is best to continue using pharmaceuticals alongside the homeopathic remedies.

COLIC

This is the dreaded word that horse owner fear hearing when they get a phone call from their livery stable in the middle of the night. If you are new to owning a horse, discuss emergency procedures for colic with your veterinary surgeon. Ask your vet how he or she prefers to be contacted in these situations. By being prepared, you will remove a lot of your fear and your judgment will be clearer should you ever be faced with this situation. It is also much better to meet your vet before an emergency situation arises—his or her familiarity will be reassuring for you.

The early warning signs of a colic episode include: passing dry, hard manure or diarrhoea; pawing the ground or standing stretched out; turning to look at either side; biting or kicking at the belly; and being restless and unable to decide whether to stand up, lie down or roll. If you believe your horse has the first symptoms of a colic attack, observe and note all of your horse's vital signs (see page 13) and seek veterinary advice immediately.

Some references recommend that you give your horse a laxative while waiting for your veterinary surgeon. Please be guided by your vet, as this is not always advisable. If your horse's symptoms are caused by an impacted, blocked bowel, a laxative could move the impaction but rupture the bowel at the same time, causing your horse's death.

While waiting for your vet there are a few things you can do to help your horse. If your horse is still eating, wet small amounts of feed with a strong infusion of Chamomile, Peppermint or Valerian tea. The homeopathic remedies Carbo Veg, Colocynthis, Colchicum, China and Nux Vomica can be of help—choose the remedy that is most appropriate for your horse's specific situation. Give your horse a 30C potency dose every hour until you see some relief. If your horse's symptoms are severe, give him a single dose of 200C instead. The tissue salt Mag Phos is very useful in most cases of colic and can be given every 30 minutes during an episode. In this situation it is best to use the tissue salts that dissolve when they come into contact with saliva, as these will cause the least distress to your horse. The Bach flower Rescue Remedy blend can be added to your horse's drinking water, and you can wipe it onto your horse's coat as many times as you like. The Bach flower remedy Water Violet is specific for colic pain. You can also massage your horse's ears, as this is a useful reflexology area when your horse has a tummy ache.

Waft essential oils under your horse's nose to help release neurochemicals that will relax his body and ease discomfort. His reaction to individual essential oils can also give you an indication of how much pain and anxiety your horse is experiencing. The best oils to help your horse cope with the stress of a painful situation are Lavender, Bergamot and Frankincense. Other oils may be massaged into your horse's abdomen to help your horse cope with pain—offer your horse a choice of Basil, Marjoram, Orange, Geranium, Fennel, Chamomile and Juniper. See which ones your horse likes most. Blend up to four of the chosen essential oils in a 2.5 per cent dilution and apply in a cold-pressed vegetable oil or Aloe vera gel carrier, and gently massage into his tummy.

After a colic attack, your horse will need continued attention. Aftercare includes making a blend of mucilaginous herbs to help soothe the intestinal tract and minimize the chance of scarring, and administering carminative herbs such as Chamomile, Peppermint and Valerian to sooth the gut. A possible blend could be equal parts of Slippery elm, Marshmallow, St Mary's thistle, Meadowsweet and Comfrey root (if available) with half a part of Licorice root. One to two tablespoonfuls of this combination can be given for up to 1 month after the episode. If you find it difficult to blend herbs this way, simply add 1–2 cups of Chamomile infusion to your horse's nightly feed for 1–2 months.

Offer your horse essential oils such as Basil, Bergamot, Fennel, Lavender, Juniper, Frankincense or Marjoram to inhale each day. If your horse has a strong attraction to one of these essential oils, place a few drops into a small amount of Aloe vera gel, offer it to him and allow him to guide you to the place on his body where he would prefer that you apply it. The poll, neck, chest and abdomen are commonly chosen areas after a colic scare.

Any horse that has suffered a severe colic attack is vulnerable to further episodes, particularly if there is scarring to the intestinal tract. As with your treatment of the acute condition, seek your veterinary surgeon's guidance and advice during the aftercare phase.

If your horse is experiencing recurrent colic episodes, this may be an indication that you need to look at and address some aspects in your own life that are not 'digestible'. Consider work, relationships and living arrangements. Are you having trouble understanding your studies or comprehending what the important people in your life are asking of you? Are you having trouble getting your point of view across? Do you have a food intolerance or are you eating foods that cause your gut to be out of balance? Don't forget to address your own issues when trying to help your horse.

DIARRHOEA

This can be a mild and easily addressed condition or, in the case of a foal, for instance, a serious situation requiring veterinary attention. A bout of diarrhoea may be caused by nerves, changed feeding patterns and any number of other things including worms, a tumour, prolonged use of antibiotics, attack by bacteria or a virus, or poisoning.

If you think your horse has diarrhoea due to overexcitement, you can address this with 1–2 cupfuls of Raspberry leaf tea poured over small. hard feeds. It is also helpful to add 10–20 drops of a Bach flower remedy such as Agrimony, Impatiens or Mimulus to his drinking water, or place approximately 6 drops of the remedy on your hand then wipe it along your horse's abdomen. Essential oils such as Bergamot will also help to address the anxiety.

A sudden change of diet may cause an episode of diarrhoea, so always take care when you make changes to your horse's feed. If you horse is glum and has a temperature, it is wise to call your veterinary surgeon as the diarrhoea may be a symptom of something more serious. Monitor your horse for dehydration if this condition continues for more than 2 days.

The quickest-acting natural remedies for most cases of diarrhoea are homeopathic remedies. Use China if the diarrhoea is violent, debilitating and involves a loss of fluids, Colocynthis if the diarrhoea is accompanied by colic and pain, and Nux Vomica if the diarrhoea has been caused by overfeeding. A 30C potency dose given twice a day is usually appropriate, though severe cases may require a single dose at a 200C potency.

You can use tissue salts with your horse if you carefully observe the colour of his stools. Use Ferr Phos if the diarrhoea is sudden and contains undigested food, or Kali Sulph if the stools are watery and yellow. Use Nat Sulph on an older horse with dark diarrhoea, Nat Phos for green, sour smelling stools, and Calc Phos for spluttery stools. If you are unsure, Calc Phos will address most unpleasant diarrhoea. When you have determined which tissue salt your horse needs, give 2 tablets every half an hour until you notice an improvement, then 2 tablets daily until your horse has settled down to a regular, healthy movement.

One to two tablespoonfuls of Slippery elm bark powder mashed into 1–2 cups of cooked pumpkin and added to your horse's feed once or twice daily will assist his recovery. A commercial probiotic can also be given to help re-establish the healthy bacteria of the bowel. Your horse may also be attracted to the aroma of Patchouli and Sandalwood essential oils at this time.

OUCH, THAT HURT

Injuries and accidents are an almost unavoidable part of owning a horse. Minor nicks and cuts can be addressed with simple ointments or essential oils such as Lavender and Tea tree oil, but prevention is obviously the best approach. Make sure your horse's stable area and paddock are clear of debris.

Accidents often happen when we wander around aimlessly without purpose. If your horse has a cut, it can point to the need to look within yourself for answers. If the cut is bleeding, the amount of bleeding can indicate you may be pushing yourself too hard. Small injuries are often little nudges to alert you to the idea that there is a problem to be faced. If there is bruising or a haematoma, you will need to look at your emotions towards these problems. If your horse develops proud flesh, this could be a sign that you are avoiding the original issue.

It is imperative that your horse is vaccinated against tetanus. Tetanus or lockjaw is a toxemia caused by the organism *Clostridium tetami* and usually occurs when a wound gets infected. Puncture wounds pose the most serious risk, but any cuts from barbed wire and punctures from nails or protrusions can cause the problem. The first sign of tetanus is stiffness in all the muscles of your horse's body. In advanced stages chewing becomes difficult, the tail and ears stay erect and the horse's reactions are extreme if frightened or startled. If left untreated, the diaphragm becomes unable to expel air from the lungs, and death usually results due to asphyxiation.

If your horse is not vaccinated for tetanus, but becomes injured and shows signs of developing this disease, contact your vet, who can administer an antitoxoid. Give your horse a 200C potency dose of Ledum, wait half an hour, then give a 200C potency dose of Hypericum. If there is a strong threat of tetanus, repeat these doses two or three times in alternation while waiting for the veterinary surgeon to arrive.

CUTS AND ABRASIONS

If your horse is bleeding from an injury, the first thing you must do is stop the bleeding. Apply a pressure bandage, and do not remove it even if the bleeding stops. Simply place a pressure pad and bandage over the top of the wound and apply more pressure. If you are unable to control the bleeding, or if the wound is very dirty or has a foreign object imbedded in it, call your vet. If an object is embedded in the wound, do not remove it. Wrap a pressure bandage around the object, not over it, and do your best to stop the bleeding without disturbing the object's position.

Homeopathic remedies can be helpful in this situation. If the bleeding is slow and the blood is dark, flowing straight from a vein, keep applying pressure and administer a 30C potency dose of the homeopathic remedy Hamamelis every 30 minutes until you notice an improvement (but give no more than six doses), or give one 200C potency dose. If the bleeding is fast and the blood is bright red, flowing directly from an artery, administer Millefolium in the same way and potencies. If the bleeding persists and your veterinary surgeon still hasn't arrived, give your horse a 200C potency dose of Phosphorus.

When the bleeding has been brought under control, you can ascertain whether your horse is suffering from shock and begin cleaning the wound. A 200C potency dose of the homeopathic remedies Arnica or Aconite can be given to address shock. Wash the wound with a bucketful of water containing 10 drops of essential oils. I recommend 2 drops of Cypress to arrest further bleeding, 4 drops of Lavender to hasten cell regeneration and 4 drops of Tea tree to address any infections. Carefully check that no foreign matter is left in the wound.

If the wound is just a small scrape, apply Comfrey or Calendula ointment to hasten healing. It is vital that no debris is left in the wound, however—these ointments heal so quickly that a stone or infection may get sealed inside. If the wound is deep and you suspect it needs stitching, bandage it firmly to reduce swelling while waiting for your vet.

Remember the Bach flower combination Rescue Remedy throughout this entire time. It can be added to compresses and bandages, wiped on your horse's body and added to your horse's drinking water.

As your horse is recovering, use herbs to support the healing process and help the immune system prevent or fight any infection. Echinacea, Garlic and Pau d'arco are useful for addressing infection. Devil's claw or White willow help the healing process and lessen any pain. Rosehips will support the tissue through the healing process, and you can use Valerian to help address the bruising. If your horse has suffered significant blood loss, you can help the recovery process along with a daily dose of the tissue salt Ferr Phos. The homeopathic remedies Hypericum or Calendula can be given daily in 30C potency doses for a few days to assist the healing, too.

BRUISES AND HAEMATOMAS

A bruise is usually caused by a kick from another horse or a collision with a fence post in the paddock, or is sustained during competition. Bruises occurs when small blood vessels rupture. In bad cases, signs of inflammation such as heat, pain and swelling will be present. In cases when your horse has been bruised by the impact of a blunt object, there may be internal damage that requires veterinary attention. The warning signs of this are a dull appearance, laboured breathing and a loss of appetite.

Most bruises subside over 3–4 days. Any one of the homeopathic remedies Arnica, Phosphorus or Hamamelis can be given in a 30C potency dose twice daily for a few days or even up to a week, until the bruising has cleared. Your horse would also benefit from a topical application of Aloe vera gel containing 6 drops of the Bach flower remedy Star of Bethlehem or Agrimony along with the essential oils Geranium, Lavender and Marjoram in a 2.5 per cent dilution.

A large blood-filled swelling known as a haematoma can sometimes develop as a result of a sudden blow or needle jab. Small haematomas can be reabsorbed by the body, and you can assist this process with a dose of 3 tablets of the tissue salt Kali Mur given daily and Raspberry leaf tea used as a compress. Larger swellings can get as large as a basketball and may need to be drained by your veterinary surgeon. This is usually done about a week after the incident, to ensure that the internal bleeding has ceased. A compress with Cypress and Lavender essential oils can be used before the draining has begun and during the healing process afterwards.

To guard against infection while a haematoma is draining, give your horse herbs such as Echinacea, Garlic or Pau d'arco. Rosehips are also useful for restoring healthy tone to tissue.

PROUD FLESH

Proud flesh is granulate tissue that forms quickly over a wound to protect it while the original tissue, which is slower to heal, is repaired from beneath. It is a form of scar tissue, but does not have blood supply. Normally the proud flesh is shed when the tissue below has sufficiently healed, but sometimes it remains as a permanent accumulation of tough tissue. This excessive production of protective tissue is relatively common on the limbs where cuts and trauma most often occur. Proud flesh becomes a problem when it interferes with other tissue and restricts the movement of tendons and joints. The removal of excess proud flesh must be done surgically by a veterinary surgeon.

To encourage the healing process, try to increase the circulation of blood to the area. One cupful of herbs such as Ginkgo and Fenugreek combined and given once or twice a day in feed will help with this. Comfrey, given daily as 1–2 cupfuls of tea or a generous handful of fresh leaves added to feed, for up to a week, will promote healing with less scarring. It is best to keep your horse stabled if he has an injury that is likely to develop proud flesh, as exercise will aggravate the wound and increase the likelihood of your horse developing this condition.

Homeopathically, Calendula can be used to encourage healing and discourage infection, and Silicea can be used to help rebuild tissue and expel foreign matter or pus. The dose required depends on the severity of the wound: Simple cuts and abrasions can be addressed by a 30C potency dose of Calendula given twice daily for up to 3 days, or a 12C potency dose given three times a day for up to 4 days. Severe injuries, particularly deep or exposed wounds, can be addressed by 30C potency doses given twice daily for up to a week. Silicea can also be given in 30C potency doses twice a day for up to a week if pus is present or foreign matter is in the wound. To minimize the development of proud flesh, a 200C potency dose of Silicea can be given twice a week for 2–3 weeks.

INJECTIONS

Some horses experience a reaction to vaccinations and either develop symptoms of the disease or have a reaction to the stick of the needle. Homeopathic remedies can be used to minimize the risk of an adverse reaction. The day before your horse is due to be given an injection, administer a morning dose of Ledum at 200C potency followed between 30 minutes to an hour later by a dose of 200C potency Hypericum. Repeat this in the afternoon or the next morning, before the veterinary surgeon arrives. Ledum will minimize your horse's reaction to the puncture, Hypericum will minimize his reaction to the pain, and both remedies will address any adverse reaction to the vaccination process.

If it is not possible for you to give your horse this homeopathic treatment before the injection, and your horse does develop a reaction afterwards, administer a 200C potency dose of Ledum, then 20 minutes later a 200C potency dose of Hypericum. You may repeat this treatment every 1–2 hours, up to three times. If your horse continues to have other adverse side effects, seek the advice of a professional as your horse may need follow up treatment with another post-vaccination homeopathic remedy such as Thuja or Silicea.

FROM THE GROUND UP

Your horse's feet provide a vital foundation for your horse's health and movement. The hooves support your horse's weight, absorb shock, provide traction, conduct moisture, help to pump blood around the body and are partly responsible for the style and action of your horse's movement. It is extremely important that your horse's feet are kept healthy and strong, as any weakness can contribute to and cause health problems in other parts of your horse's body, such as a sore back or muscular pain. Pick out your horse's feet before and after exercise. Stable bedding should also be kept clean and dry to avoid problems such as thrush.

If your horse is showing signs of lameness, the first place to look is at all four of your horse's feet. Lameness can be difficult to diagnose, even for a veterinary surgeon, but as the scientific understanding of horse health and treatment of horse health problems is becoming more specialized, clinics with experts in each part of the horse are being established. If you and your local veterinary surgeon are unable to find the cause of your horse's lameness, it is worth transporting your horse to one of these facilities.

Your horse's body weight rests on his legs, which act as supporting columns. His legs in turn rest on his hooves. It is important to work with your farrier to maintain a balanced distribution of your horse's body weight.

Occasionally when your horse is shod, a nail may come too close to the White Line or penetrate the soft tissue of the hoof. Have your farrier remove the shoe then rest your horse until you are satisfied that the injury has healed and he is sound. Any nail prick warrants the administration of a tetanus antitoxin. A poultice of Slippery elm bark powder and epsom salts will help to heal the injury. You can support the healing process by giving Silica tissue salts internally. Two tablets can be given two to three times daily for up to 3 weeks.

Problems with your horse's feet often reflect the direction that you and your horse are taking in life, and how you feel about this direction. Pigeon toes usually indicate you have narrowed the path of your life away from the direction you truly desire. Outwardly turned toes usually hint at fears about your direction. Thrush, with its offensive odour, indicates that the direction you have chosen may be offensive to you on some level and that you may be stuck in a paradigm of old concepts. If the hoof itself becomes brittle, it could be a sign that you are avoiding stepping into your own power and reaching your potential. If your horse is frequently throwing his shoes, you need examine your life to see if you lack the ability to follow through on promises.

CORNS AND BRUISED SOLES

A corn is a specific type of bruise that occurs at the angled point of the hoof wall on the heel. (This area is often referred to as the Seat of Corn.) Corns can be caused by unevenly trimmed hooves, poor hoof conformation and shoes that are too small for the hoof or have been left on for too long. Bruised soles often occur when the horse treads on a stone or sharp object, but can sometimes be caused simply by working on hard ground. Your horse will be reluctant to put weight on a corn or bruised sole, and you may notice that his action is a bit 'choppy'.

Use the homeopathic remedy Arnica in a dose ranging from 30C for a mild case of bruising to 200C for more severe bruising. You can also soak your horse's hoof in epsom salts dissolved in water to help draw out the bruising. To increase the effectiveness of this soak, add 3–4 drops of Lavender or Geranium essential oils to this solution. If you use the common treatment of iodine spray to toughen your horse's feet, add a few drops of Bergamot and Tea tree essential oils to the spray to help guard against infections. If the bruising is only slight, the tissue salt Ferr Phos can be given daily until the bruising has cleared. Severe bruising may require 2–3 tablets given three times daily for 10 days.

If your horse has a soft frog or flat feet, you can supplement his feed with herbs such as Bladderwrack, Hawthorn and Rosehips, to give the feet more strength. This must be done for a minimum of 3 months to bring about any real change. If your horse seems to find the condition painful, you can use Devil's claw as a supplement to address inflammation. Stop using Devil's claw after a week and wait to see if the foot is still sore after a few days. If it is, you should look look beyond the visible symptoms to see if there is a worse problem underlying the condition.

ABSCESSES

If the bruising develops into an abscess, it will have to be opened up and cleaned by your farrier or vet. While the abscess is healing, use the homeopathic remedy Silicea or Hepar Sulph depending on your horse's symptoms. Silicea is the best remedy to use if the abscess has a thin, white discharge. Hepar Sulph is best for painful, infected, pus-filled abcesses that are very sensitive to touch. A poultice or hoof packing made from Comfrey leaf, Slippery elm bark powder or Marshmallow root can be useful for drawing out the bruising and reducing the pain.

THRUSH

This disease is caused by a bacterium that infects the frog, on the sole of the foot. Its most distinguishing symptom is a black discharge with a strong, offensive odour. To avoid this disease, keep your horse's feet clean and his stall and paddock as dry as possible. (This is easier said than done in some seasons and climates!) Thrush does not usually cause lameness, except in severe cases which have been left untreated. If the disease has been allowed to develop this far, your horse will need veterinary attention.

Using a stiff brush, scrub your horse's feet with water daily. Add 10 drops of Tea tree oil to your bucket of water to help address the infection. Make a poultice of Slippery elm bark powder, Comfrey leaves or Marshmallow root and add up to 10 drops in total of Bergamot, Lavender or Tea tree essential oil, to help fight the infection. Support your horse with 2 Silica tissue salt tablets given three times a day for 10 days, then 2–3 tablets once a day for a further 3 weeks. In serious cases, you can continue giving 2 or 3 tablets once a day until the condition clears.

Homeopathically, your horse is most likely to respond to a 30C potency dose of Hepar Sulph given daily for 5 days. This may be followed by a 200C potency dose of Silicea to help strengthen the hoof tissue. If your horse has a severe case of offensive, purulent thrush, consider using a 200C potency dose of Kreosotum once a week for a month, though this remedy should only be used in consultation with a professional.

In severe cases where your horse is lame and has been assessed by a vet, you can support your horse with herbs that will boost the immune system and increase circulation to the feet. A mixture of equal parts Echincaea, Cleavers, Bladderwrack, Meadowsweet and Burdock should be given to your horse for 3–4 weeks. If you cannot obtain all the herbs in the powdered form, combine the dried, cut form of Echinacea, Cleavers and Meadowsweet in equal parts and give your horse 1 cupful of this mixture twice daily with feed. Combine powdered Bladderwrack and Burdock and add 1 tablespoonful of this mixture to your horse's feed, too. If the problem persists after this, consult your vet again.

LAMINITIS

Laminitis is an extremely painful condition where reduced circulation and blood supply to your horse's feet causes inflammation and congestion of the sensitive laminae of the hoof. This condition is most common in ponies, but it can affect any type of horse. The most common cause is carbohydrate overload, but repetitive work on hard surfaces, endotoxemia, dehydration, shock and pharmaceutical drugs such as corticosteriods have also been known to trigger the condition. The horse's feet become hot and tender, causing him to shift his weight frequently, and stretch away from the sore foot or feet in an effort to place as little weight as possible on the place where it hurts. You need to work closely with your farrier and veterinary surgeon in the treatment of this disease. Laminitis can also be a sign of another underlying internal disease such as Pituitary Gland Dysfunction (Cushings Disease).

The homeopathic remedy for acute cases or episodes of this condition is Belladonna. A 200C potency dose can be given once a day for 3 days. As the symptoms begin to ease and the first intense inflammatory period has calmed down, stop giving Belladonna and use Bryonia instead, in 30C potency doses, three times a day for 3–4 days. As soon as you notice that the horse appears to improve when he is moving, change to Rhus Tox in 30C potency doses, once a day for 3–4 days. If you do not see good results within this time, consult a professional.

A blend of herbs including White willow to address pain, Comfrey to heal and Garlic, Nettle, Dandelion and Fenugreek to help your horse regain mobility, can be made into an infusion. Up to 3 cupfuls a day can be given poured over a small amount of hay or chaff. When the condition has 'cooled' down, support your horse with a blend of herbs such as Burdock, Hawthorn berry and Celery seed combined in equal parts as a powder and added to feed. A cupful of Chamomile tea poured over feed can also be helpful. Further support can be given with 2 tablets of Silica tissue salts given daily for up to 3 months.

Don't forget to use Rescue Remedy whenever this condition is causing stress to your horse. Add 10 drops to his drinking water every time you fill his water bucket, and wipe it on him at least once a day.

LEG INJURIES

It is very likely that at one time or another you will discover lumps or small swellings on your horse's legs. Your horse may even have developed these in the care of a previous owner. Lumps and swellings may or may not be accompanied by lameness, but they are usually a sign of strain or injury. They may have been caused by working in unfavourable conditions (particularly hard ground), unbalanced movement where one leg is working harder than the others, stepping into a hole, or the impact of another horse's kick or a knock on a fence. Bumps and swellings are common on the legs of young racehorses that have begun race training before their growth plates are fully closed, and horses that have not been sufficiently prepared and conditioned for a demanding competition. Many leg problems can be easily prevented with careful conditioning and training.

Lameness often moves upwards from the hoof. After any hoof problems have been diagnosed, you need to pay close attention to your horse's legs. A poorly balanced hoof, for example, can lead to unnatural strain being placed on certain muscles of the leg. Never ignore splints and arthritic changes. It is best to have a vet assess your horse and address any initial inflammation. Once this inflammation has healed, careful management of any of the conditions discussed in this section should result in your horse's performance being unaffected in the long-term. While lumps and bumps are considered to be aesthetically undesirable in some disciplines, they often don't have a long-term effect on the horse's soundness and capabilities, and serve as a useful reminder to the owner that the area has been weakened.

A series of ground-based exercises based on the renowned Feldenkrais technique can help you recognize any imbalance and stiffness in your horse's legs. A good introductory guide is *Let's Ride* by Linda Tellington Jones (see Further Reading, page 229).

Problems in our horses' legs can be a reflection of our own fear of moving beyond our normal comfort zone into a new area of our lives. Try to break some of your usual daily routine and start making a habit of not being habitual. Little variances in our day can help prepare us for times when we are faced with life's larger challenges, by reducing the fear factor.

SPLINTS

This bony growth occurs between the canon and the splint bones when too much stress is placed on the inside aspect of the lower legs, particularly the forelegs. This stress causes inflammation of the periostium of the splint bone, which triggers the production of new bone growth in an effort to protect the area. Splints can be caused by working on hard ground, inadequate nutrition, a kick from another horse, poor conformation or faulty trimming of the hoof. They can be difficult to detect in the early stages of their development, though intermittent lameness is a common symptom at this time.

Prevention is better than cure. It is important that your horse's feet are trimmed by a good farrier to avoid an imbalance that could cause uneven weight distribution. It is also important that young horses do not become overweight before their bones have matured.

Hosing with cold water and applying Comfrey ointment and support bandages will lessen some of the bony changes. Silica tissue salt can help to curb the excess bone development. Two tablets can be given twice daily while heat is present. After the heat has subsided, give 2 tablets once a day for a further 3 weeks. Address the inflammation with 2 tablespoonfuls each of powdered Devil's claw and White willow bark, combined. During the initial stages of a developing splint, the homeopathic remedy Ruta Grav can be given in 6C potency doses three times a day for up to a week. In the later stages of development, Symphytum can be given as one 30C potency dose daily for 3–4 days, then the same potency once a week for 3–4 weeks.

STRAINED OR BOWED TENDONS

A bowed tendon is the result of a severe strain that causes a rupture of the tendon fibres. It is caused by exertion: usually jumping, racing or the sudden stops, starts and turns expected of rodeo or eventing horses. Conformation faults and insufficient conditioning before beginning heavy work can also leave your horse vulnerable to tendon strain. The most common signs of this condition include heat, pain, swelling and lameness.

Call out a vet to attend to your horse. In the meantime, apply a coldpack to the affected leg or legs and rest your horse. If you are present when the injury occurs, immediately give your horse one 200C potency dose of Arnica. The severity of the injury will determine the kind of veterinary treatment required and how long your horse will be rested from work.

The Bach flower remedies Vervain or Impatiens can be added to your horse's drinking water and applied directly to the injury. Comfrey leaf compresses are useful, and Lavender and Lemongrass essential oils in a 2.5 per cent dilution can be applied daily before bandaging the leg, to aid healing. Homeopathic remedies for long-term use in the healing process are Arnica, Ruta Grav, Symphytum and Rhus Tox in potencies of 30C. Choose the remedy most suitable for your horse's symptoms. Immediately after the injury occurs, give a 30C dose of Arnica twice a day for 2–3 days.

WINDGALLS

Windgalls or windpuffs are small, puffy swellings that can develop on each side of the tendon or suspensory ligament just above the fetlock. They rarely cause lameness and in themselves are relatively harmless— although they are one of nature's early warning signs that the joint is beginning to wear or may have suffered a twist.

Homeopathically, the condition may be addressed with Apis Mel, Ruta Grav, Bryonia, Rhus Tox or Silicea depending on other symptoms (refer to individual remedy entries in the Homeopathy chapter). A low potency dose of 6C may be given twice daily or a 30C potency dose given once a day for 1–2 weeks to stimulate the healing process. Herbs such as Dandelion, St Mary's thistle and Cleavers and the tissue salts Nat Mur or Calc Fluor may help reduce puffiness.

A blend of essential oils such as Patchouli, Lavender and Grapefruit in

Aloe vera gel can be applied to the affected areas on your horse before and after exercise. If deeper tissue involvement is suspected, add Lemongrass essential oil to the blend and use either cold-pressed vegetable oil, Aloe vera gel or clay as your carrier.

ARTHRITIS

The terms arthritis and rheumatism are often used loosely to describe pain that becomes worse with work. Arthritis refers to pain in joints, whereas rheumatism refers to pain in muscles, tendons or ligaments. Older horses are more likely to develop arthritis and rheumatism; however, crooked legs or hooves that turn in or out may place uneven pressure on your horse's legs and cause bony changes to develop earlier in life. Horses that have been raced as two-year-olds are also likely to develop arthritis at an early age. Joints that have suffered an injury in the past are vulnerable to the development of both these conditions and should be well monitored.

Early detection is important, as both diseases cause degeneration of the affected joint or tissue. Warning signs include heat or swelling around the joint, pain when the joint is flexed and varying degrees of lameness. Your veterinary surgeon can use an X-ray to eliminate other possible causes such as a fracture, bone chip, or foreign body, and confirm and determine the extent of the arthritis.

While the pain is acute, herbs such as Devil's claw, Meadowsweet and White willow can be used to address the pain. Two tablespoonfuls of a powdered blend of these herbs can be given daily, in feed. After 3 weeks, stop administering these herbs and observe your horse's condition to ensure that your treatment is not masking any other symptoms. Other herbs that may be used for long-term support to warm and detoxify the body include Feverfew, Celery seed, Bladderwrack and Ginger. You will need to assess your horse's changing needs every 3–4 months and modify the blend of herbs to suit the change of seasons.

A blend of the essential oils Bergamot, Rosemary, Juniper and Lavender in a 2.5 per cent dilution in olive oil has an analgesic action that lasts for up to 24 hours. It can be applied to arthritic areas if the pain becomes debilitating. Do not use it constantly, however, as the blend is so effective that you may be lulled into a false sense of the problem being cured.

Homeopathically, your horse may benefit from Bryonia or Rhus Tox given as a 30C potency dose once a day for 5 days, while the symptoms are active. For ongoing management of the condition, 2 Nat Phos tissue salt tablets given daily for 3 weeks will slow down the rate of degeneration. After this time, stop giving the salts and observe your horse's symptoms for a week. If necessary, the salts can then be given this way for a further 3 weeks.

MUSCLE SORENESS

When training a horse, you are also developing his muscles to keep him working at his peak and helping him reach his full potential. A horse in training will have many small aches and pains which occur regularly and go unnoticed. Other aches and pains will need to be addressed, though, as they may affect your horse's movement. In some cases, these aches and pains are a warning that your horse is not coping with the tasks you are setting or needs treatment before the workload is increased.

Addressing muscle soreness calls upon your massage skills. As your sense of touch and feel develops, you will begin to recognize spasms and tears in your horse's muscles. A spasm is usually triggered when a muscle is overstretched. Initially just a few small fibres spasm, then rigidity builds up in the surrounding fibres, resulting in a full muscle spasm that reduces the elasticity of the muscle and its movement. Sometimes a muscle is stretched past its limit and the fibres tear, producing an inflammatory response with heat and swelling. If left untreated, tears may develop scar tissue that inhibits the function of the muscle even further.

Offer your horse Basil, Rosemary, Geranium, Lavender, Chamomile, Marjoram, Mandarin, Juniper and Fennel essential oils, one at a time. Select the three or four oils your horse enjoys most and add 20 drops in total to 20 millilitres of a cold-pressed vegetable oil or Aloe vera gel. You may find that your horse's selection of essential oils changes as the muscles respond to treatment.

A Bach flower remedy can also be added to your aromatherapy muscle blend or liniment. Impatiens assists in the relief of muscular tension, Rock water is useful for tight muscles and joints and Water violet can help to ease stiffness and tension. Add 3–6 drops to the blend.

Arnica is the homeopathic remedy of choice when the injury first happens. A 30C potency dose can be given daily for up to 5 days to help minimize any bruising. Rhus Tox and Ruta Grav address most muscle problems as does Bryonia—the remedy and potency you select will depend on your horse's individual symptoms. If there is nerve damage or muscle spasm and tightness is impinging on a nerve, Hypericum is an effective remedy to use. One 200C potency dose can be given, or 30C potency doses daily for up to 5 days. Calc Fluor may be given daily as a 6X potency homeopathic remedy or 2–3 tissue salt tablets, for up to 3 weeks, to help an older horse experiencing chronic aches and pains maintain freedom of movement.

Mag Phos tissue salt is specific for muscle spasm and pain. You can give your horse 2–3 tablets hourly if his aches and pains are severe; however, 2 tablets given twice a day for up to 3 weeks will address most muscle hurts.

Chamomile is an excellent herb for relieving muscle spasms and helping muscle heal with less likelihood of further injury. While your horse is recuperating, add a cupful of the fresh or dried flower heads or 1–2 cupfuls of a strong infusion to your horse's evening feed. Devil's claw or White willow can be used to address pain, while Celery seed, Burdock and Dandelion can be used to help your horse deal with any toxins in the muscles that may be slowing his recovery.

Horse's muscles often reflect horse owner's feelings of guilt. If your horse has a one-off muscular injury, you may be feeling uncomfortable about something you said to someone, or a white lie you told. If your horse is continually sore, look at areas in life where you may be cheating, and even cheating yourself. You may feel that you are not performing at your best, or at the standard of your peers—this can create feelings of guilt that make your muscles and your horse's muscles vulnerable to damage.

TYING-UP

Tying-up, or azoturia, is a serious condition causing stiffening and spasms of muscles throughout the horse's body. Although its causes are not yet fully understood, it is often associated with physical exertion and hard feed. A horse experiencing this condition will seem stilted and unable to walk normally. A severe case of tying-up can be frightening, as the horse is in obvious pain, sweating heavily and likely to panic. During this stage the affected muscle fibres are actually breaking apart, so avoid moving your horse if possible. The horse's urine may get darker while his heart rate, respiration rate and temperature all become elevated. These symptoms may come on quickly before your horse has done any significant exertion, or gradually after work. Because the symptoms of tying-up are easily confused with the symptoms of colic, it is important that you call your veterinary surgeon and get a reliable diagnosis.

While waiting for your veterinary surgeon, keep your horse as still, calm and warm as possible and ensure that he has easy access to fresh water. Give your horse a 200C potency dose of Arnica to avoid further muscle damage. Two other remedies which are not discussed in this book but may be worth using in consultation with a professional are Bellis Perennis, if there is deeper muscle spasm, and Berberis, if there is a darkening of urine. The Bach flower remedy Vervain is particularly useful for congested muscles. It can be added to your horse's drinking water and wiped over the affected muscles three times a day while the symptoms are intense, then once a day as your horse's recovery progresses. Most horses will not tolerate massage while this condition is painful; however, hot compresses with a blend of Grapefruit, Juniper, Lavender and Geranium essential oils will help to relax the muscles and encourage the removal of excess toxins.

It is important to address the whole horse, not just the symptoms, when treating this condition. Always consult your veterinary surgeon; if the problem is not treated properly, your horse could suffer kidney failure. Ask your veterinary surgeon to help you determine which vitamin supplements could help your horse. Your vet should test your horse's blood and urine, monitor your horse's plasma muscle enzyme activities and recommend the most appropriate electrolytes for your horse. Horses susceptible to this condition do not always tolerate hard feed. Three tablets of the tissue salt Nat Phos can be given daily for 3 months, and a probiotic is often recommended to support the horse's internal health. Herbs such as St Mary's thistle, Bladderwrack, Marshmallow, Dandelion root and Cleavers can be used to boost your horse's metabolism. Mild cases of tying-up are quite common, as it can be difficult for riders to recognize the fine line between what is necessary for building muscle and stamina in the equine athlete, and overexertion.

After an episode of azoturia, careful treatment should usually see the horse recover within 12–36 hours, but seek a veterinary opinion before you recommence ridden work. It is important that a susceptible horse is kept in regular daily exercise. If this is not possible, try to turn your horse out for as long as possible on rest days. Monitor the amount of feed your horse eats and make sure that he does not get more than he requires, especially on days of light work. Your horse should always be kept warm, so if he is kept at grass he will need to be rugged and given shelter. Encourage your horse to keep moving by placing his feed and water at different sections of the paddock.

MOODY MARES

Hormonal problems tend to complicate the life of a mare. Her personality is often labelled 'mareish', and any behavioural problems are blamed on hormones. The owner should become aware of his or her mare's individual pattern and cycles. This is an important factor in being able to distinguish between a training issue or a hormonal problem. If you try any of the suggestions here and have no success after 6–8 weeks, there may be deeper physiological problem involved requiring a vet's diagnosis.

Young fillies often come in and out of season frequently as they mature. Use only mild herbs such as Chamomile, Lemon balm and Raspberry leaf with these younger horses. If the imbalances that occurred as a filly continue after the mare has reached 5 years of age, you may use stronger herbs such as Dong quai and Licorice root with those previously mentioned. It is also important to have the mare examined for cysts on the ovaries, as the pain these may cause during ovulation can turn a pleasant mare into a horror horse. Most of these herbs do not need to be given continuously; they can be used to address problems when they arise and help the horse adjust internally. In other cases, you may need adopt a more regular approach. Be guided by your mare's behaviour.

Mares are polyoestrous. During the warmer months of the year, the average mare is fertile every 20–22 days. Her cycle may disappear during winter, but be suddenly tricked into ovulating by unseasonably warm days. It is important to know your mare's reaction to her cycle. It may vary from slight irritability during one cycle to very aggressive behaviour in the next cycle, which can make it difficult to find a pattern.

Wild yam is a useful herb for addressing hormonal imbalances, and can safely be given for long periods of time. If your mare is very aggressive, consider giving her the calming herb Passion flower—or even Valerian at her worst times. Many hormonal imbalances respond to herbs that support the liver, such as Nettle, Dandelion, St Mary's thistle, Chickweed, Burdock and Yellow dock.

Consult a professional if you wish to use homeopathic remedies to help address a mare's hormonal upsets, as the symptom picture can be complex and may require remedies not listed in this book.

Consider using the tissue salts Mag Phos and Kali Phos. Mag Phos is the best choice if you suspect your mare is experiencing pain with her symptoms. Choose Kali Phos if she is sensitive and nervous. Two tablets given twice a day will support your efforts to work with your mare.

The Bach flower remedy Mustard is useful when your mare is behaving badly due to hormonal imbalances. It can be added to her feed and water and wiped across her loins twice daily to help address these symptoms.

Essential oils have a particularly useful role to play in this situation thanks to their action on the limbic system after being inhaled and their subsequent effect on the endocrine glands. Offer your mare Geranium, Fennel, Orange and Ylang ylang essential oils. Depending on which ones she chooses, apply the oil in an Aloe vera gel to the part of her body she requests. Chamomile and Lavender essential oils are useful for calming, Mandarin can help her deal with frustration, and Grapefruit can lift her above depression.

If your mare's moods fluctuate, you should look at your own state of balance. Is your personality steady and consistent when you are with your horse or are you unpredictable, carrying a dark cloud with you on some visits? Mares tend to hold onto an emotional state for longer than geldings, so your assistance in relieving these often long-term 'grudges' is vital. Your own premenstrual tension can indicate a deep fear of living and being able to give and accept love freely. The first step in addressing these issues is to recognize the small things you like about yourself and make a daily effort to compliment yourself on your appearance or an effort you have made. Your love of self will slowly increase, and your mare's moodiness may decrease as a reflection of this.

PREGNANCY

Larch Bach flower remedy is for the mare or stallion reluctant to mare. It is wise to avoid giving herbs to a mare in the early stages of pregnancy. Some herbs can be given throughout pregnancy, but only under the guidance of a professional. The Bach flower remedy Elm is useful for a couple of months before and during pregnancy to help with the production of folic acid. Add 10 drops to the mare's drinking water daily during the first trimester. In the last 75 days of pregnancy, a combination of 1 cupful of boiled barley and 1 tablespoonful of Fennel seeds can be added to the mare's feed daily to enhance her milk quality and quantity. Fenugreek is another herb that may be used after the mare has foaled to encourage milk production. Do not give Garlic to a mare during the last 30 days of her pregnancy, as it may taint the taste of the milk for the foal. During the last 40 days of your mare's pregnancy, a cupful of dried, cut Raspberry leaf or a cupful of the tea can be added to her feed daily to help prepare the uterus for delivery and a quicker recovery.

Walnut Bach flower remedy can make it easier for the mare expecting her first foal to adjust to the changes in her life. Crab apple will help to expel the afterbirth.

A 200C potency dose of Arnica can be given to the mare as soon as possible after foaling, to help her cope with the shock of the experience and any bruising. If there were any complications with the birth, you should seek the advice of a professional, who will recommend homeopathic remedies that are specific for your mare's symptoms.

If your mare slips her foal, the Bach flower remedy Mustard can help her to be optimistic about becoming pregnant again.

THE NERVOUS HORSE

A horse may feel nervous for many reasons. Your horse may be in pain, or have had an experience that has undermined his confidence. He may not understand what you expect of him or he may be picking up your own worries. If your horse gets nervous in certain situations, observe when this nervousness begins. Does it perhaps correspond with your own nervousness?

If you have a nervous horse, training is the first area at which you should look. Natural therapies can be very helpful in treating behavioural problems, but they are not a replacement for patient training methods. Young horses in particular can become nervous if too much is asked of them too soon. It's important to be able to recognize signs that your horse is having problems with training and ease off for a short while. Signs to look out for include: resisting instructions, shying, an inability to focus, hypersensitive overreactions to your aids, aggressive behaviour and attempts to remove the rider. Offer your horse inhalations of Basil or Lemon essential oil before and during training sessions to help him focus on what is required.

The best way to calm your horse is to get an understanding of where his fear is based. A nervous or anxious horse often holds tension in a specific part of his body. As a guideline, anger has an affinity with the liver; frustration goes hand in hand with the pancreas; the lungs often fill with grief; and fear vibrates in the kidneys and the ears. Each muscle in your horse's body also relates to the organs and is therefore affected by your horse's feelings and emotions. Regular massage can help your horse release many of these stored undercurrents of emotion so they do not build up and manifest in the form of anxious behaviour. Massage will also have a good effect on behavioural problems caused by physical pain.

Herbal blends can be used to manage nervous behaviour, but should only be regarded as a temporary measure to help you peel away a layer or two of the behavioural symptoms and identify the underlying cause. For example, if your horse has recently been involved in an accident during travel, calming herbs such as Chamomile or Passion flower can be given (individually or in a blend) either as 1 cupful of the dried herb or as 1–2 cupfuls of an infusion, added to feed. This can be used for the first three or four trips following the accident, to help the horse overcome any fear created by the past experience and to help him to realize that there is no real threat of injury.

Chamomile has an action on the liver, and therefore helps your horse release anger and deal with any anger he is picking up from his environment. Add a cupful of Chamomile tea to your horse's feed to calm temper tantrums. Herbs such as Lemon balm, Passion flower, Wood betony, Valerian and Chamomile can be used singularly or in a blend.

Aromatherapy not only helps your horse overcome fear and anxiety, but also triggers the release of neurochemicals that help the endocrine system address sub-clinical imbalances of certain organs on a cellular level. A fearful horse will often have pain over his loins, just above the kidneys. The horse that holds fear in his body is often attracted to Juniper essential oil. Juniper, the age-old choice of scent for addressing phobias, helps balance the urinary syste, and therefore has a connection with the kidneys.

Offer your horse a selection of essential oils such as Bergamot, Frankincense, Juniper and Fennel. Your horse's choice can give you important clues about the cause of his nervousness or fear. Bergamot often appeals to a horse that feels anxious, Frankincense to a horse that is fearful, Juniper to a horse that is worried, and Fennel to a horse that feels vulnerable and unable to trust his owner. Chamomile and Lavender essential oils are very calming and can be included in the blend. It is also good to select some nurturing essential oils such as Orange or Mandarin and some uplifting oils such as Grapefruit and Ylang ylang in your blend as well. Ask your horse if he just wants to inhale the scent or if he would like it applied in a carrier to his body somewhere—he will indicate his preference.

The Bach flower Rescue Remedy combination can help lift any fear and panic that may be making your horse wary of needles and paste syringes, unmanageable for your farrier, or afraid of entering his box. Simply place a few drops in the palm of your hand, wipe it along his neck or back and repeat regularly depending on your horse's degree of internal turmoil. If you can identify the cause of your horse's fear, use Aspen or Mimulus essence in the same way as Rescue Remedy. Aspen can be helpful for irrational fears, when your horse is afraid but doesn't seem to know why. Mimulus can be useful when your horse is fearful of something specific. If you are unsure which of these two remedies is best for your horse's situation, use Rescue Remedy instead. If your horse is panicking, or suffering from an uncontrollable fear, Rock rose or Cherry plum essence may be used instead. Wild Oats is a useful essence for addressing fear of commitment and is therefore a good remedy for a showjumper having refusals.

As your horse's nervousness may have many aspects, the homeopathic possibilities are almost endless. Generally, however, Phosphorus, Belladonna and Aconite make a good starting point. Chamomilla, Valeriana and Passiflora make good calmative remedies when used in very low potencies. Arg-nit and Gelsemium are also favourites for nervous fear in anticipation of events, though these are not included in this book and should only be used with professional consultation.

The tissue salt Kali Phos is useful for the horse that is on edge or has an abusive past. Give 2 tablets two or three times a day for 10 days, then 2 tablets daily for 3 months. If your horse is nervous after a mishap, Mag Phos can be used instead. Give 2–3 tablets once or twice a day for 5–10 days to help his recovery. Calc Phos is useful for the horse that has a nervous disposition about everything in life or suffers from a long-term debilitating disease or neglect. Give 2 tablets daily for up to 3 months.

THE OLDER HORSE

It is inevitable that your horse will one day grow too old to be ridden as a performance horse. When this happens, it is important he is not placed in a back paddock and forgotten.

As your horse gets older, it is even more necessary to monitor his dental health. He is more likely to have broken or missing teeth and be prone to abscesses. Poor teeth can compromise how well your horse chews his food, and inefficient chewing can increase the risk of colic or choking.

Older horses are not able to regulate and maintain their internal body temperature as well as younger horses. Therefore, it is important to provide adequate shade and protection from heat and humidity in summer, and provide rugs and shelter from the wind during the colder months. Geriatric horses can be given herbal support in the form of circulatory stimulants such as Ginger, Gingko and Hawthorn berry. You can add 3 slices of fresh Ginger to the bottom of your horse's drinking water daily, and add half the recommended doses of both Gingko and Hawthorn berry to his feed on a daily basis. Only increase the dose to the full, recommended amount during the colder months or as his health condition requires.

An older horse is more prone to injury if he loses condition. If the horse is still sound, he should be kept in light exercise to maintain his condition and keep his joints mobile. Gentle exercise will also help keep an older horse's mind active. The Feldenkrais training methods developed by Linda Tellington-Jones (see Further Reading, page 229) are gentle yet challenging enough to keep an older horse's mind and body responsive.

Older horses have a less efficient immune system and are therefore more vulnerable to diseases. You can give your horse immune-building herbs such as Echinacea, Pau d'arco, Rosehips and Garlic during the winter months. Rosehips and Garlic can be added to the feed daily, while Echinacea can be added at any sudden onset of cold weather, and Pau d'arco added throughout the coldest months.

Older horses are more likely to be debilitated by worm infestations than younger horses, so a de-worming schedule must be maintained. Horses' longevity today has been credited to the improvement in worming products in recent years. However, your horse's feed can also be supplemented with Garlic, Fennel and Peppermint to help keep the gut less worm-friendly, and his paddock should be cleared of manure regularly. Other worm-deterring herbs not listed in this book are Wormwood, Southernwood and Rue. These are best used in a blend prepared by a professional. Homeopathically, a 6C potency dose of Cina or a 6X potency dose of Sulphur may be repeated daily for 7–10 days, every couple of months, and a chemical wormer may be used every 3 months. If you have been using these homeopathic remedies this way before each worming, then one dose of Calc Carb 200C can be given as a post-worm treatment to help maintain an internal environment that is less friendly for worms. Feeding your horse carrots can also act as a worm deterrent. Do not feed more than four or five carrots a day to an older horse, however, as carrots have a high glycaemic factor. Their high sugar content can contribute to and irritate a pituitary and adrenal condition in horses called Cushings Disease. The tissue salt Nat Phos is also indicated for the worm-infested horse, especially if he has become nervous and fretful about his other symptoms.

A good general tonic to assist the movement, digestion and his overall well-being of an older horse is a blend of Dandelion, Fenugreek, Marshmallow, Peppermint and Nettle in equal parts, with a half part Pau d'arco. Do not rely on this and ignore other symptoms, though. Older horses are vulnerable to many degenerative diseases that may cause weaknesses within the function of the kidneys and liver, and are prone to developing tumours on vital endocrine pituitary and thyroid glands. A geriatric horse may respond better to a blend of herbal circulatory stimulants including Gingko, Hawthorn berry, Chamomile, St Mary's thistle, Celery seed and Meadowsweet in equal parts, though most of these herbs can be used on their own or in other combinations to help your horse. An older horse's gut would also benefit from a commercial probiotic.

Essential oils can be made into blends to relieve stiffness in the joints. A cold-pressed olive oil carrier is best, as it is warming to the body even when used alone. Juniper, Ginger, Rosemary, Cardamom, Lemongrass and Eucalyptus are good essential oils to include in the blend. An older horse also needs a little more nurturing; when you massage him, he may select the lighter essential oils such as Orange, which will have the effect of a big hug, or Grapefruit, which will give him a bit of a lift. The calming faithfuls such as Lavender and Chamomile are useful for older horses, too.

Tissue salts can be used at varying times depending on your older horse's symptoms. Poor circulation can be stimulated with Kali Phos or Calc Phos. Kali Phos may also be a useful remedy with narcolepsy. This condition also responds to herbs such as Valerian, Rosehips and Gingko. Because it usually only affects older, non-performing horses, little research has been done into this disease.

Moon blindness, a common term for uveitis or periodic ophthalmia, is another disorder about which little is known. It is associated with recurring attacks of inflammation, which can eventually result in opacity of the eye and blindness. This condition can be addressed with one of about forty different homeopathic remedies; however, Euphrasia, Aconite and Belladonna are good choices if you catch the condition in its early stages of development. Moon Blindness should never be ignored, as it can be a sign of a viral, bacterial or parasitic attack on your horse's immune system. (In fact, all eye conditions require veterinary attendance. An injury as simple as a scratch can ulcerate and lead very quickly to blindness.) Some veterinary surgeons suggest daily doses of Bute; however, this may irritate the gut of an older horse more than a younger horse, so you may prefer to use up to 2 tablespoonfuls of Devil's claw, daily, instead. As the condition clears, the homeopathic remedy Silicea can be used to hasten the resolution of scar tissue. An eyewash made from Eyebright, Raspberry or Nettle tea can also assist your horse.

An older mare can be given the support of a blend of herbs such as Wild yam, Dong quai, Siberian ginseng, Hawthorn berry and Passion flower. These herbs will support her body as it adjusts to the changes she is experiencing in later life. These herbs can also offer support to a mare that is still being bred from late in life. Mustard is a useful Bach flower remedy for a mare that is having difficulty adjusting to the changes that accompany later life.

Several other useful Bach flower remedies for older horses include Pine for the horse who is apologizing for not being useful anymore, Walnut for the older horse who withdraws from contact when he no longer feels useful, and Honeysuckle for the older horse who misses the 'good old days' and still thinks he can do all the dressage movements or big jumps, although his body won't follow his mind.

When it comes time to say goodbye to your older horse, the Bach flower remedy Olive can restore peacefulness before euthanasia, and Oak can help the horse who just won't give in when his body has closed down. You can clear the horse's fears by gently wiping Frankincense and Juniper essential oils through his energy field and giving him a gentle massage.

This is an important decision which many owners of older horses will face. Take your time in making such a decision and be guided by your knowledge of your horse. If his quality of life is no longer comfortable, carefully plan how you would like to see him pass from this life. It is important to thank your horse for the many gifts he has brought into your life—if you cannot do this before he has passed on, then do so afterwards, in your own time.

A FINAL NOTE

I have enjoyed putting this book together. As each chapter has been completed, more thoughts have been added and refined. Even as the book was almost ready to go to the printers, I was still wondering about what else could be included to help you with your horse.

For many of you, this will be the beginning of a journey of a lifetime of learning, a journey that will lead you to discover many things about yourself. For me it was an opportunity to understand where my learning has led me and clear the way to see where it will take me next. I still learn something from each horse that I touch or ride.

Always remember that your veterinary surgeon has a vital role in caring for your horse. I have seen some owners panic and fear the worst, only to discover that their horses had minor maladies. Unfortunately, I have also seen other owners let themselves be persuaded not to call a vet, only to find that their horses had broken bones. In both situations, consultations with trusted veterinary surgeons gave clarity.

After you have obtained this clarification, work with the material I have provided in this book. The key to your success will often lie in the most simple approach. Do not underestimate each therapy in its own right. With a pinch of old-fashioned common sense, I expect you will enjoy a healthy relationship with your horse the natural way.

GLOSSARY

acute illness—an acute health situation characterized by the rapid onset of severe symptoms. Such conditions are not long-term or chronic.

catalytic response—the use of alcohol or cider vinegar in a preparation that will be administered internally can increase the rate of the desired chemical reaction of the constituents of the herb without tampering with the end reaction of the herb.

chronic illness—a chronic condition is one of long duration. It is usually characterized by a slow progression of symptoms. There is often no complete healing or 'cure' as such for these conditions, but you can offer support and it is sometimes possible to slow the speed at which the condition is developing. Most degenerative diseases, such as arthritis, are considered to be chronic conditions.

decoction—an extract obtained from a herb by simmering it in water for an extended period of time. This method of extracting the active constituents is reserved for those herbs where the medicinal properties come from denser parts of the plant, such as the bark and roots. A simple tea or infusion made with these parts of the herb would not yield enough of the active constituents to get the desired effect in your horse.

emmenagogue—an action that promotes menstruation in humans and has a stimulating effect on the uterus. Mares do not menstruate, but their hormones can be stimulated by an emmengagogue, which can cause the uterus (a large muscle in its own right) to contract. This is to be avoided if your mare is in foal, so I suggest you avoid using any herbs or essential oils that reputedly have this action on a pregnant mare. Even when given the best of care, 10 per cent of mares do not carry their foals to full term, but it is unwise to use any natural product that could be blamed for such an incident when it may simply be a coincidence. There is not enough scientific evidence to show that a herb or essential oil with an emmenagogic action can cause a premature birth; however, if there is any element of doubt, it is safer to avoid using them at all.

haematoma—a swelling or mass of blood trapped within an organ, tissue or internal space, caused by a break in a blood vessel: put in simple terms, a blood blister. A horse may develop a haematoma as a result of any sudden impact, sometimes even from an injection. Small haematomas are easily reabsorbed; however, large haematomas require veterinary treatment to assist the drainage of fluid after bleeding into the area has stopped.

healing crisis—a situation that may arise due to the use of detoxifying herbs and high potency homeopathic remedies. If your horse suffered an illness that was treated with pharmaceutical drugs in the past, and you decide to use these herbs and homeopathic remedies to treat a later illness, he may suffer a short illness (lasting 1–3 days) accompanied by heavy elimination of toxins that have built up as a result of pharmaceutical treatment. If this happens, ease off your herbal or homeopathic treatment. While a healing crisis is often considered to be a desirable response when natural therapies are used on humans, your horse does not need this stress added to his condition—you will still be able to achieve good results with smaller, gentler doses and patience.

homeostasis—a dynamic state of equilibrium in the internal environment of the body systems, mind and emotions. Your horse's body constantly seeks to regulate and maintain this balance.

limbic system—the collective parts of the brain activated by motivated behaviour and arousal. Memories, emotions and the flight/fight response are stored here. This is the part of the brain that responds to the scent of essential oils. The correct choice of essential oil can trigger a response within the limbic system that influences the endocrine and autonomic motor systems.

moon blindness—properly known as equine recurrent uveitis or periodic ophthalmia, moon blindness is a long-lasting, painful eye disease that produces inflammation in some of the deeper eye structures, eventually resulting in blindness. As the name implies, recurrent uveitis typically occurs repeatedly, which increases the risk of damage to the eye and eventual vision impairment. A bacteria called Leptospira is suspected to be involved in this disease state. The organism is hosted by cattle and can be found in soil where cattle have grazed, and can remain active in the soil for many years. Moon blindness is not prevalent amongst any particular breed of horse. It is difficult to treat effectively; however, I have seen it respond very well to homeopathic prescriptions. Call a vet if you suspect your horse is developing this condition. To delay doing so may put your horse's sight at risk.

narcolepsy—a chronic ailment involving recurrent attacks of drowsiness and sleep. The horse is unable to control these spells of sleep, but is easily awakened. If left to himself, the horse often doesn't wake until he falls to the ground. This condition can vary widely in degrees of severity. In mild cases the horse may be ridden, but the rider must be careful not give the horse any opportunity to snooze. In the most severe cases, a vet may suggest euthanasia.

navicular syndrome—the mere mention of this syndrome can create fear in most horse owner's hearts. It is a progressive, degenerative condition that may involve the navicular bone, navicular bursa and the deep digital flexor tendon. Little is known about this condition; it often goes undetected and is passed off as intermittent lameness until the damage is irreversible. By the time the horse is lame and X-rays show visible changes, the condition is well established.

nephrosis—a condition in which there are degenerative changes in the kidneys.

neuralgia—acute pain radiating along one or more nerves.

photosensitivity—there are circumstances under which a horse may become particularly sensitive to the sun and exhibit symptoms of sunburn. Some herbs and essential oils contain a photodynamic substance, that is, a substance that intensifies or induces the toxicity of sunlight. These include St Johns wort and the citrus essential oils. Even alfalfa, taken internally, can cause a photosensitive reaction in some horses. As with bad sunburn, any hairless or lightly pigmented

areas will turn pinker or redder, eventually peeling, cracking and bleeding. In more severe cases, the damaged tissue may even slough off, leaving the underlying skin very raw and exposed.

It is important that you contact a veterinary surgeon to determine the cause of the reaction and the proper course of treatment. If the reaction is caused by the horse ingesting a certain herb or weed, the horse should be removed from sunlight and remain out of the sun for at least 2 weeks (the time it takes for the herb to be removed from the horse's system). Your veterinary surgeon may also want to check your horse for liver damage, which could be causing the photosensitivity. This procedure can be done through a simple blood test.

poultice—a soft, usually heated and sometimes medicated mass of herbs or clay spread on cloth and applied to sores, lesions or muscle soreness.

proud flesh—excess granulation tissue known as proud flesh may develop over and/or around a wound. This is not to be ignored; seek veterinary advice to decide if the tissue needs to be removed. Copper sulphate is often used to do this, but it can damage healthy cells on the edges of the wound. In some cases a skin graft is required. Some people have successfully treated the condition by dressing the wound with raw honey; however, this is no replacement for veterinary consultation.

rubefacient—a substance or herb that causes redness of the skin.

stringhalt—a disease that results in an exaggerated flexion of one or both hind legs. Affected horses may show only mild signs, but the symptoms will be most noticeable when the horse is asked to rein-back or stop suddenly. In other cases, the exaggerated flexion can be so severe that the front of the fetlock may hit the belly and you may see a wasting of muscles around the gaskin. If both back legs are affected, a bunny-hopping type of gait may develop. Stringhalt may be caused by ingesting a toxin which affects some of the long nerves in the body. The pasture weed Catsear (*Hypochoeris radicata*) has been associated with many outbreaks; however, researchers are not sure if it is the plant or a spore that it hosts on the underside of its leaves that is the most likely culprit. Recovery may take a few days or up to 18 months. Thoroughbreds seem to be more susceptible than other breeds.

succussion—the process of potentizing a substance by vigorously shaking a properly diluted homeopathic remedy. The vial is held in one hand and struck against the palm of the opposite hand or down on a heavy book at least ten times. The more times a remedy is succussed and diluted, the more potent that remedy will be.

sweet itch—an irritating skin condition caused by a small insect. The horse may rub the affected areas raw in an attempt to ease the itch. In northern regions of Australia, it is caused by tiny insects of the Culcoides species. Similar conditions occur in other countries—Summer Sores in France, Dhobie Itch in the Philippines and Kasen disease in Japan—but all of these are caused by a different species known as Onchocerca.

systemic—a word used to describe a preparation or an approach that may use a combination of preparations which will act on a particular body system or certain interacting systems, rather than just the specific localized area that seems to be affected. For example, if you suspect your horse has a blood disorder, you can give a supplement to build the blood; however, a more systemic approach would address the whole circulatory system, including the heart and blood vessels. It could then involve looking deeper to see which organs may also be involved, such as the liver and kidneys, and finding an approach that will address the major organs of the body and thus the whole body system. A systemic approach may be specific to an individual body system or the whole body as a system in itself.

tincture—a solution made from herbs for medicinal benefit which is in an alcoholic menstruum. A menstruum is a substance that dissolves a solid or holds it in suspension. When the term is used in reference to herbal medicines, it means the original plant matter has been percolated with a solution of 60 per cent alcohol.

FURTHER INFORMATION

HERBS AND HERBALWARE

Frontier Natural Products Co-op
P.O. Box 299
Norway, IA 52318
United States
Tel: 800 786 1388/Fax: 800 717 4372
www.frontierherb.com

The Herbal Apothecary
103 High Street
Syston, Leicestershire LE7 1GQ
United Kingdom
Tel: 0116 2602690/Fax: 0116 2602757

Lavender Lane Inc.
7337 Roseville Road Suite No. 1
Sacramento, CA 95842
Tel: 888 593 4400/916 334 4400
Fax: 916 339 0842
www.lavenderlane.com

Mayway Corporation
1338 Mandela Parkway
Oakland, CA 94607
United States
Tel: 800 262 9929/510 208 3113
Fax: 800 909 2828/510 208 3069
www.mayway.com
or
Mayway UK Limited
43 Waterside Trading Centre
Trumpers Way
Hanwell W7 2QD
United Kingdom
Tel: 181 893 6873/Fax: 181 893 6874
www.mayway.demon.co.uk

Meadowsweet Acre Herbs
Patti Duffy-Salmon
181 Wildcreek Road

Shelbyville, TN 37160
United States
Tel: 931 684 8838
Email: psalmon@cafes.net
www.meadowherbs.com

Midland Herbs Supply Co Ltd
1a Formans Trading Estate
Pentos Drive
Sparkhill
Birmingham, West Midlands B11 3TA
United Kingdom
Tel: 0121 7785771/Fax: 0121 7771348

Starwest Botanicals, Inc.
11253 Trade Center Drive
Rancho Cordova, CA 95742
United States
Tel: 916 631 9755/Fax: 916 853 9673
www.starwest-botanicals.com

ESSENTIAL OILS AND CLAYS

Appalachian Valley Natural Products
132 Walnut Street
P.O. Box 515
Friendsville, MD 21531
United States
Tel: 800 342 6546/301 746 5084
Fax: 301 746 4437
www.av-at.com

Elixarome Limited
Hop Pocket Lane
Paddock Wood
Tonbridge, Kent TN12 6DQ
United Kingdom
Tel: 01892 833334 /Fax: 01892 833335
Email: oils@aroma-oils.co.uk
www.aroma-oils.co.uk

HOMEOPATHIC REMEDIES

Ainsworths Homeopathic Pharmacy
36 New Cavendish Street
London W1N 7LH
United Kingdom
Tel: 0207 9355330/Fax: 0207 4864313
www.ainsworths.com

Dolisos America, Inc.
3014 Rigel Avenue
Las Vegas NV 89102
United States
Tel: 800 365 4767

Helios Homeopathic Pharmacy
89-97 Camden Road
Tunbridge Wells, Kent TN1 2QR
United Kingdom
Tel: 01892 537254/Fax: 01892 546 850
www.helios.co.uk

Homeolab USA
78 East Airport Road
P.O. Box 717
Swanton, VT 05488
United States
Tel: 800 404 4666
www.homeolab.com

MASSAGE AND THERAPY COURSES

Homeway Farm
Lyn Palmer
Westhay Road
Meare
Glastonbury, Somerset BA6 9TL
United Kingdom
Tel: 01458 760287
Email: homewayfarm@aol.com

Tellington-Touch Training, TTEAM/TTOUCH
Maggie Moyer
9899 Loop Road
Seven Valleys, PA 17360
United States
Tel: 717 428 1514
Email: tmsaki@nfdc.net
www.brassringhorsemassage.com

Catherine Bird can be contacted at:

Healthy Happy Horses, Naturally
PO Box 670
Randwick NSW 2031
Australia
Email: happyhorses@hartingdale.com.au
www.happyhorses.com.au

FURTHER READING

The Body is the Barometer of The Soul, 8th ed., Annette Noontil, self-published, 2000.

The Complete Herbal Handbook for Farm and Stable, Juliette de Bairacli Levy,
Faber and Faber, London, 1991.

Emotional Healing for Cats, Stefan Ball and Judy Howard, The C W Daniel Co. Ltd, UK, 2000.

Equine Massage: A Practical Guide, Jean-Pierre Hourdebaigt, Hungry Minds Inc, 1997.

Equine Science Health and Performance, Sarah Pilliner and Zoe Davies, Blackwell Science
Inc, UK, 1996.

Horse Nutrition and Feeding, 2nd ed., Sarah Pilliner, Blackwell Science Inc, UK, 1999.

Lame-Horse Causes Symptoms and Treatments, James R. Rooney, Wilshire Book Co, 1992.

Let's Ride! with Linda Tellington-Jones: Fun and Teamwork With Your Horse or Pony,
Linda Tellington-Jones, et al, Trafalgar Square, 1997.

Modern Herbalism Dictionary: A Comprehensive Guide to Practical Herbal Therapy,
Simon Y. Mills, Fine Communications, 1997.

Riding Success Without Stress, Joni Bentley, J A Allen & Co Ltd, UK, 1999.

Treatment of Horses by Homeopathy, George MacLeod, Beekman, 1979.

INDEX

HURON COUNTY LIBRARY

Date Due

AUG 15 2002		
AUG 2 8 2004		
FEB 2 4 2005		
SEP 2 4 2005		
SEP 2 6 2005